Participatory Evaluation in Education

The Falmer Press Teachers' Library

The Falmer Press Teachers' Library: 8

Participatory Evaluation in Education:
Studies in Evaluation Use and Organizational Learning

Edited by

J. Bradley Cousins
and
Lorna M. Earl

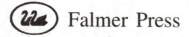 Falmer Press

(A member of the Taylor & Francis Group)
London • Washington, D.C.

UK   The Falmer Press, 4 John Street, London WC1N 2ET
USA   The Falmer Press, Taylor & Francis Inc., 1900 Frost Road, Suite 101, Bristol, PA 19007

First published in 1995

A catalogue record for this book is available from the British Library

Library of Congress Cataloging-in-Publication Data are available on request

ISBN 0 7507 0402 0 cased
ISBN 0 7507 0403 9 paper

Jacket design by Caroline Archer

Typeset in 9.5/11 pt Times by
Graphicraft Typesetters Ltd., Hong Kong.

Printed in Great Britain by Burgess Science Press, Basingstoke on paper which has a specified pH value on final paper manufacture of not less than 7.5 and is therefore 'acid free'.

Contents

Contents

List of Tables and Figures

Foreword

Schools are dragging themselves, ponderously for the most part, into the era of restructured organizations. For many large corporations, this has meant '... outsourcing, delayering, and deconstruction ... a radical downsizing' (Burgess quoted in Naisbitt, 1994). In contrast, school restructuring is best characterized as a form of superficial tinkering often initiated by governments intent on being seen by the public to be 'doing something' in the name of greater accountability. Many of the changes advocated in the name of school restructuring involve either 'doing more of the same' only harder or in a marginally refined way (like setting student performance standards or replacing educational 'goals' with 'outcomes'!). Other school restructuring initiatives appear to be advocated for reasons that have little to do with improving the learning of students; involving parents in site-based decision making is probably the most widely advocated of this type.

Such superficial responses to a world of turbulent change could well spell the demise of public schooling as we know it, at least at the secondary level. Realistically, how can schools in anything like their present form withstand the onslaught of private competition, niche marketing, and a gradually declining share of public revenues? In their present form, how are they to cope with individual home access to the information highway? What will they do in response to the erosion of consensus about educational purposes and values brought on by a growing tribalism around issues of language, culture, religion, and ethnicity?

Few people claim to know the answers to these crucial questions and those who do probably will turn out to be wrong. But there is a compelling case to be made that schools *redesigned as learning organizations* would engage in processes likely to discover those answers. A learning organization is a group of people pursuing common purposes (individual purposes as well) with a collective commitment to regularly weighing the value of those purposes, modifying them when that makes sense and continuously developing more effective and efficient ways of accomplishing these purposes; this is a '... process of improving actions through better knowledge and understanding' (Fiol and Lyles, 1985, p. 803). The specific content of the answers resulting from these processes, however, would differ considerably across schools as they began to learn the lessons already discovered by other organizations of comparable size: large is cumbersome; one solution (or educational policy) does not fit all; the boundary between you and your customers should be seamless, and the like.

Very little is known about the design of schools as learning organizations or about organizational learning processes in schools and how those processes are enhanced or inhibited (indeed, Huberman, in this volume, expresses some skepticism about the concept itself). But there is an urgent need to fill these gaps in our knowledge and that is what the work reported in this book begins to do. In particular, this work starts from the sensible premise that the adequacy of an organization's learning is substantially dependent on the quality of the information its members use to inform their thinking. Based on this premise, the authors propose a model of 'participatory evaluation'. This model provides general guidelines or principles for collecting information of better quality than is typically available for school-level decision making: it also offers means of ensuring greater use of that information than is typically the case with information provided through conventional forms of research and evaluation.

With its roots in contemporary knowledge utilization and change theory, participatory evaluation promises to add some much needed structure to the process of collaborative decision making in schools. Collaborative decision making and the development of professional cultures which support such collaboration are processes critical to the success of most school change initiatives. But the practical meaning of collaboration is in danger of becoming a vacuous mantra without structures such as those provided by participatory evaluation.

Participatory evaluation also provides a forum for more explicitly and, yes, 'rationally' (not really a bad word) negotiating (sometimes) contrary courses of action suggested by the many different forms and sources of knowledge bombarding school staffs as they deliberate about what to do. Traditional forms of research and evaluation provide what Lindblom and Cohen (1979) refer to as *professional social inquiry* knowledge. While such knowledge has the potential to contribute critical and unique insights, its value in organizational decision making usually pales in comparison with the mountain of 'ordinary', tacit, highly contextualized knowledge on which people rely to inform their day to day actions. Participatory evaluation provides a means for increasing the relevance of professional social inquiry knowledge to organizational concerns and for more systematically integrating directions suggested by both ordinary and professional social inquiry knowledge.

Much of the impact of participatory evaluation rests on its bringing together, on a level playing field with the same agenda, two groups of people who have usually marched to quite different drummers – school practitioners and professional evaluators. What transpires when this happens is what the ten chapters in the book describe. It isn't always pretty, as Shula and Wilson teach us in Chapter 8, and as King documents in two of three case studies of participatory evaluation in Chapter 6. Sometimes the impact seems disappointing in spite of well functioning evaluation processes as Cousins description of a 'marginally successful' case in Chapter 4 illustrates. But there are impressive successes: both Earl (Chapter 2) and Lafleur (Chapter 3) offer us such examples. Indeed, the real value of the book hinges on the variety of participatory evaluation experiences available from which to learn.

What is it, in particular, that can be learned from this book? Most chapters have something very useful to say about the contributions of participatory evaluation to organizational learning, and the different forms that participatory evaluation can take. Most chapters also clarify the conditions that foster and inhibit useful forms of participatory evaluation. Many describe changes in the role of the evaluator necessitated by participatory evaluation. This is neither a good news nor a bad news story. It is a real story, richly representative of the complexities involved in any effort to effect educational change. Similarly, the chapters are neither simply case studies nor theoretical musings. They offer a relatively rare example of mostly qualitative explorations of the many facets of a promising theory by an array of people each of whom brings a somewhat unique perspective to bare on that theory: this includes a skeptical perspective on some of the key concepts in the theory provided not only by Huberman in Chapter 7 but also, refreshingly, by the editors themselves in their concluding chapter.

Participatory Evaluation In Education makes an important contribution to our understanding of what it will take to begin to transform schools into learning organizations.

Kenneth Leithwood

References

FIOL, C. and LYLES, M. (1985) 'Organizational learning', *Academy of Management Review*, **10**, pp. 803–813.

LINDBLOM, C.E. and COHEN, D. (1979) *Usable Knowledge*, New Haven, Yale University Press.

NAISBITT, J. (1994) *The Global Paradox*, New York, Avon Publishers.

Preface

This is a book about change in educational organizations. Specifically, it is about the conscious integration into the normal operations of schools and school systems of very deliberative processes of systematic inquiry and applied research methods. In it we explore what it is that researchers, either those employed internally within the systems or in some capacity external to them, can bring to the change process and how what is brought is received. Our intention throughout the book is to reflect critically on the processes we advocate. At the outset, we adopt a posture that acknowledges the deficiencies of merely describing, however enthusiastically, our success stories and sharing our opinions about the role of applied research and researchers in the educational organizational context. We have compiled an original set of empirical studies with data collected, in the most part, from teachers, school administrators, district administrators and researchers; the people directly involved in or affected by the collaborative research processes of interest. It is through their eyes and voices that we add to our knowledge about the sensibility and the potential viability of 'participatory evaluation' as an approach to organizational change in education.

Though most certainly of interest both to applied researchers and academics, this book is written for educators. It is written for teachers and administrators. Those who have had some prior exposure to or involvement in applied research activities, and those who have not. Especially, this book is written for those who are intrigued by the possibilities of applied research as a change lever and, in some sense, are seriously considering this route.

Part 1 begins with an overview of what we describe as participatory evaluation, couched in a conceptual backdrop of theory, research and practical experience. Chapter 1 culminates with an agenda for research and a challenge to researchers. Our first step toward meeting this challenge was to organize a symposium at the annual meeting of the American Educational Research Association (Division H, School Evaluation) held in Atlanta, Georgia, April 1993. At the symposium, five independent empirical studies spanning a wide range of educational contexts and locations were presented. In each of these studies, now presented in Part 2 (chapters 2 through 6 written by ourselves and Clay Lafleur, Linda Lee and Jean King), applications of participatory evaluation were critically considered from different perspectives. At the symposium, Michael Huberman and Marvin C. Alkin provided critical syntheses of the papers. Subsequently, Michael Huberman presented his ideas in chapter 7 and Marvin Alkin's ideas were passed along in written correspondence and incorporated into chapter 10. Along the way to drawing together the themes and ideas emerging from the studies we encountered fortuitous opportunities to enhance the collection with additional empirical studies that add to the richness of the evidence we present and consider. Chapters by Lyn Shulha and Bob Wilson and by Donna Mertens, Terry Berkeley and Susan Lopez appear in Part 3 and help to develop our understanding of participatory evaluation by collectively mani-pulating the contextual unit of analysis from a single school (Shulha and Wilson) to a cross-cultural national education system (Mertens *et al.*). Part 4 of the book consists of our systematic attempt to look across the studies, their different contexts, their different foci and to extract themes and patterns emerging from them. Here we draw and comment on ideas from Huberman and Alkin and attempt to capture what we have learned from these studies and what that learning says about applied research in schools and school systems. We conclude with a set of exercises and challenges for educators and students of participatory evaluation to consider. It is our sincere hope that responses to these challenges are readily informed by the evidence and messages provided in the collection.

We would like to express our gratitude to the contributors to this volume for their thoughtful and illuminating chapters, for their willingness and eagerness to respond to our feedback and for their patience over a somewhat protracted editorial process. Thanks also to Ken Leithwood for providing some very insightful opening remarks, at the symposium and in the Foreword, and to Ivor Goodson for inviting us to add to the *Teachers' Library* series and for his editorial comments and suggestions. Much of this work was made possible by a research grant from the Social Sciences and Humanities Research Council of Canada (Grant # 410–92–0983): the opinions expressed within the final product are those of the authors and do not necessarily reflect council policy. Margaret Oldfield provided us with very helpful editorial comments on previous drafts of many of the chapters. Carolyn Brioux handled the word processing and formatting chores with high levels of conscientiousness and speed. Support staff at the University of Ottawa, notably Monique Carrier, also participated on these tasks. Thanks to one and all for helping bring this project to fruition.

J. Bradley Cousins and Lorna M. Earl
January 1995

Part 1

Why Participatory Evaluation?

In 1992 we published an article in Educational Evaluation and Policy Analysis *that provided a conceptual foundation for our ideas on participatory evaluation. In the paper, we described participatory evaluation and prepared a justification for it from a review of empirical and theoretical research. We then presented some preliminary thoughts about the conditions necessary in order for participatory evaluation to be effective, and an agenda for research. One of the blind reviewers for that article called it the best paper in evaluation he or she had seen in several years. Many of the ideas presented in that 1992 article are revisited an chapter 1, but the chapter extends them by grounding the case more directly in the context of considerations important to the process of change in educational organizations. Also, we elaborate our ideas about organizational learning, a theoretical orientation with natural appeal for utilization-oriented participatory evaluation. Finally, we end up with a set of questions that require investigation, a natural point of departure for the remainder of the book.*

Chapter 1

The Case for Participatory Evaluation: Theory, Research, Practice

J. Bradley Cousins and Lorna M. Earl

'Show Me'

The teacher's role has and will continue to evolve at a rather sharp pace as schools persevere into the next century with a variety of tensions and conflicts. There seems to be little question that norms of privacy and isolation from peers and colleagues are under siege. At the same time, teachers' resolve to protect longstanding interests and to maintain a territorial stance on classroom decision making is pervasive and strong. Teachers are just plain unwilling to make a fundamental shift simply because a new idea sounds good. Blind acceptance of new direction and expansion in the role is not enough. Not unlike Missouri state automobile licence plates that proudly convey to the world the state's nickname and a people's disposition toward 'high falutin' proposals and ideas, teachers are saying 'show me'.

This book is about the acceptance of a relatively new direction and expansion of the role for educators. In particular, the focus for discussion, debate and deliberation is teachers' and principals' involvement on school- and system-based applied research projects; activities that clearly fall outside traditionally defined teaching roles. All things considered, why on earth would teachers and principals want to become involved in applied research activities, ventures that are entirely likely to spell hard work, heightened anxiety, tension and stress, and general disequilibrium? We have some distinct ideas about the answer to this question. The basis for our ideas is several years of experience working in schools and school systems with educators on applied research projects of local interest. We have seen the benefits and we have seen the pitfalls. We have hurdled obstacles and we have run into brick walls. But we continue to pursue with alacrity, opportunities to work in partnership with our practice-based colleagues and we absolutely delight in their invitations to come back. We understand and accept that our delights are not sufficient to persuade others. We also appreciate that by merely presenting our rationale for embracing collaborative research projects, no matter how coherent, attractive or 'high falutin', we will not even begin to persuade the uninitiated. We know that the proud message of the hearts and licence plates of Missourans defines the path that we must take. That message provides both the starting point and the impetus for this book.

J. Bradley Cousins and Lorna M. Earl

Professionalization as Inquiry Mindedness

The tensions, pressures and influences confronting schools are many, highly varied and pervasive. As others have cogently considered these influences (see, for example, Glickman, 1993; Leithwood, Begley, and Cousins, 1992; and Murphy, 1991) we will not belabor them here. Suffice it to say that such forces as: rapid movement from industrial to technology-based economies; aging populations; cultural, religious and ethnic diversity; individual rights and freedoms; and the evolving role of the family and its implication for children's educational experiences, provide the dynamic and turbulent backdrop for contemporary schooling. These forces continue to have significant implications for schools, especially in defining the impetus for change and reform.

'Restructuring', yet another over-used and overworked term in educational circles, provides the current handle for intended significant and sustained planned change and school improvement. Restructuring and reform, of course, are by no means peculiar to educators; organizations in both the public and private sector are globally embracing the rhetoric for change. Restructuring in business and industry, however, implies something different from the common understanding in education. There the term suggests a focus on innovation and new product development with the expressed purpose of enhancing competitiveness in the global marketplace. In education, on the other hand, restructuring tends to imply the reconfiguration of organizational roles, relationships, and structures, often in the context of some locally defined and valued end. Elmore and associates (1990) describe what they see as three basic thrusts in educational restructuring:

1 raising educational standards, reflected predominantly in calls for 'back to the basics', closer monitoring (testing) of student achievement, and heightened accountability demands on educators;
2 involvements of members of the school community as legitimate and true partners in the educational process, reflected in shared governance initiatives, provision to parents of latitude in selecting their children's school, and general efforts to engage families as working partners in their children's educational experience; and
3 the professionalization of teaching.

This third thrust provides the overarching framework for the present book.

The so-called professionalization of teaching implies significant reform in what teachers do and think. The concept is a slippery one that means different things to different people. Perhaps fundamental to our way of thinking about professionalization is the cultivation and development of a posture of 'inquiry-mindedness' regarding technical core activities, manifest in teachers' genuine participation in the determination of school goals and the means adopted to achieve those goals. The thinking among teachers as professionals transcends the bounds of procedural knowledge or the drive to develop more fully an understanding of 'how' one embraces instructional tasks, and extends more deeply to questioning the very reasons for doing the task at all. Calls for reform in classroom practice and the introduction of educational innovations are not accepted at face value, nor are they rejected out of hand within a general mood of frustration and cynicism. Rather, new ideas are critically evaluated against professional wisdom, a collective understanding of educational purpose and school-specific goals, and a clear and articulated sense of underlying assumptions and values. The emphasis on asking 'why?' invariably precedes questions of technical fidelity.

4

Organizations as Learning Entities

If we embrace an image of professionalization as inquiry-mindedness, what are the implications for our view of what organizations are and how they operate? One set of theoretical principles called 'organizational learning' provides a suitable framework within which to consider this question.

Although relatively new to the study of educational administration, organizational learning concepts have been considered in the broader study of organizational theory for quite some time (Cousins, in press; Huber, 1991; Louis, 1994). They are premised on the assumption that learning in organizations is not merely the sum of organization member learnings. Herbert Simon (1991, pp. 125–6) comments on the synergistic qualities of learning at this level:

> Human learning in the context of an organization is very much influenced by the organization, has consequences for the organization and produces phenomena at the organizational level that go beyond anything we could infer simply by observing learning processes in isolated individuals.

We see here the natural link to the fundamental notions of social interactionism and Bandura's foundational work on social learning theory (1977; 1986). The underlying premise is one of an interactional model of causation in which personal factors associated with individuals, environmental events and behaviors operate as interacting determinants of one another. To follow, we summarize the key features of organizational learning theory as a conceptual context for considering strategies or interventions designed to enhance the learning capacity of organizations.

- *Knowledge representation* Knowledge is represented in organizations in a variety of ways. Theorists (e.g., Argyris and Schön, 1978) differentiate between espoused theories such as one would find in organizational policy documents and spoken utterances and theories-in-use, the image of organizational processes and structures and the causal relationships among them that are held by organization members. When such mental representations are widely held among members, organizational learning capacity is greater. Knowledge in organizations is also captured by organizational routines, codes, documents, stories, jokes, and other symbolic representations. Theorists differentiate between locally created or 'generative' knowledge and knowledge acquired from the environment or 'adaptive' knowledge.
- *Actions versus thoughts* Some organization theorists maintain that organizational learning is reflected in the 'change in the range of potential organization behaviors' (Huber, 1991), but others argue that learning occurs through repetitive error detection and correction, and as such cannot occur unless observable organizational actions are apparent (Argyris, 1993).
- *Levels of learning* Low level, incremental, or 'single loop' organizational learning occurs when the organizational response to stimulus for change is manifest in attempts to build upon existing mental conceptions of operations and their consequences. High or 'double-loop' learning occurs when organization members surface, articulate and reflect on deeply held assumptions about purposes and processes (Argyris and Schön, 1978; Fiol and Lyles, 1985; Lundberg, 1989). This sort of learning is non-incremental because the

5

organizational response will occur within a newly formulated 'mental map'. At an even higher level, one might consider the organization's capacity to learn how to learn, or what Argyris and Schön (1978) call 'duetero learning'.

*   *Structural versus interpretive influences* Organizational learning theorists maintain that an organizational response to stimuli for change can and, depending on circumstances, will vary from highly rational, deductive and logical to highly interpretive, non-linear and non-rational (Daft and Huber, 1987; Lovell and Turner, 1988). This perspective provides a better fit with what we know about how organizations operate and is a distinct improvement on the highly rational image of organizations portrayed in much of the program evaluation literature, for example.

*   *Organizational memory* A significant feature associated with organizational learning is the organization's capacity to order and store information for future retrieval and, indeed, its capacity to retrieve desired information as the need arises. Organizational memory and production systems are held by organization members and thus susceptible to rapid decay with personnel turnover and forgetting and by physical record keeping and management information systems set up to perform the function (Levitt and March, 1988; Simon, 1991; Tiler and Gibbons, 1991). While the efficacy of storage and retrieval systems is generally regarded as a key dimension in explaining organizational learning, an organization's ability to 'unlearn' is also viewed as being critical (Hedberg, 1981; Nystrom and Starbuck, 1984).

Organizations such as schools can engage in a variety of strategies and processes designed to enhance organizational learning capacity and generative and adaptive knowledge bases. Strategies designed to enhance a school's generative knowledge might include, for example, local experimentation or systematic trial and error; ongoing monitoring of performance; simulation and gaming; and general strategies designed to improve internal communications. Strategies designed to enhance adaptive learning, on the other hand, include personnel recruitment; general and focused searches of the school's environment; vicarious learning by observing other schools through, for example, inter-school personnel exchange and visitation; and imitative or mimetic learning (copying). Some strategies such as program evaluation and needs assessment can be thought of as organizational strategies designed to add to either generative or adaptive knowledge bases.

Collaboration as the Key

The implications for schools of moving toward an image of professional and organizational inquiry-mindedness are considerable. Key to this movement is a fully developed conception of teachers' joint work reflected by collaborative curriculum decision making; genuine and direct participation in non-curricular, managerial or organizational governance processes; frequent collegial exchange; and the general dissipation of norms of isolation and privacy when it comes to classroom-based activities. Zahorik's (1987) observation that 'collaboration stops at the classroom door' (p. 391) would give way to norms of professional sharing, joint implementation, and collegial observation and feedback. But if educators accept this image and embrace it as worthy of pursuit they will find the transition to contemporary norms to be fraught with obstacles and challenges.

Researchers in many countries have described the persistence in schools of teacher norms of privacy (Little, 1990), noninterference (Feiman-Nemser and Floden, 1986; Huberman, 1990; Lortie, 1975; Nias, Southworth and Yeomans, 1989), individualism (Hargreaves, 1990), and lack of commitment to opportunities for school-wide decision making (Duke and Gansneder, 1990; Duke, Showers and Imber, 1980; Hallinger, Murphy and Hausman, 1991). These conditions are not particularly consistent with the establishment of collaborative culture as a vehicle for school reform. Huberman (1990) characterized teachers as 'tinkerers' who operate independently in adherence to norms of noninterference, and rely more on their personal, practical knowledge in thinking about their teaching than on interaction with peers. Leinhardt and Greeno (1986) amplify the notion of teacher independence by elucidating expert teachers' preference for on-the-spot decision making with minimal pre-planning. Hargreaves (1990) developed an explanation of persistent teacher isolation based on the merits of individualism rooted in an ethic of care and service. The demand on teachers' time away from class was suggested to be a sufficient deterrent to collaboration. Some researchers (e.g., Campbell and Southworth, 1990) even go so far as to say that teachers are ill prepared to collaborate and lack the capacity to work in groups.

Some critics of collaborative activity as a reasonable route to desired change in schools, have framed their arguments in terms of reward structures, suggesting that collaborative work will diminish intrinsic rewards available to teachers. Intrinsic rewards are defined as feelings of satisfaction arising from personally meaningful intangibles such as pride in student achievement, collegial stimulation and support, the glow of service, and enjoyment of teaching activities (Feiman-Nemser and Floden, 1986). Extrinsic rewards are defined as organizational mechanisms for benefiting individuals, such as pay awards, and promotion to positions of added responsibility that confer prestige and/or power. Such rewards are virtually nonexistent in the 'flat' teaching career (Feiman-Nemser and Floden, 1986). Indeed, leadership strategies focused on the distribution of extrinsic rewards (Blase, 1990; Sergiovanni, 1989), including merit pay and career ladder systems installed to enhance teachers' performance through incentives have met with less than satisfactory results (Bacharach and Conley, 1989; Shedd and Bacharach, 1991; Tyack, 1990). What is not clear is whether intensified teacher–teacher interaction will act to curtail the availability to teachers of intrinsic rewards, or, indeed, to enhance them.

Some would argue that under the right conditions, teachers' joint work may either enhance the availability of intrinsic rewards for teachers or provide an additional source of them (e.g., Feiman-Nemser and Floden, 1986). Empirical support for this proposition is beginning to accumulate. In an interview study, for example, Lytle and Fecho (1989) reported that teachers involved in a cross-visitation program found their own classes more intellectually challenging, changed their own routines, tended to learn more from students, received validation of their own skills, became more reflective, and improved their view of the teaching profession. Kushman (1992) came to similar conclusions in stating that, 'Rewards were derived from meaningful adult contact, from working together with one's colleagues to solve daily problems' (p. 28). He concluded, as did Rosenholtz (1989) and Louis and Smith (1991), that teachers' joint work can enhance their commitment to the organization. Other intrinsically satisfying activities include participating in the initiation of new programs, witnessing the motivation of others to experiment, and the generation of new ideas through brainstorming (Little, 1987; Nias *et al.*, 1989; Rosenholtz, 1989).

Another outcome attributable to collaborative work cultures is the development of shared meaning of program implementation and a collective theory of work (Little, 1990; Nias *et al.*, 1989). In the UK, Nias and her associates found that, 'everyday talk was the medium through which shared meanings first evolved and then were continuously and implicitly reinforced' (p. 79). Barth (1989) connected collaborative activity to teacher learning, and Rosenholtz and her associates (Rosenholtz, 1989; Rosenholtz, Bassler and Hoover-Dempsey, 1986) concluded that the ease with which teachers give and receive collegial advice is directly related to their acquisition and development of skills. The link between teacher–teacher interaction and student growth has not been well established (Little, 1990; McCarthy and Peterson, 1989), but some evidence suggests that an indirect link may exist through enhanced teacher efficacy and satisfaction (Ashton and Webb, 1986; Kushman, 1992; Newmann, Rutter and Smith, 1989; Rosenholtz, 1989; Sarason, 1990).

In Canada, we studied a sample of three successful schools (Cousins, Ross and Maynes, 1994) and found that individual and organizational benefits derived from teachers' joint work were to some extent a function of 'depth of collaboration' or the type and degree of sharing among teacher colleagues. For example, deeper, more penetrating forms of collaborative implementation of educational innovations were found to be associated with increased understanding of educational innovations, clarity of interpretation and goals, enhanced communication among teacher colleagues, better knowledge and understanding of students, and the development of confidence, self esteem and sense of belonging within the organizations. These outcomes for teachers were seen to be distinct from, and perhaps in addition to, the normal instrumental benefits of joint work, such as division of labour and time saving, equitable distribution of resources and the development of collectively owned and supported products (curriculum materials, innovations, decisions, etc.). If we concede that under the right circumstances, collaborative activities among teacher colleagues are desirable, then it remains to be seen which sorts of activities will be most beneficial and useful. Collaborative involvement in applied research activities, we propose, constitutes one form of joint work worth a close look.

The Case for Participatory Evaluation

What is Participatory Evaluation?

By participatory evaluation we mean applied social research that involves trained evaluation personnel (or research specialists) *and* practice-based decision makers working in partnership (Cousins and Earl, 1992). Usually decision makers are organization members with program responsibility or people with a vital interest in the program – in Alkin's (1991) terms, 'primary users'. Participatory evaluation is best suited to formative evaluation projects that seek to understand innovations (programs) with the expressed intention of informing and improving their implementation.

In participatory evaluation, the evaluator helps to train key organizational personnel in the technical skills vital to the successful completion of the research project. Essentially, practitioners 'learn on the job' under the relatively close supervision of the expert evaluator while both parties participate in the research process. Such learning is crucial to the participatory model since it is intended that key organization members develop sufficient technical knowledge and research skills to take on the coordinating role on continuing and new projects, and need to rely on the evaluator for consultation about technical issues and tasks, such as statistical analysis, instrument design, technical reporting, and the like.

Participatory evaluation is likely to be responsive to local needs, while maintaining sufficient technical rigor so as to satisfy probable critics, thereby enhancing use within the local context. This feature differentiates participatory evaluation from other similar practice-based research activities.

How is Participatory Evaluation Different?

Participatory evaluation is conceptually distinguishable from various forms of action research and other types of collaborative inquiry on two important, although not independent, dimensions: interests (goals) and form (process). First, traditional action research orientations advocate the simultaneous improvement of local practice *and* the generation of valid social theory (Cochran-Smith and Lytle, 1993; Whyte, 1991). More contemporary 'practitioner-centred' instances of action research (e.g., emancipatory, critical, educative) are explicitly normative in form and function and have as a goal the empowerment of individuals or groups or the rectification of societal inequities (e.g., Carr and Kemmis, 1992; Gitlin *et al.*, 1992; McTaggart, 1991). Such interests are beyond the scope of participatory evaluation. The approach that we advocate is not ideologically bound, nor is it devoted to the generation of social theory. Rather, participatory evaluation has, as its central interest, seeking to enhance the use of evaluation data for practical problem solving within the contemporary organizational context. A second dimension, form, takes shape in participatory evaluation by having the researcher working in partnership with members of the community of practice. Whereas researchers bring a set of technical skills to the research act, practitioners bring a thorough knowledge of context and content. The researcher works as coordinator or facilitator of the research project but fully shares control and involvement in all phases of the research act with practitioners. This thrust is distinguishable both from traditional forms of action research where control of the research process is maintained by the researcher (e.g., Whyte, 1991), and from practitioner-centred approaches (e.g., teacher research) where such control lies completely in the hands of the practitioner group (e.g., Elliot, 1991; Hustler, Cassidy and Cuff, 1986).

Participatory evaluation boils down to an extension of the conventional 'stakeholder-based' evaluation model best characterized by the following features:

- The stakeholder model attempts to engage a large number of potentially interested members of the organization in order to create support. The participatory model involves a relatively small number of primary users.
- The stakeholder model involves organization members in a consultative way to clarify domains and establish the questions for the evaluation or research project. The participatory model engages the primary users in the 'nuts and bolts' of problem formulation, instrument design or selection, data collection, analysis, interpretation, recommendations and reporting.
- In the stakeholder model, the researcher is the principal investigator who translates the institutional requirements into a study and conducts that study. In the participatory model, the researcher is the coordinator of the project with responsibility for technical support, training, and quality control. Conducting the study is a joint responsibility.

Why Participatory Evaluation?

The underlying justification for this approach is problem solving in professional work which is closely tied to Schön's (1983) terms: reflection-in-action and reflection-on-action. Through participatory evaluation, organization members may be surprised by what they observe and moved to rethink their professional practice. Unlike emancipatory forms of action research, the rationale for participatory evaluation resides not in its ability to ensure social justice or to somehow even the societal playing field but in the utilization of systematically collected and socially constructed knowledge. Our orientation toward evaluation utilization (Cousins and Leithwood, 1986) suggests that under certain conditions evaluation or applied research data will be used either in providing support for discrete decisions within the organization (e.g., decisions about program continuation or termination, and decisions associated with program management) or in educating organization members about program operation and consequences of program practices. These uses of evaluation data are known to be dependent on two main categories of factors: features of the evaluation itself including its timeliness, relevance, quality and intelligibility; and features of the context in which data are expected to be used, such as organizational need for information, political climate, and receptiveness toward systematic inquiry as a mode to understanding (Cousins and Leithwood, 1986).

This framework for understanding participatory evaluation is inadequate in at least two respects. First, it links the use of data to an undifferentiated individual called the decision maker. To assume that organizational decisions supported by data are the product of single individuals processing information and translating it into action is, at best, tenuous, and probably not representative of decision making in most organizations. Rather, decisions made explicitly or implicitly are the product of some form of collective discourse, deliberation or exchange (Kennedy, 1984; Lindblom and Cohen, 1979). As such it is eminently preferable to envision the nature and consequences of participatory evaluation within the context of organizational groups, units, subunits, and the like. A second inadequacy is that the evaluation utilization framework as described fails to recognize the powerful influences of various forms of interaction between practice-based and researcher-based communities. Considerable evidence is accumulating to show the benefits of combining the unique sets of skills brought to projects and tasks by both researchers and members of the community of practice, regardless of whether or not the tasks are research-based.

In a recent article (Cousins and Earl, 1992) we provide a thorough review of a variety of lines of research-based evidence in support of the participatory research process. A brief summary of the conclusions within each is presented in table 1.1. These findings underscore the importance of social interaction and exchange and the need to conceive of organizational processes in collective and social terms. They also support the integration of research and practice specializations as a means to stimulating enduring organizational change. An appropriate theoretical framework within which to situate participatory evaluation then will be one that adheres to such principles. The perspective on organizational learning and teachers' joint work described above provides such a framework.

Participatory evaluation, viewed from within this perspective, is a strategy or intervention that will produce adaptive knowledge to the extent that it monitors and provides an opportunity for the interpretation of program outcomes and generative knowledge such that interpretations lead to enlightenment or the development of new insights into *program* operations or effects, or especially *organizational* processes and

Table 1.1   Research-based evidence supporting the participatory research process

Line of Research	Source	Themes and Conclusions
Conceptions of Use	Kennedy (1984) King and Pechman (1986) Weiss and Bucuvalas (1980)	• Conceptualizations, research use are too simplistic, not sensitive to dynamic complexities • Non-use of research is a legitimate outcome of organizations • Interpretations of facts are used rather than facts themselves • Knowledge is socially constructed
Participation and Linkage	Cousins and Leithwood (1993) Greene (1987, 1988a, 1988b) Hargreaves (1984) Huberman (1987, 1990) Louis and Dentler (1988)	• Ongoing contacts and connections between researchers and practitioners regarding research projects will create organizational conditions for sharing and thinking about the meaning of data • Participation helps develop in practitioners skills to do research
Prior Training	Green and Kvidahl (1990) McColskey, Altschuld and Lawton (1985) Walker and Cousins (1994)	• Prior training in research methods enhances practitioners' receptiveness to research, and consumption and use of research
School–University Partnerships	Goodlad and Soder (1992) Vivian (1989)	• Partnerships are mutually beneficial to school-based and university-based personnel • Teachers in partnering schools are more likely to participate in school visitations, professional conferences, review research, form new strategies and alliances
Internal Evaluation	King and Pechman (1984) Mathison (1991)	• Internal research units and functions are increasing • Such units likely to be highly useful given emphasis on formative issues and proximity to program issues and matters • Empirical research in its infancy

consequences. In schools, we see participatory evaluation as a powerful learning system designed to foster local applied research and thereby enhance social discourse about relevant school-based issues. When applied research tasks are carried out by school and district staff their potential for enhancing organizational learning capacity will be strengthened. This requirement of direct involvement in the research process and learning about technical research knowledge will heighten opportunities for staff to discuss process and outcome data and to rethink their conceptions and challenge basic assumptions in ways not previously available. Making explicit underlying assumptions about practice is a necessary precursor to individual and group learning (Senge, 1990). Participatory evaluation will also develop within staff their propensity to be consumers of local applied research conducted by colleagues or others. Partial turnover in personnel from one evaluation project to another will naturally engage more and more organization members in the process and increase the likelihood and the potential for organizational learning.

While we have provided a strong rationale for participatory evaluation from available research-based evidence and from a theoretical standpoint we have arrived only at a starting point. Much remains to be known about participatory evaluation as a learning system, particularly concerning its fit with the organization and culture of schools. The case studies in this book represent a variety of different forays into schools and school systems viewed through the lens of participatory evaluation. Through them we hope to achieve a better understanding of how, and even whether, this approach can be useful to schools on the road to continuous improvement. In this quest, we have many unanswered questions that we hope to explore. We are particularly interested in the changes a participatory evaluation model will require in the way schools operate and in the role of evaluators and researchers.

Unanswered Questions

Participatory evaluation offers a powerful approach to the improvement of educational organizations by creating learning systems that enhance organizational learning and, consequently, lead to better informed decisions. Required, however, are a number of predispositions and adjustments on the part of both the schools and evaluators working with them. At least some of these conditions are likely to be integral to the success of participatory evaluation as school or school district learning systems.

What is Required of Schools and School Systems?

For participatory evaluation to become viable, certain organizational realities must be taken into account. We have identified five requirements that seem especially important. First, and perhaps key, evaluation and local applied research must be valued by schools and districts. There is considerable evidence to support the suggestion that organizational decisions are made in non-rational, haphazard, politically sensitive ways and that evaluation, which assumes a rationalistic model of organizations, necessarily will have limited impact (C.H. Weiss and Bucuvalas, 1980; C.H. Weiss, 1988). Yet evaluation activities appear to be flourishing. In Ontario, Canada, for example, many school systems are operating on a cycle of curriculum review, development, and implementation (Fullan, Anderson and Newton, 1986; Leithwood, 1987), which identifies an integral role for evaluation. Argyris and Schön (1978) refer to a similar cycle of discovery–invention–production–generalization in their description of requirements of effective organizational learning systems. Such patterns suggest that organizations, though not entirely rational, want to use evaluation information and strive to systematize their assessment of information through review or discovery. While routine use of data may not currently be within the organizational culture of schools and school systems, there is reason to suspect that change in this direction is both desirable and possible.

Second, the administration must provide the time and resources required. This requirement is somewhat, although not exclusively, dependent upon the first. The level of involvement of teachers and school administrators in the research process will be necessarily substantial. Anyone who has participated in a serious applied research project from start to finish will have a clear understanding of this verity. But it must be assumed that these folks are extremely busy coping with the daily pressures of their own roles: teachers, for example, are continually being asked to do more in less time (Sarason, 1990). It is vital, then, that organizations sufficiently free up primary users from their routine tasks in order for them to meaningfully participate in the research.

Third, and also dependent upon the first requirement, school districts need to be committed to organizational learning as a route toward improvement. This implies a need to improve *organizational memory* concerning the applied research process. The participatory evaluation process is likely to be highly technical and somewhat foreign to the normal role of teachers and administrators (Walker and Cousins, 1994). While it will work toward developing within schools the capacity to carry out these complex tasks, unless organizational memory is enhanced through, for example, assigning key personnel to subsequent projects in a cascade approach, or explicitly documenting procedures and processes to be followed, such development is unlikely to occur.

Fourth, teachers and administrators participating in evaluation activities must be motivated. These people are likely to face significant challenges and relatively tight time-lines. Are they fully cognizant of the scope of the endeavor before agreeing to participate? Can they afford to be away from their organizational function to the extent that would be demanded by the evaluation? Freeing up personnel from their routine duties may be a source of resentment for some, the consequences of which ought not to be taken lightly. What are the personal benefits to be accumulated? What are the assurances that a useful contribution can be made? What will be the consequences of participation for relationships with others within the school and district (i.e., subordinates, peers, superordinates)?

Fifth, and finally, it is necessary to assume that staff likely to participate in evaluation activities do not have sufficient research experience and knowledge to carry out such tasks, but that they have the ability to learn given appropriate training. In educational contexts, for example, it is well documented that teacher training involves, at best, only cursory exposure to measurement principles or evaluation techniques (Schafer and Lissitz, 1987). Given the nature of teachers' work, it is unlikely that they would have substantial access to technical research knowledge in their normal routines. Since their initial participation is likely to be in the role of apprentice, and since only some would continue on subsequent research tasks, it is not necessary to have all participants develop extensively their research skills. However, it is pivotal that at least some primary users have the potential to do so quickly and have the leadership skills to aid in carrying out subsequent coordinator roles.

What will be the Role of Researchers?

The role of trained researchers in participatory evaluation is a significant departure from more traditional views of the role. We have identified six requirements of evaluators that must be met in order for the organizational benefits of participatory evaluation to be realized. First, evaluators must have the necessary training and expertise in technical research skills. Since evaluation and applied research have flourished as legitimate enterprises since the 1960s the availability of such expertise to school systems is not likely to be problematic.

A second dimension of availability may be more troublesome. Evaluators must be accessible to organizations for participatory activities. Whether located internally within the organization or externally to it, significant demands on evaluators' time will be generated by the participatory model. Furthermore, time will be required for researchers and practitioners to develop a shared language. The critical importance of effective communication cannot be understated.

Third, resources necessary to the research process (e.g., access to support services, budget for incurred costs) must be made available. This assumption is specific not only to participatory evaluation, but, of course, is inextricably tied to organizational needs and administrative commitment to the process. Again, needs will vary depending upon the organizational location (i.e., internal versus external) of the evaluator.

A fourth consideration is an emerging instructional role for evaluators in the participatory process. Although the conception of 'evaluator-as-teacher' is not new (Anderson and J. Weiss, 1983; J. Weiss, 1989; Wise, 1980), we refer here to teaching *about* evaluation rather than teaching *through* evaluation. In the participatory context, evaluators must be capable of training practice-based staff in the skills of systematic inquiry. An important consideration, however, is that the circumstances under which such training would occur probably will be less than ideal from an instructional standpoint (e.g., interruptions, time pressures, competing priorities). Evaluators must be sensitive to principles of adult learning and ought to have the appropriate interpersonal and communication skills. Since a significant portion of the training is likely to take place as projects unfold, the exercise is likely to be grounded within contexts familiar and meaningful to practitioner participants.

Fifth, evaluators must be motivated to participate. The goal of empowering teachers and administrators with the technical knowledge and skill to conduct useful applied research is vital and needs to be explicitly acknowledged and accepted by all. Evaluators who are able to transcend an edict of expert–novice professional relationships, and who are willing to share and instruct about their technical expertise will be more likely to experience success.

Sixth, and finally, and also related to the foregoing discussion, evaluators ought to have significant tolerance for imperfection. The training task, as a rule, will be a significant challenge particularly where staff not grounded in prior research experience and training are concerned. Evaluators must acknowledge and accept that errors and mistakes are likely to be common. It is incumbent upon them to anticipate and deal with such mistakes so as to maintain the integrity and necessary standards of technical quality for the research process.

Concluding Remarks

Participatory evaluation in education, then, at first blush, has a bright future. It holds the promise espoused by advocates of collegial work, it is likely to provide a practical and cost-effective alternative and it appears to offer a distinct approach for schools and school systems wishing to develop organizational learning capacity. But the current bank of empirical data is much too thin to warrant unreflective change in this direction. In the presentation and critical synthesis of the original empirical studies to follow we hope to add substantially to this knowledge base.

References

ALKIN, M.C. (1991) 'Evaluation theory development II', in McLAUGHLIN, M.W. and PHILLIPS, D.C. (eds) *Evaluation and Education: At Quarter Century*, (Ninetieth Yearbook of

National Society for the Study of Education) Chicago, University of Chicago Press, pp. 91–112.

ANDERSON, S. and WEISS, J. (1983; April) 'The pedagogical potential of case studies: Considerations for evaluation practice.' Paper presented at the annual meeting of the American Educational Research Association, Montreal.

ARGYRIS, C. (1993) *Knowledge for Action: A Guide to Overcoming Barriers to Organizational Change*, San Francisco, CA, Jossey-Bass.

ARGYRIS, C. and SCHÖN, D.A. (1978) *Organizational Learning: A Theory of Action Perspective*, Reading, MA, Addison-Wesley.

ASHTON, P. and WEBB, R. (1986) *Making a Difference: Teachers' Sense of Efficacy and Student Achievement*, New York, Longman.

BACHARACH, S.B. and CONLEY, S.C. (1989) 'Uncertainty and decisionmaking in teaching: Implications for managing line professionals', in SERGIOVANNI, T.J. and MOORE, J.H. (eds) *Schooling for Tomorrow: Directing Reforms to Issues that Count*, Boston, Allyn and Bacon, pp. 311–29.

BANDURA, A. (1977) *Social Learning Theory*, Englewood Cliffs, NJ, Prentice Hall.

BANDURA, A. (1986) *Social Foundations of Thought and Action: A Social Cognitive Theory*, Englewood Cliffs, NJ, Prentice Hall.

BARTH, R.S. (1989) 'The principal and the profession of teaching', in SERGIOVANNI, T.J. and MOORE, J.H. (eds) *Schooling for Tomorrow: Directing Reforms to Issues that Count*, Boston, Allyn and Bacon, pp. 227–50.

BLASE, J.J. (1990) 'Some negative effects of principals' control-oriented and protective political behaviour', *American Educational Research Journal*, **27**, 4, pp. 727–53.

CAMPBELL, P. and SOUTHWORTH, G. (1990; April) 'Rethinking collegiality: Teachers' views'. Paper presented at the annual meeting of the American Educational Research Association, Boston, MA.

CARR, W. and KEMMIS, S. (1992) *Becoming Critical: Education, Knowledge and Action Research*, London, Falmer Press.

COCHRAN-SMITH, M. and LYTLE, S. (1993) *Inside/Outside: Teacher Research and Knowledge*, New York, Teachers' College Press.

COUSINS, J.B. (in press) 'Understanding organizational learning for educational leadership and school reform', in LEITHWOOD, K.A. (ed.) *International Handbook of Educational Leadership and Administration*, Boston, Klewer Academic Publishers.

COUSINS, J.B. and EARL, L.M. (1992) 'The case for participatory evaluation', *Educational Evaluation and Policy Analysis*, **14**, 4, pp. 397–418.

COUSINS, J.B. and LEITHWOOD, K.A. (1986) 'Current empirical research on evaluation utilization', *Review of Educational Research*, **56**, 3, pp. 331–64.

COUSINS, J.B. and LEITHWOOD, K.A. (1993) 'Enhancing knowledge utilization as a strategy for school improvement', *Knowledge: Creation, Diffusion, Utilization*, **14**, 3, pp. 305–33.

COUSINS, J.B., ROSS, J.A. and MAYNES, F.J. (1994) 'The reported nature and consequences of teachers' joint work in three exemplary schools', *Elementary School Journal*, **94**, 4, pp. 441–65.

DAFT, R.L. and HUBER, G.P. (1987) 'How organizations learn: A communication framework', *Research in the Sociology of Organizations*, **5**, pp. 1–36.

DUKE, D. and GANSNEDER, B. (1990) 'Teacher empowerment: The view from the classroom', *Educational Policy*, **4**, 2, pp. 145–60.

DUKE, D.L., SHOWERS, B. and IMBER, M. (1980) 'Teachers and shared decision making: The costs and benefits of involvement', *Educational Administration Quarterly*, **16**, 1, pp. 93–106.

ELLIOT, J. (1991) *Action Research of Educational Change*, Milton Keynes, Open University Press.

ELMORE, R. and ASSOCIATES (eds) (1990) *Restructuring Schools: The Next Generation of Educational Reform*, San Francisco, Jossey-Bass.

FEIMAN-NEMSER, S. and FLODEN, R.E. (1986) 'The cultures of teaching', in WITTROCK, M.C.

Handbook of Research on Teaching, New York, Macmillan Publishing Company, pp. 505–26.

Fiol, C.M. and Lyles, M.A. (1985) 'Organizational learning', *Academy of Management Review*, **10**, pp. 803–813.

Fullan, M.G., Anderson, S. and Newton, E. (1986) *Support Systems for Implementing Curriculum in School Boards*, Toronto, The Queen's Printer for Ontario.

Gitlin, A., Bringhurst, K., Burns, M., Cooley, V., Myers, B., Price, K., Russell, R. and Tiess, P. (1992) *Teachers Voices for School Change*, New York, Teachers' College Press.

Glickman, C.D. (1993) *Renewing America's Schools: A Guide for School-based Action*, San Francisco, Jossey-Bass.

Goodlad, J.I. and Soder, R. (1991) 'School-university partnerships: An appraisal of an idea', Occasional Paper No. 15. Seattle, Wash. Institute for the Study of Educational Policy, College of Education, University of Washington.

Greene, J.C. (1987) 'Stakeholder participation in evaluation design: Is it worth the effort?', *Evaluation and Program Planning,* **10**, pp. 375–94.

Greene, J.C. (1988a) 'Communication of results and utilization in participatory program evaluation', *Evaluation and Program Planning*, **11**, pp. 341–51.

Greene, J.C. (1988b), 'Stakeholder participation and utilization in program evaluation', *Evaluation Review*, **12**, 3, pp. 91–116.

Green, K.E. and Kvidahl, R.F. (1990; April) 'Research methods courses and post-bachelor education: Effects on teachers' research use and opinions'. Paper presented at the annual meeting of the American Educational Research Association, Boston, April.

Hallinger, P., Murphy, J. and Hausman, C. (1991; April) 'Conceptualizing school restructuring: Principals' and teachers' perceptions.' Paper presented at the annual meeting of the American Educational Research Association, Chicago, IL.

Hargreaves, A. (1990; April) 'Individualism and individuality: Reinterpreting the teacher culture', Paper presented at the annual meeting of the American Educational Research Association, Boston, MA.

Hargreaves, A. (1984) 'Experience counts, theory doesn't: How teachers talk about their work', *Sociology of Education*, **57**, pp. 244–54.

Hedberg, B. (1981) 'How organizations learn and unlearn', in Nystrom, P.C. and Starbuck, W.H. (eds) *Handbook of Organizational Design: Vol. 1. Adapting Organizations to their Environments*, New York, Oxford University Press, pp. 2–27.

Huber, G.P. (1991) 'Organizational learning: The contributing processes and the literature', *Organizational Science*, **2**, 1, pp. 88–115.

Huberman, M. (1990) 'Linkage between researchers and practitioners: A qualitative study', *American Educational Research Journal*, **27**, pp. 363–91.

Hustler, D., Cassidy, T. and Cuff, T.E. (1986) *Action Research in Classrooms and Schools*, London, Allen & Unwin.

Kennedy, M.M. (1984) 'How evidence alters understanding and decisions', *Educational Evaluation and Policy Analysis*, **6**, 3, pp. 207–26.

King, J.A. and Pechman, E.M. (1984) 'Pinning a wave to the shore: Conceptualizing evaluation use in school systems' *Educational Evaluation and Policy Analysis*, **6**, 3, pp. 241–251.

Kushman, J.W. (1992) 'The organizational dynamics of teacher workplace commitment: A study of urban elementary and middle schools', *Education Administration Quarterly*, **28**, 1, pp. 5–42.

Leinhardt, G. and Greeno, J.G. (1986) 'The cognitive skill of teaching', *Journal of Educational Psychology*, **78**, 2, pp. 75–95.

Leithwood, K.A. (1987) 'Using the principal profile to assess performance', *Educational Leadership*, **45**, 1, pp. 63–6.

Leithwood, K.A., Begley, P.T. and Cousins, J.B. (1992) *Developing Expert Leadership for Future Schools*, London, Falmer Press.

LEVITT, B. and MARCH, J.G. (1988) 'Organizational learning', *Annual Review of Sociology*, **14**, pp. 319–40.

LINDBLOM, C.E. and COHEN, D.K. (1979) *Usable Knowledge*, New Haven, CT, Yale University Press.

LITTLE, J.W. (1987) 'Teachers as colleagues', in RICHARSON-HOEHLER, V. (ed) *Educators Handbook: A Research Perspective*, New York, NY, Longman, pp. 491–518.

LITTLE, J.W. (1990) 'The persistence of privacy: Autonomy and initiative in teachers' professional relations.' *Teachers' College Record*, **91**, 4, pp. 509–36.

LORTIE, D. (1975) *Schoolteacher: A Sociological Study*, Chicago, University of Chicago Press.

LOUIS, K.S. and DENTLER, R.A. (1988) 'Knowledge use and school improvement', *Curriculum Inquiry*, **18**, 10, pp. 33–62.

LOUIS, K.S. (1994) 'Beyond bureaucracy: Rethinking how schools change', *School Effectiveness and School Improvement*, **5**, 1, pp. 2–24.

LOUIS, K.S. and SMITH, B. (1991) 'Restructuring, teacher engagement and school culture: Perspectives on school reform and the improvement of teacher's work', *School Effectiveness and School Improvement*, **2**, 1, pp. 34–52.

LOVELL, R.D. and TURNER, B.M. (1988) 'Organizational learning, bureaucratic control, preservation of form: Addition to our basic understanding of research utilization in public organizations', *Knowledge: Creation, Diffusion, Utilization*, **9**, 3, pp. 404–25.

LUNDBERG, C.C. (1989) 'On organizational learning: Implications and opportunities for expanding organizational development', *Research in Organizational Change and Development*, **3**, pp. 61–82.

LYTLE, S.L. and FECHO, R. (1989; March) 'Meeting strangers in familiar places: Teacher collaboration by cross-visitation'. Paper presented at the annual meeting of the American Educational Research Association, San Francisco.

MATHISON, S. (1991) 'What do we know about internal evaluation?', *Evaluation and Program Planning*, **14**, pp. 159–65.

McCARTHY, S.J. and PETERSON, P.L. (1989; March) 'Teacher roles: Weaving new patterns in classroom practice and school organization'. Paper presented at the annual meeting of the American Educational Research Association, San Francisco.

McCOLSKEY, W.H., ALTSCHULD, J.W. and LAWTON, R.W. (1985) 'Predictors of principals' reliance on formal and informal sources of information', *Educational Evaluation and Policy Analysis*, **7**, 4, pp. 427–36.

McTAGGART, R. (1991) 'Principles for participatory action research', *Adult Education Quarterly*, **41**, 3, pp. 168–87.

MURPHY, J. (1991) *Restructuring Schools: Capturing and Assessing the Phenomena*, New York, Teachers' College Press.

NEWMANN, F.M., RUTTER, R.A. and SMITH, M.S. (1989) 'Organizational factors that affect school sense of efficacy, community, and expectations', *Sociology of Education*, **62**, pp. 221–38.

NIAS, J., SOUTHWORTH, G. and YEOMANS, R. (1989) *Staff Relationships in the Primary School: A Study of Organizational Cultures*, London, Cassell.

NYSTROM, P.C. and STARBUCK, W.H. (1984) 'To avoid organizational crises, unlearn', *Organizational Dynamics*, **12**, pp. 53–65.

ROSENHOLTZ, S.J. (1989) *Teachers' Workplace: The Social Organization of the School*, New York, Longman.

ROSENHOLTZ, S.J., BASSLER, O. and HOOVER-DEMPSEY, K. (1986) 'Organizational conditions of teacher learning', *Teaching and Teacher Education*, **2**, 2, pp. 91–104.

SARASON, S. (1990) *The Predictable Failure of Educational Reform*, San Francisco, Jossey-Bass.

SCHAFER, W.D. and LISSITZ, R.W. (1987) 'Measurement training for school personnel: Recommendations and reality', *Journal of Teacher Education*, **38**, 3, pp. 57–63.

SCHÖN, D.A. (1983) *The Reflective Practitioner*, New York, Basic Books.

SENGE, P.M. (1990) *The Fifth Discipline: The Art and Practice of Organizational Learning*, New York, Doubleday.

SERGIOVANNI, T.J. (1989) 'Science and scientism in supervision and teaching', *Journal of Curriculum and Supervision*, **4**, 2, pp. 93–105.

SHEDD, J.B. and BACHARACH, S.B. (1991) *Tangled Hierarchies*, San Francisco, Jossey-Bass.

SIMON, H.A. (1991) 'Bounded rationality and organizational learning', *Organizational Science*, **2**, 1, pp. 125–34.

TILER, C. and GIBBONS, M. (1991) 'A case study of organizational learning: The UK teaching company scheme', *Industry and Higher Education*, **5**, 1, pp. 47–55.

TYACK, D. (1990) '"Restructuring" in historical perspective: Tinkering toward Utopia', *Teachers College Record*, **92**, 2, pp. 170–91.

VIVIAN, H.W. (1989; March) 'Improving schools through application of "effective schools" research', Paper presented at the annual meeting of the American Educational Research Association, San Francisco.

WALKER, C.A. and COUSINS, J.B. (1994; October) 'Influences on teachers' attitudes toward applied educational research'. Paper presented at the annual meeting of the American Evaluation Association, Boston, MA, November.

WEISS, C.H. (1988) 'Evaluation for decisions: Is anybody there? Does anybody care?' *Evaluation Practice*, **9**, 1, pp. 5–19.

WEISS. J. (1989) 'Evaluation and subversive educational activity', in MILBURN, G., GOODSON, I. and CLARK, R. (eds) *Re-interpreting Curriculum Research: Images and Arguments*, London, Falmer Press, pp. 121–31.

WEISS, C.H. and BUCUVALAS, M.J. (1980) *Social Science Research and Decision Making*, New York, Columbia University Press.

WISE, R. (1980) 'Evaluator as educator', in BRASKAMP, L.A. and BROWN, R.D. (eds) *Utilization of Evaluative Information: New Directions in Program Evaluation*, **5**, pp. 11–18, San Francisco, Jossey-Bass.

WHYTE, W.F. (1991) *Participatory Action Research*, Newbury Park, Sage.

Zahorik, J.A. (1987) 'Teachers' collegial interaction: An exploratory study', *The Elementary School Journal*, **87**, 4, pp. 385–96.

Part 2

Participatory Evaluation in Schools and School Systems

The Atlanta AERA symposium in which the original five studies of applications of participatory evaluation were presented was very well attended and culminated in a lively exchange among presenters, discussants and members of the audience. We knew that we were on to something worth exploring further.

Here we present revised versions of those original papers. Lorna Earl begins with her study of internal collaborative evaluation within a large metropolitan school district (77,000 students). Two major evaluation studies of school improvement activities – one for the secondary panel and one for the elementary – were coordinated by the research department and involved the direct participation of school and central board office administrative and consulting staff. Clay Lafleur then reports on a similar model of evaluation but in a smaller school district (46,000 students) and a smaller research shop. Lafleur interviews and surveys participants in several collaborative projects carried out over the past several years.

Brad Cousins introduces an approach to participatory evaluation that involves the evaluator working in an external organizational context; a non-fee for service, school–university partnership arrangement. He shares with us his views on two projects with apparently differing degrees of success.

Each of the above chapters provides rich data concerning the impact of participatory evaluation and factors influencing observed impact. Linda Lee and Brad Cousins report on Linda's work with a charitable foundation as an evaluation consultant to secondary schools competing for and managing external funds for 'home-grown' school improvement projects. While data were collected too early in the process to report on longer term effects, the chapter has much to say about the nature of the process and its effects on participants, both educators and the researcher.

Finally, Jean King provides some insightful reflections on past and current projects. She begins by offering a framework for thinking about collaborative work and then locates her own projects within. Jean comments on both progress and effects. Michael Huberman then summarizes his remarks delivered at the Atlanta symposium and offers some keenly honed theoretical insights prior to examining each of the models of participatory evaluation in terms of what they do and do not offer.

Chapter 2

District-wide Evaluation of School Improvement: A System Partners Approach

Lorna M. Earl

Introduction

The Scarborough Board Research Unit is an internal evaluation unit that loosely operates on a decision-oriented research model presented by Cooley and Bickel (1986) – that is, educational research that is designed to be directly relevant to the current information requirements of those who are shaping educational policy or managing educational systems. In this role, we have the ongoing responsibility for research and evaluation in the organization and are an integral part of the management activity within the district. Although the Research Unit has historically operated in a somewhat isolated capacity, the last decade has seen a decided shift in focus away from a detached research stance towards an emphasis on forming partnerships with educators and providing high-quality information to contribute to institutional decision making and enhance organizational learning. This philosophy has brought us into the mainstream of cutting-edge initiatives and controversial decisions. As Love (1991) pointed out:

> effective internal evaluation requires forging a common mission and positive relationship between managers and evaluators . . . evaluators must forge strong bonds with managers.

This paper describes two related evaluation studies undertaken within the Scarborough Board that involved using 'participatory evaluation' methods (Cousins and Earl, 1992) to increase understanding, commitment and utilization on the part of both the evaluator and the clients. Both of these studies focused on school improvement efforts in a large suburban school district.

The Scarborough Board of Education serves a district with 75,000 students in a city that is one of six making up the Metropolitan Toronto area. It operates with a school improvement model that utilizes a balance between central control and local decision making. This model emphasizes: (a) change is an ongoing process; and (b) advances in curriculum require the collaborative and cooperative effort of a large number of 'system partners'.

The focus for the implementation of change in Scarborough secondary schools has been on each school establishing a school-wide Curriculum Management Plan which is unique to that school and recognizes that many schools have been involved in school improvement initiatives for many years.

School improvement initiatives, however, are not exclusively school-based and the curriculum management plans have not been developed by schools in isolation from the school board administration. In order to facilitate development of the curriculum management plans, the program department has provided considerable leadership and support over a period of years and has established the framework for change but has left the specification of the end result to each school.

After several years of supporting schools in their efforts, the district administrators with responsibility for curriculum sensed that the schools were responding positively to the decentralized process of curriculum management and, as would be expected, were responding in many different ways. It was difficult to assess, however, how successful the efforts of the past few years have been in actually creating changes and improvement in individual schools. It was also becoming more difficult to decide what kinds of resources and assistance should be provided to assist the schools in implementing their own unique improvement project. Hence it was time to stand back as a system and evaluate the process that was in place. At this point the Curriculum Review Development Implementation (CRDI) Committee invited the research centre to conduct a study. The study was designed to:

1 assess the extent to which the CRDI school improvement activity was actually being implemented in the secondary schools;
2 describe the kind of school improvement activity ongoing in the secondary schools; and
3 identify factors that facilitate and impede school improvement activity in the secondary schools.

The School Improvement Evaluation Process

The initial invitation to undertake an evaluation came as a simple request for me as director of the research unit to attend a meeting of an ad hoc committee and help design a questionnaire for principals to provide information about their school initiatives. As the committee (made up of two secondary principals, two central office administrators, a department head, a centrally assigned curriculum coordinator, and myself) discussed the issues and as I asked questions, it became clear to the committee that the range of initiatives and school-based activities were relatively complex and that the principals might not be familiar with all that was happening and that a questionnaire might not be able to capture the full range of information. After several meetings, in which there was much discussion about the nature of the evaluation problem, and consideration was given to possible alternative ways of gathering valid information and the potential anxieties among staff, we agreed that this committee should be formalized as the Needs Assessment Committee (NAC) and take ongoing responsibility for conducting the evaluation. The evaluation itself took the form of focused interviews with the group of people who were responsible for CRDI in each school. Since CRDI and school improvement are very complex issues that require knowledgable interviewers, and because the NAC wanted to emphasize the importance of this interview, well-respected, centrally assigned staff and school personnel (mostly coordinators, principals, and vice-principals) were trained as interviewers. In teams of two they conducted interviews in each of the twenty-five Scarborough secondary schools in May and June of 1989, using a scripted preamble and interview protocol.

As it developed, this process became a model with three levels of participation: a school could participate by having a team that was interviewed; school-based administrators could serve as interviewers in other schools; and a few administrators were among the members of the core focused interview planning team, the NAC. The participation for teams being interviewed consisted of meeting together; considering their own school's plan for improvement; reflecting on their accomplishments, concerns and future directions; and engaging in a structured dialogue about their unique improvement approach. The interviewers had the additional involvement of a two-day training session in focused interview techniques, the experience of interviewing and getting a 'birds-eye view' into several other schools as they described their plans, and a follow-up debriefing session to consider the reports and the recommendations before they were released. The core focused interview planning team had a major role to play from the very conception of the project. They defined the problem; identified the constraints and problems in gathering the data; brainstormed a process that was considered to be unorthodox but seemed to provide direct and indirect benefits to the system; considered the data summaries and established a reporting format; wrote the executive summary and recommendations; and became the key presenters of the results. Several of them also participated in the data analysis.

Two reports were generated as a result of this study: a research report that contained the methodology and results, and an executive summary with key findings and recommendations for action. These reports were released in the fall of 1989. At that time, it seemed quite clear that something of significance had happened in this project. Although I had often worked with committees in a stakeholder-based evaluation model, to ensure that the evaluation was consistent with system needs, this was the first time that participation had been so intense and widespread. I was fascinated to observe that, by the time the recommendations had gone through the routine bureaucratic channels, many of them were already well on their way to implementation and even completion. There were many positive comments in other forums about the value of the process. I had a number of letters from participants thanking me for the opportunity to be either 'listened to' or to 'be involved in real educational discussions' or to 'learn more about interviewing and about research'.

The core team (NAC) was perhaps the most interesting because its members saw the project as 'theirs' and, for them, the obvious route for distribution and communication of the results was for them to be the ambassadors. Except for presentations at research meetings (and I have always taken an NAC member to these), I have never

---

One of the curriculum coordinators, a flamboyant, garrulous man, burst through my door after having conducted an interview in one of the secondary schools and announced:

> *You would have been so proud of me. They told me that the (his subject) program was in shambles and I just nodded, wrote it down and said 'uh huh.' I really wanted to know what was going on and they knew it. They knew I'd been trained to get the information and not be judgmental or try to fix. And I didn't, I just let them tell me the way it is. You know what, I learned a lot more than I would have it I'd just arrived and talked to the head.*

> *More than a year after the training a comment at a meeting of district administrators went something like this:*
>
> > *One of the most valuable training sessions that I ever had was the training in interviewing that we did for the CRDI project. Before that I had no idea that I could use interviews to get good information about things. I used them more like gab sessions to put people at ease and I depended on my intuition to know what was really going on. Now, I find I use interviews all the time when I'm reviewing schools and I go back to that training a lot. I try to plan before hand so I know what I'm interested in and I really focus on giving people a chance to tell me what they're doing.*

> *One member of the elementary core team, a principal, used the focused interview as a jumping off point for school planning but wasn't satisfied to continue without good data about their process and progress. She let me know that she was interested in getting as much information as she could for the staff to use as they approached school restructuring in this middle school. I arranged for two different researchers (both teachers in the district, also working on post-graduate degrees) to work with her and conduct interviews with staff in this school to describe their efforts at collaboration and integrating curriculum. Their reports have generated considerable discussion among the staff and spawned new initiatives, as well as consolidating and fine-tuning existing ones. Not to be stopped, this principal and the staff applied for and got funding for a small research grant to continue the research efforts in their school, as a way of documenting their activity and providing a basis for future planning.*

> *When it came time to decide about the value and the constraints associated with a school-based staff development pilot project, two members of the secondary core committee conducted their own focused interviews with staff from schools who were participating in the pilot. With very little assistance, they used the skills they had developed to create the interview questions, conduct the interviews, analyse the data and write the report.*

been asked to present the report although it has been presented and discussed throughout the district many times. Certainly, my perception, and the perception of the key central office administrators, was that this process had a major impact on the school improvement initiatives in the secondary schools, and on those people who were involved as interviewers and on the NAC. Unfortunately, we had no formal documentation of our beliefs.

One unanticipated outcome of the study came from the elementary schools. News about the project and the enthusiasm it had generated brought representatives from the elementary school teams clamoring for implementation of the same process in all of the elementary schools. This was a much more daunting task because Scarborough has 140 elementary schools. We agreed to embark on such a project and started with the formation of an elementary focused interview planning team to create a proposal. This team was made up of six elementary principals, three centrally assigned curriculum coordinators, a research associate and myself. Although a central office senior administrator was assigned to the team, competing commitments prevented his active involvement in the process.

The elementary committee operated very much like the secondary NAC had done and the members accepted their role as the 'evaluation' committee. They quickly established that, because the elementary schools were different from the secondary schools they could not use precisely the same process and went about the business of developing a unique plan suited to their needs. Although, in its final form, it is not so very different from the one used in the secondary schools, these decisions were arrived at after considerable debate and wrangling. For example, sampling was suggested as a possible way of decreasing the magnitude of the task. The group grappled with the technical problems of sampling schools and generalizability. They also considered the issue from a political and staff development perspective and came to the decision that all school teams needed to experience the interview process as a way to reflect on their practice and that elementary staff would also benefit from the focused interview training. The result was that teams of four to seven staff were interviewed in each school and fifty-one elementary principals, vice-principals and centrally assigned staff were trained as interviewers and conducted the interviews in teams of two during May of 1991.

The report from this study was somewhat more complicated to write because of the enormous amount of textual data. The data was initially organized by a research associate who read, categorized and coded all of the information. Once she had established initial categories, the committee met for a number of working meetings to consider her analysis, reread the protocols and discuss the categories. These discussions once again included much attention to issues surrounding data management and interpretation. Once the categories were finally agreed upon, the committee moved on to the task of interpreting the results and deciding what the text of the report should contain. They labored over the problem of providing readable, accessible reports without trivializing the information. The final decision was to write two reports, similar to the secondary reports: a research report, and an executive summary with recommendations. Unfortunately, the analysis process took a good deal longer than for the secondary study and the reports were not completed until the spring of 1992. Although the committee was concerned that the information might not be considered fresh, they decided that the reports should be distributed to the system by members of the core team at area principals' meetings in the spring of 1992 in time for consideration as part of planning the 1992–93 school year.

Once again, I was impressed by the dedication and interest of the participants in this project. The interviewers requested a debriefing session and an opportunity for input to the analysis categories. The core team was willing to come before and after school to consider the data and to engage in thoughtful and sometimes intellectually stimulating debate about not only the meaning of the data, but about the evaluation methods themselves. I began to hear questions like, 'How far can we push our interpretation without violating the data?' or 'I think we're getting better agreement about what people meant by talking this through', (an issue of reliability in my world) or 'I wonder how we should write the report so that our colleagues will use it? How much detail do they need?' As I listened, I was becoming even more curious about the impact that the participation process was having on the participants. Here was a second group of talented educators willing to do the work and feeling very much invested in the process and responsible for its use. It seemed like a question worth pursuing.

Evaluating the Evaluation

Method

Since the CRDI Committee was interested in investigating the use of the report, we decided to circulate a simple questionnaire to the curriculum management teams (CMTs) of all of the elementary schools so as to gather information, *albeit* limited, about involvement in the process, opinions about the process and utilization of the research report and the executive summary and recommendations. I took advantage of this follow-up process to gather some information about the relationship of participation to utilization. A questionnaire with forced-choice and open-ended questions was sent to each school. With the school as the unit of analysis participation ranging from low to high was categorized as either 'Our team was interviewed'; 'Someone on our team served as an interviewer'; or 'Someone on our team was a member of the focused interview committee and participated in writing the report.' The use of the data was assessed in four questions: 'How did your team feel about the interview process?' 'Has the CMT or any members of it, spent time reviewing the reports?' 'Have you used any of the information from the reports in planning this year?' and 'How likely are you to use these documents in your future planning?' The questionnaire also allowed the respondents to indicate the overall impact that they thought the focused interview process and the reports have had or will have on the planning in the school. This questionnaire was distributed to the principal of each school in the fall of 1992, after most schools had completed their planning for the school year.

Results

Response rate Ninety-three schools responded to the survey for a response rate of 66 per cent. Although the responding schools were representative of the district in some respects, the observed response rate raises some concern that the non-respondents could represent different opinions or behaviors than those expressed by the respondents. In almost all of the schools, the team had been interviewed (three schools were newly opened and had not existed when the interviews were conducted). In sixteen of the schools (17 per cent of the total), at least one person had served as an interviewer. Since thirteen of the interviewers were centrally assigned staff, it is possible that as many as twenty-two of the interviewers were either in schools that did not respond or that their new assignments put them in schools with other interviewers. All six of the schools with school-based committee members responded to the survey.

Feelings about the interviews 94 per cent of the schools indicated positive or very positive feelings about the interview process. This opinion was expressed by virtually all (99 per cent) of those who had participated in the process as interviewers or core team members. Over half of the schools (54 per cent) made open-ended comments to this question. Most of the comments were positive, although some indicated a neutral response and two schools said it was not particularly useful. The most frequent kinds of comments were that it:

- provided an opportunity to confirm and validate accomplishments (thirteen schools);
- provided an opportunity to discuss and reflect (eleven schools);
- gave direction and focus to the process (seven schools);
- provided positive feelings and encouragement (six schools); and
- provided an opportunity to share (four schools).

Several actual quotations are quite informative in understanding the value of the interview to school teams. For example, one respondent indicated that 'this was a great chance to review and reiterate our school plans', while another remarked 'we could blow our own horn'.

Utilization of the reports The reports (full report and executive summary) had been reviewed by 80 per cent of the schools.[1] Overall, 46 per cent of the school teams indicated that they had used the information from the report for planning for the 1992–93 school year and 86 per cent said they may or are likely to use the documents in future planning. School teams with interviewers or core team members were only slightly more likely (no statistical difference) to respond affirmatively to these questions (54 per cent and 96 per cent, respectively). The most frequent kinds of written comments following these questions were:

- we got hints, suggestions and ideas to help our planning (six schools);
- the reports increased collaboration and communication (four schools);
- it helped us plan staff development (four schools); and
- the reports gave us structure and focus (three schools).

Again, some actual quotations are revealing: 'the data [were] sometimes astounding and made us double check our plans in relation to other schools'; '[they] stressed the importance of planning for effective change'; and '[they were] particularly helpful in recognizing the areas we have worked well in and also pointing out to us the components we needed to work on'.

As was noted above, the respondents were also asked to describe their perception of the impact of the focused interview and the reports on their planning: 74 per cent responded. The respondents from schools who were interviewed but did not have anyone serving as an interviewer or planning team member generally expressed that the impact was positive (78 per cent). There were a number of comments from this group, however, that indicated that there would be no impact (12 per cent) and some made neutral comments (10 per cent). *All* of the schools that had interviewers or team members said that the impact was positive. The most frequent kinds of comments were that it:

- consolidated ideas, reaffirmed achievements (sixteen schools);
- sharpened the focus of improvement efforts (twelve schools);
- provided direction, suggestions, information and insight (nine schools);
- made the team aware of need to articulate and structure plans (nine schools);
- influenced future planning (nine schools);

- provided positive feedback (eight schools);
- provided a way of evaluating our progress (seven schools); and
- provided an opportunity to share (seven schools).

The flavor of the responses from the teams about overall impact is captured by the following quotes: 'increased involvement of all teachers has led to a greater focus on how our students will benefit from our project'; 'in the future, we will conduct focused interviews ourselves in the school'; 'at first I thought the process consumed too much time but after talking to the team it became evident that the time was essential for us to plan cooperatively and effectively'; 'allowed us to reflect as a group on what was done and where we are going and gives you [central office] a global picture'; and 'the interviews brought our team together [and] helped us look at what we were doing in the school and helped us do less and do it better'. One interviewer wrote:

> as an interviewer at six other schools, I found the process very beneficial in providing leadership at home. This should be considered as routine professional development for principals.

Discussion and Implications

The major focus of this paper is the role of participatory evaluation methods in enhancing engagement and use of the results of evaluation studies. In my role as internal evaluator, I have endeavored to explore the issue through active engagement in the process, always with an eye to investigating and understanding the internal dynamics of the decision-making process and to exploring questions that we have raised elsewhere about participatory evaluation (Cousins and Earl, 1992). In this instance, I was looking in particular at the questions of utilization of evaluation results and the effect of in-depth participation on both the participants and their use of the data. Taken together, these two evaluation studies really constitute a single case example, utilizing a similar approach with different groups on different occasions. The particular model included three levels of participation: school teams that were interviewed; school administrators who also acted as interviewers in other schools; and administrators who served on the core committee and participated in analyzing the data and writing the report. Overall, the results lend credence to the power of participation in the process as a contributor to influence on participants and their use of the information.

Participatory Evaluation and Utilization

One powerful possibility in internal evaluations is that utilization can be larger than responding to the results of the evaluation report. The process itself can be an important contributor to 'organizational learning'. It is important not to overlook the full range of possible forms of utilization. The follow-up survey with elementary school teams showed that the process of interviewing school teams, summarizing results and reporting those results was an effective strategy. There was strong consensus that, not only was participation in the interview a positive experience, but there has also been and will continue to be widespread use of the reports. These results confirmed my informal feedback (through letters, phone calls and incidental conversations) that, long before the reports were available, the focused interview process had an impact on the participants.

The process generated considerable initial anxiety and concern. The response directly following the interview process suggested something more like a catharsis. Generally, the team members that I talked to were excited and impressed by the system's interest in them and by the importance that was being attached to their opinions. I had begun to think of it as the 'somebody finally asked me' syndrome. But it was not just a self-aggrandizing exercise. The process allowed the school-based improvement teams to galvanize their own plans and to engage in the kind of collaborative discussion that allowed them to reflect on their practice and challenge their beliefs and their actions. This process occurred during the interview and it continued when the reports were released. The open-ended responses from the survey suggest that the reports provided the same reflective opportunity drawing on a broader range of alternatives that may not have occurred to the team before.

Effects of In-depth Participation

This study included two relatively deep levels of participation. Some people served as interviewers and a few played major roles as part of a core 'evaluation team'. The results from the follow-up survey give some support to the belief that in-depth participation may enhance the use of the evaluation results. Although the present results were only slightly more favorable for teams with in-depth participants than for teams without in-depth participants, the qualitative information in the comments provided additional insights. It is also important to note that the survey was addressing the use by the school team in planning, not the impact of participation on the individuals involved. Once again, the comments were consistent with data that I received in less formal ways. During the interview process, the interviewers expressed interest and dismay about how we would be able to summarize such a massive amount of data into anything that would be useful. When the reports were in draft form, these people insisted on an opportunity to meet and discuss the analysis procedures, to consider the reports before they were released and to offer suggestions about changes to the reports and about dissemination. Several interviewers have asked for additional information about interviewing and about creating interview questions that are unbiased and really get at the issues they want to investigate. The research unit regularly receives draft copies of questions from members of this group to consider and offer suggestions for improvement and many of these participants have made interviews with staff (and even students and parents) a routine part of their annual planning cycle.

Perhaps the most interesting groups were the core teams. Although they did not stand out in the follow-up interview, two of the seven who were in schools at the time of the survey were in newly constructed schools and had not yet established the culture or organizational structures to benefit from the evaluation. Once again, utilization has to be seen in a broader context. In both the secondary and the elementary core teams, the level of commitment and of involvement was very high. They were highly motivated to participate and, when the demands of the project began to interfere with their 'real' jobs, they chose to meet after hours. As I mentioned earlier, when the reports were released, the core team members became the key disseminators. Throughout the analysis and report writing process, they continually expressed their enthusiasm and excitement about the things they were learning and speculated about the ways in which they might use their new skills. Several of them (from the secondary team) have subsequently carried out their own formative evaluation of a school-based staff development project, using focused interviews. The report from this study was released as an official

> *Evaluation has become an important part of the district culture with educators at all levels saying things like:*
>
> > *We can't carry on with this discussion until we know what is in the literature and have an idea how we're going to evaluate what we do. The Research team has to be part of the planning. (district administrator)*
> >
> > *I am going to interview key stakeholders in the district before I take over the job to find out what they expect and how they will judge my success. (new chief education officer)*
> >
> > *We need to know what our students think about coming to this school before they come and then check the same thing afterwards. (secondary school vice-principal)*
> >
> > *If we're going to implement an expensive program like this, we have to know that it makes a difference. (district administrator)*

report of the research department, even though our only involvement was as technical consultants to the project. Another member of a core team (elementary) has established a research group within her school and has applied for a small research grant to conduct a school-based research/evaluation project.

New Questions

These formative evaluations of school improvement have offered support for participatory evaluation approaches as a way of increasing utilization and of enhancing 'organizational learning', through the learning and the influence of the participants. They also leave some questions unanswered and raise some new ones. I am curious about the schools who did not respond to the follow-up survey. Did they have a very different view of the process and the results? Were their opinions similar but they were too busy to respond or were they negatively affected and unwilling to share their opinions? Perhaps the whole thing was irrelevant to them? It would be useful to have data from these schools, especially those that have administrators who served as interviewers, to help us better understand the total picture of the impact of the evaluation process. Without this further knowledge, it is difficult to examine the full range of effects of evaluating school improvement initiatives using participatory evaluation methods.

The differences between the two studies has raised a new set of questions for me. Although both studies appear to have resulted in the use of new knowledge, my sense has been that the elementary process was not as successful as the secondary one in engaging the educators in action. There may be a number of reasons for this difference: perhaps the reports arrived too late to be seen as useful; perhaps the absence of a central office administrator on the core team (therefore, no key decision maker) made it less likely that schools would view the reports as important; perhaps there are differences in the way elementary and secondary schools operate that contribute to differential use. This seems to me to be a worthwhile area for further study.

Final Thoughts

It seems quite clear that participatory evaluation methods can produce considerable 'organizational learning' by engaging a large number of key players in the evaluation process. This can be particularly valuable when 'what is being evaluated' is itself a process that requires educators to engage in an inquiry process and reflect on their own behaviors. In many ways, the focused interview process itself served a valuable purpose in highlighting the importance that the district placed on the school improvement process and legitimizing the involvement in systematic analysis and reflection about their initiatives. The reports that followed allowed for another round of discussions, gave a broader base of information for planning and gave clear direction for action in the form of recommendations.

Whatever else has occurred as a result of these participatory formative evaluations of school improvement, focused interviewing has become a system pastime. It is sometimes difficult to convince committee members that it is not always necessary and certainly not efficient to use interviews for data collection. Even the newly appointed Chief Education Officer (CEO) engaged the assistance of the research department and conducted his own focused interviews with a broad-based sample of key stakeholders as a basis for his 'entry plan'.

If, as we maintain in chapter 1, knowledge is socially constructed and organizations can develop through developing shared 'mental maps', the studies examined here offer further evidence that participatory evaluation can be a powerful vehicle for

---

The research staff have become critical players in almost all of the key district initiatives with an evaluation role to play in strategic planning, restructuring schools, accountability, and staff development. This makes us very busy people. We are finding that this focus reinforces a number of in-house needs. First, we have to remain current in our own field so that we have a number of methods and approaches at our disposal as we work with educators to define the problems. One researcher commented recently:

> *I don't know if I'll ever feel confident that I'm making the best suggestions for the evaluation when I'm thinking on the fly, but I guess I have to trust that it will continue to develop and I can bring more ideas later. That's a lot different than sitting in my office planning the whole thing from start to finish.*

It is also fascinating to see the increasing respect that the researchers and educators have for one another. The research staff routinely note that they feel more like the professionals that they are and less like glorified gophers, and they have a much increased tolerance for the realities of school and classroom life. As people share the problems of doing a useful evaluation, both worlds become more clear. Although this is often positive, it also points out the differences in priorities. Some researchers experience considerable discomfort with the ambiguity and free-wheeling styles of some educators. They also hate to give up control of what has been, traditionally, their turf. There are many skills to learn to be partners not consulting 'experts'.

---

creating new methods for acquiring information as well as providing a forum for sharing the information that exists within the district. However, participatory evaluation is a time-consuming, and sometimes expensive, proposition. It is critical that we examine conditions under which participatory evaluation is likely to pay off.

With a school district as large as Scarborough, it is often difficult to create ways to distribute knowledge beyond a few players. In as many studies as possible, particularly any that allow for discussion and reflection on important educational issues, I am leaning toward a 'system partners' approach to evaluation, and extending participation, in varying degrees, to a wide variety of groups (e.g., parents, teachers, administrators and curriculum staff). An important component of these participatory evaluations will be 'evaluating the evaluation' to enhance our understanding of the complexities and the dynamics of knowledge use under different conditions.

Note

1 It was reviewed by 81 per cent of the schools that contained interviewers but only 71 per cent of those with core team members because two of these members were in new schools and, at the time of the present survey, were just beginning their usual spring planning activities. These groups did not differ from one another in their views about report usage.

References

COOLEY, W. and BICKEL, W. (1986) *Decision-oriented Educational Research*, Boston, Kluwer-Nijhoff Publishing.

COUSINS, J.B. and EARL, L. (1992) 'The case for participatory evaluation', *Educational Evaluation and Policy Analysis*, **14**, 4, pp. 397–418.

LOVE, A. (1991) *Internal Evaluation: Building Organizations From Within*, Newbury Park, CA, Sage Publications.

Chapter 3

A Participatory Approach to District-level Program Evaluation: The Dynamics of Internal Evaluation

Clay Lafleur

Background and Introduction

For the past several years I have been the sole educational researcher for a medium-sized school district in one of the largest counties in Ontario, Canada, containing approximately 4,800 square kilometres of territory. The school district currently has approximately 48,000 students and 3,100 teaching staff in eighty-two elementary and fifteen secondary schools. The 1992 expenditure budget was $290,300,000 Cdn.

During the 1980s a major program focus for all school systems in Ontario was the implementation of provincial curriculum guidelines. The ensuing evaluation, development and implementation cycle (Leithwood, 1987) resulted in a more visible role for program evaluation. Consequently, we developed a model for conducting program evaluation to guide internal evaluation activities in this school district (Lafleur, 1990).

Evaluation comprises an accountability component and a formative component which inform decision making. One purpose of the program evaluation model is to engage primary users in as many phases of the evaluation process as possible. For example, all internal evaluations rely on an evaluation team that involves team members in the 'nuts and bolts' of the problem formulation, instrument design or selection, data collection, analysis, interpretation, and reporting. Members of this team typically include senior administrators, program support staff, school administrators, teachers, and the school district researcher. In addition, a range of staff members or people are often involved in specific working groups related to the evaluation process, such as data collection, analysis and interpretation of the findings.

Participants who are members of the evaluation team or of the various evaluation working committees include staff who actually use the findings of the program evaluation to improve implementation. Such 'primary users' may, for example, make decisions related to the implementation of the program at a system level or may make daily decisions related to the achievement of student outcomes at the classroom level. In other words, primary users are defined as those who are in a position to use the findings of the program evaluation to make decisions about the implementation of the program.

The current focus on educational change (Fullan with Steiglebauer, 1991), school improvement (Stoll and Fink, 1992), and restructuring (Murphy, 1991), as well as the continuing public concern for accountability, ensures a continued role for program evaluation in this school district. In the current economic climate, it is increasingly obvious that high expectations of the education system by the public will continue, in a context of very limited resources. Internal evaluation, such as that described by Love (1991) and Mayne (1992), emphasizes working within the organizational context, but also highlights the organization's responsibility. Consequently, the present study provides data that permits critical reflection on existing program evaluation strategies used in this school district.

This research study acknowledges the work of Alkin (1991), who spoke of the importance of identifying primary users and then engaging them in the evaluation enterprise. Work by Cousins and Leithwood (1986), Greene (1988), Weiss (1988) and Huberman (1990) was particularly helpful in highlighting the potential value of involving primary users in the evaluation process. The substantial evaluation of the literature that was recently completed by Cousins and Earl (1992), however, provided a cogent and extremely useful overview of participatory evaluation that caused the present author to reflect upon past program evaluations. In fact, the design of the research study reported here uses many of the ideas developed by Cousins and Earl and deliberately operationalizes a number of their key concepts.

The emphasis given by Cousins and Earl to organizational learning seems to make a great deal of sense in the current context of educational change and restructuring. Bolman and Deal (1991) and Schein (1991), for example, have provided extensive documentation that helps us examine and consider some of the issues related to organizational cultures. It seems reasonable, for example, to conclude that the way organizations do business influences the form and impact of program evaluation.

The power relations and existing structures of the organization are the practical, everyday realities that may or may not match its stated beliefs and values. It may be critical, as Shavelson (1988) suggests, to try and understand the mind-frames of policymakers, and practitioners. By understanding better the perceptions and demands on policymakers, the likelihood of improving evaluation and the utilization of findings may be increased.

Greene (1992) also focuses on the relation between participatory evaluation and the organization. She suggests, however, that 'the more difficult challenge . . . is just how a collaborative inquiry process can catalyze and develop the structural capacity to act' (p. 7). Weiss' views (1988) that evaluation is a political act and that decision making is not always a rational enterprise also challenge evaluators to critically consider how they can best assist individuals in participating more wisely.

A case study by Pugh (1990) illustrates the difficulties of evaluation utilization. Despite quality work, Pugh believes that '. . . significant findings and/or policy implications are not acted upon due to the combination of economic considerations, political realities and public relations impact'.

Cousins and Earl (1992) have provided an excellent synthesis of the literature on participatory evaluation and evaluation utilization. Their work occurs at a critical time in the evolution of the evaluation enterprise. It acknowledges the increasing democratization of evaluation by respecting the roles and responsibility of the individual and the organization. In addition, evaluation is growing up in an environment that is more tolerant, accepting and even demanding of methodological diversity. As we deal with new and emerging educational paradigms, the challenges to the evaluation enterprise will continue.

Methods

The present research study was designed as a retrospective examination of this school district's approach to program evaluation. In particular, the study set out to examine the relation between the participatory nature of the evaluation process and the utilization of the findings. It was also designed to provide information about how well the current model for internal program evaluation is being implemented in a medium-sized school district where the author is the sole person employed in a research capacity. In addition, information was required about the strengths and weaknesses of current evaluation practices and needed changes.

This research study collected data on the perspectives of primary users who were involved in a number of internal evaluations that were completed over the past several years. The actual research activities, including the development of instruments, the administration and collection of data, the analysis of data, the interpretation of findings, and the writing of the report were coordinated and undertaken by the author.

In order to obtain the most reliable and valid information related to the impact of the participatory evaluation approach, complementary research approaches were used in this study. Initially, data was obtained from written correspondence initiated by the author with several primary users who had participated in previous school district evaluations. One person – either the chairperson or an individual who had played an active role in past program evaluations – was identified for each evaluation team from each of eight program evaluation projects. Seven of the eight persons wrote back, reflecting on the pros and cons of the evaluation process. Questionnaires were then used to collect further information from a wider range of primary users. A stratified sample, comprising one third of all primary users involved in previous school district program evaluation teams, was obtained in this second phase of the study. These individuals responded to a set of predetermined questions based on previous research in this area, particularly the recent work of Cousins and Earl (1992). Finally, a group discussion was undertaken with the cadre of primary users who had participated in the initial written correspondence. The intent here was to have participants publicly reflect upon the strengths and weaknesses of the program evaluation process, and discuss a number of issues related to their involvement and the subsequent merit and worth of the evaluation approach used in the school district. The remaining part of this method section describes the techniques associated with each of the different approaches that were used in the study.

Method One: Written Correspondence

The intent of the written correspondence was to gather initial information and, at the same time, involve a small cadre of individuals in the present retrospective research study. This method was chosen as an unobtrusive and manageable way of encouraging a small, select group of individuals to reflect on their involvement in previous program evaluations and to reconstruct significant features of their participation.

Although the eight persons initially approached agreed to participate, other commitments precluded one person from participating in the written correspondence phase of the study; consequently, the author corresponded with seven individuals. Four of these people had been chairpersons of program evaluation teams: one was a principal, two were vice-principals and one was a department head. Of the remaining three persons, two were school district curriculum specialists and one was a department head. In two instances, one written exchange occurred. In each of the remaining five cases, two or three letters passed back and forth. Following a period of about six weeks, the written correspondence phase of the study was concluded. Replies were then analyzed for emerging themes and issues.

Method Two: Questionnaires

The use of questionnaires is one way of collecting data from a large number of individuals in a relatively short time span. In this research study, a questionnaire was used to focus on the perceptions of a selected group of primary users who had been involved in previous program evaluations.

The exploratory nature of this study, and the time and resource restrictions, precluded the involvement of all primary users who had participated in past evaluations. Consequently, it was decided to use a stratified sample of primary users who had participated in evaluation teams only. Every third person on a master list of all individuals who had been members of internal evaluation teams during the past several years (including those who participated in the written correspondence phase of this study) was asked to complete a questionnaire. The group was selected to represent nine internal evaluations that had been completed in the school district within the last eight years. The focuses of these evaluations were: technical education; behavior; grade 4–6 mathematics; French as a second language; special education identification and placement; guidance (student) services; library services; grade 7–10 mathematics; and grade 7–10 history and contemporary studies.

The questionnaire items explored the participatory approach to evaluation and the utilization of the findings. Some of the issues that emerged during the written correspondence phase of the present study were incorporated into the questionnaire. Following Cousins and Earl (1992), a series of questions dealt with the quality of the evaluation and factors affecting utilization. In addition, some questions contained a number of Likert items about the views of primary users on the participatory evaluation process, their involvement in the evaluation activities, and the organizational culture of the school district relative to evaluation.

The questionnaire was developed, and returned responses were analyzed by the school district researcher. Twenty-eight individuals were given questionnaires to complete. Twenty-four responses were received and included in subsequent analyses. Descriptive statistics and comments were compiled for all questions. In addition, correlations were undertaken to examine the relations among some of the variables.

Method Three: Group Discussion

Within two weeks of the questionnaires being distributed, the eight persons who had been asked to participate in the written correspondence were invited to participate in a group discussion. All eight individuals agreed to be involved and spent approximately 90 minutes sharing their ideas about the value and effect of internal program evaluation. Field notes were taken and summaries made of key ideas and suggestions.

Findings

The findings are presented under three headings, each corresponding to the approaches described in the method section. It should be stressed that these results represent the outcomes of a study undertaken within a limited time frame and with limited resources. The study was designed to be a retrospective examination of an internal program evaluation model (Love, 1991) and its limitations must be acknowledged when examining the findings.

Findings One: Written Correspondence

The written correspondence provided a unique opportunity for several primary users to reflect upon their involvement in previous evaluations. For a few, this meant revisiting activities that took place up to eight years ago. Others were able to base their comments on either recently completed or current evaluation activities.

All participants identified their experiences as positive and worthwhile. All indicated that they had learned more about the inquiry process and the program in question. On the other hand, most were guarded in their assessment of the actual impact of the evaluations, indicating limited success in the development and implementation of the resulting action plans.

The positive role of the school district researcher was mentioned in most of the written comments. The researcher's ability to connect with members of the evaluation team, to establish a close working relationship, and to bring a degree of credibility to the study are highlighted in the following comments:

> Since the beginning, the researcher has been closely connected to program personnel. Initially, this occurred formally when the researcher had coordinating responsibilities for some subject areas. . . . Also, the researcher met regularly with other program department members. . . . As such, research has never been outside the program. Rather, it has been integral to it. For example, the Document Implementation Plan which guides our system has program evaluation as part of the process. . . .

> An evaluation steering committee was struck to oversee this project. Although the researcher did not chair the committee, the membership looked to him for leadership and direction. . . . Throughout the project the researcher laid out the blueprint . . . leading us through the process. . . . In summary, the term 'collaborative effort' might be used to describe the relationship.

> One of the major strengths was the gathering of a variety of data in diverse ways. The information diversity gave the impression (an accurate one) that this was a very thorough evaluation covering a wide range of areas and leading to a workable action plan. The mix of people on the committee . . . and the fact that the committee was chaired by a secondary school principal, gave a high degree of credibility to the group and led to strong feelings of team membership. The fact that we also had a high degree of credibility at the provincial level was a positive factor for everyone involved.

Team building was reflected in several written exchanges. Members of the evaluation team learned to work cooperatively and cohesively together, throughout the evaluation.

> As we continued into the next phase of our task it seemed to me that we were working cohesively. . . . We would bring to each committee meeting our ideas and share them with the group. Ideas were accepted, challenged or modified in a very open manner . . . using consensus the group would agree, approve, revise. . . .

Ownership of the evaluation study also seemed to emerge as the evaluation process evolved.

> As a committee we were very proud of the work we had done, the interest we had generated and the suggested courses of action that we had developed. Perhaps I should start by indicating that I am a very strong believer in providing the opportunity for teachers to accommodate their 'ownership' of the particular issue at hand. Only by having their input and a sense that they are part of the decision will change occur. I believe that I, along with other evaluation team members, was given the opportunity and latitude to effect a constructive and meaningful evaluation.

It became clear that primary users were not generally familiar with the intricacies and politics of the program evaluation process. The following quotations illustrate the possible culture clash that may have existed for some:

> I think that our problem is that evaluations are foreign to us. Teaching has largely been a very private endeavor between teacher and student. There has been little monitoring, supervision and dialogue even within the same school.

> In both evaluations, for different reasons, the system did not take much action to put in specific items from the evaluation. The two evaluations were started for purposes that did not fit the realities of political commitment. Generally speaking, the evaluations had a fairly large agenda to 'sharpen up' some aspects of the system. Additional, but minor, agenda items were to gather information and to give future direction. . . .

The role and impact of the senior administration permeates all of the written replies. From the initial task of formulating evaluation questions to the utilization of the findings, the power and influence of senior administrators is evident. Although senior administrators supported programe valuation in principle, their need to control these evaluations was problematic for primary users.

> Much of the time in the beginning stages was spent formulating the criteria/ questions for the evaluation. . . . After each meeting our work would be scrutinized by the superintendent of program. Areas that were deemed by him as not applicable to the evaluation were dropped. Other than that the evaluation team set its own goals for the evaluation.

> [What happened next] was to be our biggest disappointment of the whole process. . . . Delay after delay ensued. . . . No indication as to where our report would go was given to us. . . . Letters by various members of the committee

inquiring into the status of the evaluation or release of the evaluation to the system were not answered.

When I think about the action plan developed after the evaluation and the changes that have been made because of it, I'm a little disappointed . . . many óf the suggested courses of action have not been followed.

I also detect signals . . . that the action plan was laid on from 'above' and that this plan criticized [teachers'] credibility and therefore they tended to be on the defensive. . . . Having said this, slowly but surely change is occurring as a direct result of the evaluation.

Involvement heightened the overall awareness of primary users of the many complexities of doing an evaluation. As well as enhancing understanding, the process was also empowering, and led to the establishment of significant (and enduring) personal and professional friendships.

I learned a lot about the following: the system process and hierarchy, capturing and analyzing valid data, the structure of an evaluation, the structure of the program department and the involvement of system representatives in the evaluation. Some of the very positive things that came out of the evaluation . . . were never publicized or brought forward in any way. That [particular] information was a very pleasant surprise for many of us working on the evaluation team and the kind of information that needed to be conveyed to the system.

. . . the first thing that comes to mind is the connection I was able to make with [certain evaluation team members].

I learned a lot about the evaluation process and I met and befriended some wonderful people, especially the evaluation committee members. . . . My involvement was influential with other principals because principals tend to accept requests associated with other principals. Also, the influence and involvement of principals and teachers in the training workshop for collecting observational data was invaluable.

From the beginning I felt that it was important that there be some 'accountability' to the [implementation] process and therefore I was pleased that the evaluation was an integral part of implementation.

Finally, the next quotation illustrates the changing roles of the school district researcher and a primary user who had already participated in a previous program evaluation. During the second evaluation the researcher adopted a consultative role, while the primary user assumed a more pronounced leadership role. In other words, the researcher blended into the background enabling the primary user to take a more active role, using newly developed confidence and competence relevant to the evaluation enterprise.

Whether or not it was the nature of the [second evaluation] project . . . there was less direct involvement by the researcher. In spite of the more 'arms-length' approach by the researcher this should not be interpreted as a

Table 3.1 Means and standard deviations of program evaluation characteristics and intercorrelations

Characteristic	Mean[1]	SD	Correlations							
			(1)	(2)	(3)	(4)	(5)	(6)	(7)	(8)
(1) Quality	5.79	1.18								
(2) Credibility	6.46	.93	.22							
(3) Relevance	6.08	1.10	.54*	.34						
(4) Communication	4.96	1.78	.39	.36	.53*					
(5) Findings	5.88	.95	.78**	.34	.56*	.44				
(6) Timeliness	5.63	1.25	.03	.25	.40	.42	.08			
(7) Time line	5.29	1.55	.37	.18	.83**	.35	.45	.59*		
(8) Utilization	3.96	1.84	.23	.28	.51*	.63**	.19	.37	.32	

[1] A seven-point Likert scale was used to rate program evaluation characteristics (1–low and 7–high)
* 1–tailed significance $p < .01$
** 1–tailed significance $p < .001$

less valued contribution. The researcher was a valued consultant to the planning committee . . . the relationship between myself and the researcher was different. . . . The difference would be in the roles and responsibilities. . . . I feel that the 'training' I received in the [first evaluation] project allowed me, consciously or otherwise, to rely less heavily on the researcher.

Findings Two: Questionnaires

The purpose of this section is to present the findings from the questionnaire responses. Descriptive statistics and correlation analysis were used to examine the responses to closed-ended items. Key themes and issues were identified from the open-ended comments.

Characteristics of the program evaluations A seven-point Likert scale was used to assess the seven characteristics of the program evaluations (Cousins and Leithwood, 1986). Descriptive characteristics and correlations for these variables appear in table 3.1. Credibility and relevance of the evaluations received the highest overall ratings. The extent to which the findings matched expectations, the overall quality of the evaluations and the timeliness of the findings for decision-making were also rated highly. The nature, amount and quality of communication of the results were given a low rating. In addition to these seven characteristics, the utilization of the program evaluations was assessed and it received the lowest mean rating.

Relevance of the program evaluations significantly correlated with most of the other characteristics of them. Utilization, on the other hand, significantly correlated with two other characteristics: the nature and quality of communication; and the relevance of the study.

Factors influencing utilization Respondents were asked to use a seven-point Likert scale to indicate the level of influence of nineteen items on the utilization of program evaluation findings. Descriptive statistics and correlations appear in table 3.2. The involvement of primary users; the commitment and resolution of program staff and the

Table 3.2   Means and standard deviations for factors deemed to influence utilization and correlations with utilization

Factor	Mean[1]	SD	Correlation with Utilization
(1) *Quality*	5.93	1.67	.58*
(2) *Credibility*	5.69	1.29	.46
	5.82	1.65	.45
(3) *Relevance*	5.23	1.69	.60*
(4) *Communication*	5.14	1.61	.70**
(5) *Findings*	5.38	1.99	.54
(6) *Timeliness*			
Commitment of:			
(7) *The ministry*	3.80	1.24	.43
(8) *The director*	4.05	1.53	.46
(9) *Senior staff*	4.71	1.55	.44
(10) *Program superintendent*	5.67	1.53	.83**
(11) *Program staff*	6.00	1.27	.54
(12) *Principals*	5.14	1.62	−.02
(13) *Teachers*	5.00	1.81	.08
(14) *Parents*	4.10	1.70	−.14
(15) *Students*	4.00	1.82	.08
(16) *Community*	3.95	1.66	.23
(17) *Evaluator*	4.95	1.83	.39
(18) *Primary user involvement*	6.14	.85	.55*
(19) *External factors*	4.81	1.91	.41

[1] A seven-point Likert scale was used to rate program evaluation characteristics (1–low and 7–high)
* 1–tailed significance $p < .01$
** 1–tailed significance $p < .001$

superintendent of program; and the quality, credibility and relevance of the evaluation received the highest overall ratings. In addition, five factors were identified as correlating significantly with the utilization of previous school district evaluations. The two factors having highly significant correlations with utilization were the extent to which the findings agreed with the expectations ($r = .70$) and the commitment and resolution ($r = .83$) of the school district's superintendent of program. Three additional factors that correlated significantly with utilization were the overall quality of the evaluation, the nature and quality of communication, and the involvement of primary users in the evaluation.

Evaluation process   Eighteen statements documented the process used in program evaluations. Table 3.3 presents descriptive statistics and correlations of these variables with utilization and characteristics of the evaluation. Based on responses using a five-point Likert scale, those statements receiving positive ratings were technical assistance provided by the school district's researcher; joint responsibility among evaluation team members; primary users who learned on the job; primary users who were involved in the 'nuts and bolts' of the evaluation; and the partnership between a trained evaluation person and primary users. In addition, primary users were seen to support the evaluation's goals and activities. They also valued the interpretation part of the evaluation process. Lowest ratings indicated that the action plan was not well implemented and that primary users were rarely involved in developing the action plan.[1]

Table 3.3 Means and standard deviations of statements about the evaluation process and correlations with evaluation characteristics

Statement	Mean[1]	SD	Correlations							
			Quality	Credibility	Relevance	Communication	Findings	Timeliness	Time line	Utilization
(1) This evaluation had a positive impact on the system.	3.96	1.25	.00	.49	.38	.59*	.03	.37	.22	.66**
(2) Primary users, that is, practice-based decision makers or those who had responsibility for program implementation, were involved in planning the evaluation.	4.38	1.06	.36	-.28	.24	.31	.51*	-.12	.24	.13
(3) This evaluation featured a partnership between trained evaluation personnel and primary users.	4.71	.69	.63**	.12	.59*	.36	.66**	-.17	.42	.29
(4) Primary users were involved in the 'nuts and bolts' of the problem formulation, instrument design or selection, data collection, analysis, interpretation and reporting.	4.75	.85	.63**	-.12	.52*	.25	.64**	-.18	.41	.23
(5) The board's research officer provided technical support and assistance.	5.00	.00								
(6) Conducting the evaluation was a joint responsibility involving all members of the program evaluation team.	4.83	.82	.72**	-.13	.62**	.36	.68**	-.06	.47	.36
(7) Practitioners who were involved in the evaluation process 'learned on the job' under the guidance of the board's research officer.	4.83	.38	.35	-.02	.17	.11	.44	.05	.40	-.01
(8) Primary users who were involved in the evaluation were supportive of the evaluation's goals and activities.	4.42	.72	.66**	.19	.68**	.32	.71**	.31	.66**	.37

(9) Interpretations resulting from discussion, not facts only, resulted in shared meaning about the value of the evaluation.	4.42	.65	.31	-.01	.49*	.07	.47	.46	.64**	.09
(10) From the very beginning it was clear that this evaluation was going to make an important contribution to the program.	3.96	1.00	.41	.14	.76**	.52*	.53*	.55*	.73**	.53*
(11) External reasons such as budget considerations, contract negotiations and/or other restrictions limited the utilization of the evaluation findings.	3.64	1.18	-.37	-.06	-.03	-.24	-.26	.28	.17	-.32
(12) Primary users were able to use formative findings of the evaluation and affect decisions as an ongoing part of program implementation.	3.64	.95	.25	-.33	.27	.37	.21	.31	.33	.51*
(13) Primary users contributed to the writing of suggested courses of action as part of the evaluation process.	3.92	.97	.58*	.17	.49	.42	.64**	.33	.55*	.44
(14) The development and implementation of a final action plan for the evaluation was determined and controlled by senior staff of the board.	3.96	1.26	-.24	-.22	-.05	-.33	-.22	.16	.17	-.51*
(15) Primary users were involved in developing a final action plan to implement the findings of the evaluation.	3.17	1.40	.21	.22	.27	.56*	.23	.13	.07	.64**
(16) The final action plan dealt with most of the findings of the evaluation.	3.78	1.17	-.10	.37	.06	.49	-.12	.12	-.11	.71**
(17) The evaluation's action plan has been implemented.	3.00	1.27	.09	.19	.57*	.46	.04	.37	.50*	.79**
(18) Primary users were involved in implementing the final action plan.	3.44	1.44	.17	.19	.32	.61*	.11	.15	.16	.80**

1 A five-point Likert scale was used to rate program evaluation characteristics (1-Strongly Disagree to 5-Strongly Agree)
* 1-tailed significance $p < .01$
** 1-tailed significance $p < .001$

Knowing that the evaluation is going to make an important contribution to the program correlated significantly with six characteristics of program evaluations. Similarly, having primary users support the evaluation's goals and activities correlated significantly with four characteristics of program evaluations. Five other statements about the evaluation process were correlated significantly with three characteristics of program evaluations. Several statements correlated significantly with utilization. Most notable was a cluster of four statements with highly significant correlations that related to the development and implementation of the action plan.

Involvement of primary users A five-point Likert scale was used to document responses to thirteen statements relating to the involvement of primary users in the evaluation. Descriptive statistics and correlations with utilization and characteristics of the evaluation appear in table 3.4. The findings indicated that primary users learned a great deal about the 'nuts and bolts' of doing an evaluation, viewed their involvement as a valuable staff development process, and considered the evaluation to be a positive experience. In addition, they learned more about the program, developed a stronger relationship with the internal evaluator as well as at least one other member of the evaluation team, and believed that they made a worthwhile contribution to the evaluation process. On the other hand, respondents reported few subsequent opportunities to use their new-found expertise, and indicated that they had received limited recognition for their efforts.

The thirteen statements about primary user involvement have very few significant correlations with the characteristics of program evaluations. However, four significant correlations did occur with the statement describing membership on the evaluation team as a positive experience. None of the statements about primary user involvement correlated significantly with utilization.

Organizational culture Eleven statements related to the organizational attitude of the school district toward program evaluations were also rated on a five-point Likert scale. Descriptive statistics for the variables and correlations with utilization and characteristics of the evaluation appear in table 3.5. Ratings were consistently lower than those given to items related to the evaluation process and primary users' involvement in the evaluation process. There was, however, general agreement that primary users were given support to participated in the evaluation, that primary users were motivated to participate, and that the evaluation was an integral part of the implementation process. Respondents, however, were less inclined to rate the school district as committed to organizational learning, or inquiry as a way of enhancing learning and empowering staff. Furthermore, most primary users were not fully aware of the scope of the task before they agreed to participate in an evaluation.

The statement describing the school district as committed to organizational learning correlated significantly with five characteristics of program evaluations. Two statements correlated significantly with four characteristics of program evaluations. They were 'evaluations are valued by the system' and 'the system wants to use evaluation information to inform decision making'. Four statements about organizational culture correlated significantly with utilization.

The open-ended questions on the questionnaire were used to clarify further the issues related to participatory program evaluations. Key themes are summarized here.

Pros and cons of using a participatory approach There was overwhelming evidence favoring participation as a valuable professional development. In addition, empowerment, increased understanding, and ownership of the evaluation process, were identified as important outcomes. Respondents believed that it was important to involve those who were ultimately responsible for making changes. The participatory approach was also seen as a way of keeping the evaluation practical and honest.

On the other hand, the participatory approach requires a great deal of time. Also, involvement of primary users does not seem to guarantee utilization. Responses highlighted the need for commitment by senior administration; the process must be valued and used to inform decision making.

Issues related to the utilization of evaluation findings Budgets were identified several times as a limiting factor, especially in a time of limited resources. Several respondents mentioned the need for evaluation to be seen as an integral part of the decision-making process. This includes a commitment to follow through with and implement the action plan. Related to these issues is a commitment to the evaluation process and the resulting action plan by system and school administrators, as well as school staff. Respondents suggested that this commitment is generally lacking in this system. The need for better communication both about the evaluation process and the findings was also stressed.

Factors mentioned most often in the responses included limited budget; lack of commitment of senior staff; commitment of key individuals; commitment of the evaluation team; and lack of system commitment to the action plan process.

Conditions likely to benefit the system and primary users Several respondents mentioned improving the development and implementation procedure associated with the action plan. In addition, more commitment, support, understanding, and involvement of senior staff were seen as important. Several persons indicated that the system must value and use the results of the evaluation studies. There should also be more effort to support the release of primary users from other duties, as well as the involvement of primary users in framing and implementing the action plan.

Value of participatory evaluation Previous evaluations in the school district were generally characterized as highly credible and reliable. In addition, the ratings for findings and evaluation quality and timeliness were relatively high. On the other hand, evaluations were rated lower in terms of communication and time taken to complete the study. Utilization was deemed to be generally low.

There were a number of comments expressing gratitude for the opportunity to be involved and stressing the positive nature of the experience. Comments were very supportive of the evaluation process. There was, however, concern about the lack of, or inappropriateness of, follow-up activities, especially related to the action plan.

Findings Three: Group Discussion

The group discussion involved several primary users in a discussion about the value and impact of participatory evaluations in this school district. Individuals based most of their comments on the specific evaluation and context that they had experienced.

Once again, the value of primary user involvement in program evaluation as professional development and as a collaborative learning experience was emphasized. The sense of competence and empowerment that accrued characterized each evaluation project. Without exception, there was support for the variety of data collection methods and the perceived relevance of the data collected. Primary users welcomed the opportunity to participate in the evaluation process and to collect data that could be used as the basis for action.

Table 3.4 Means and standard deviations for statements about primary user involvement and correlations with evaluation characteristics

Statement	Mean¹	SD	Quality	Credibility	Relevance	Communication	Findings	Timeliness	Time line	Utilization
(1) Being a member of the evaluation team was a positive experience.	4.75	.85	.72**	-.18	.66**	.34	.58*	.08	.58*	.34
(2) I learned a great deal about the 'nuts and bolts' of undertaking a program evaluation.	4.83	.48	.59*	-.11	.05	.09	.25	.04	.14	-.01
(3) I learned more about the program as a result of my involvement in the evaluation process.	4.63	.88	.23	-.09	-.25	-.10	.01	.04	-.09	-.16
(4) Participating in the program evaluation was a valuable staff development process.	4.79	.51	.19	-.22	-.21	-.07	.05	-.11	-.04	-.27
(5) The evaluation process helped me better understand the way decisions are made in this board.	3.75	1.42	-.08	.29	.14	.19	-.14	.32	.19	.19
(6) I believe that I made a worthwhile contribution to the program evaluation process.	4.46	.66	.37	-.08	.43	.15	.47	.18	.59*	-.02
(7) As a result of participating in the evaluation I have a stronger relationship with the board's research officer.	4.58	.65	.28	.16	.14	.17	.14	.15	.31	-.02

(8) As a result of participating in the evaluation I have a stronger relationship with at least one other member of the evaluation team.	4.54	.66	.03	−.07	−.09	−.32	−.19	−.06	−.07	−.37
(9) In general I think that my involvement in the evaluation was unnecessary and a waste of time.	1.17	.38	−.40	.09	−.29	−.13	−.23	−.10	−.25	−.14
(10) I felt part of the decision-making process during all phases of the evaluation.	4.25	.99	.49	−.01	.47	.25	.48	.07	.48	.29
(11) As a result of my participation in the evaluation I have been able to play a leadership role in and facilitate other similar projects in the board.	3.30	1.30	.20	.09	−.15	.11	.22	−.11	−.18	−.13
(12) Participating in the program evaluation was an empowering experience for me.	4.00	1.22	.47	−.14	.07	.13	.44	−.01	.15	−.02
(13) My involvement in the evaluation resulted in positive recognition and acknowledgements.	3.67	1.24	.23	−.20	.31	.05	.17	.26	.45	.04

¹ A five-point Likert scale was used to rate program evaluation characteristics (1–Strongly Disagree to 5–Strongly Agree)
* 1–tailed significance $p < .01$
** 1–tailed significance $p < .001$

Table 3.5 Means and standard deviations for statements about organizational culture and correlations with evaluation characteristics

Statement	Mean[1]	SD	Correlations							
			Quality	Credibility	Relevance	Communication	Findings	Timeliness	Time line	Utilization
(1) Evaluations are valued by the system.	3.50	1.06	.32	.21	.58*	.61*	.15	.37	.59*	.61*
(2) The system wants to use evaluation information to inform decision making.	3.42	1.28	.18	.36	.54*	.67**	.19	.48	.50*	.65**
(3) The system provides adequate time and resources to do program evaluations.	3.33	1.13	.39	-.07	.03	.04	.32	-.10	.14	-.29
(4) The system supports inquiry as a way of enhancing learning and empowering participants.	3.54	1.06	.33	.24	.58*	.45	.26	.35	.62*	.34
(5) Primary users are given sufficient support to participate meaningfully in program evaluations.	4.17	.87	.66**	-.05	.40	.09	.65**	.20	.47	.04
(6) The system is committed to organizational learning as a route to improvement.	3.58	.97	.62*	.09	.71**	.59*	.42	.43	.71**	.62*

(7) The system encourages primary users to collaborate about program evaluation issues and findings.	3.42	1.06	.22	.11	.54*	.60*	.10	.47	.62*	.48
(8) The experience and skills of those who have participated in program evaluations are used in subsequent projects.	3.44	.79	.26	.28	.25	.13	.08	−.15	.07	.47
(9) Primary users who participate in program evaluations are motivated to do so.	3.75	.85	.42	−.04	.37	.20	.48	.26	.47	.17
(10) Primary users who participate in program evaluations are fully cognizant of the scope of the task before agreeing to participate.	2.83	1.31	.34	.33	.53*	.45	.32	.49	.62*	.27
(11) Evaluations are viewed as an integral part of the program implementation process.	3.75	1.15	.33	.38	.47	.50*	.15	.21	.40	.50*

[1] A five-point Likert scale was used to rate program evaluation characteristics (1–Strongly Disagree to 5–Strongly Agree)

* 1–tailed significance $p < .01$

** 1–tailed significance $p < .001$

A few comments from the group discussion demonstrate how the involvement of some primary users in the program evaluation process contributed to individual professionalism.

> Before I became involved in any evaluation I had a very crude understanding of what was involved. If I were to have tried to do one it would have been full of holes – in terms of methodology and the way to negotiate the evaluation questions. I knew very little about designing evaluations, choosing the best ways to get data, and asking questions on a survey. Not that I now have a sophisticated level of expertise, but I at least know what the components of a sound evaluation should look like. Professionally, I'm more competent and more critical of evaluations. If people are doing surveys or interviews or using other methods to gather data, I now have the ability to apply a critical eye.

> When I had to develop a questionnaire for the grade 9 and 10 health program – and I'm not sure how much I consulted with [the researcher] – but I felt very confident in doing it because of the things I had learned and experienced in previous evaluations. I sort of knew what had to be done so that the data that I would get back would be meaningful. And in a way that included both quantitative and qualitative data. Data that could be analyzed meaningfully. I wasn't just going to end up with a bag full of stuff that I couldn't make any sense out of. And I reflected on that afterwards and when I had to develop this health study and a questionnaire I knew I could do it. And that was a result of working with [the researcher] and being part of evaluations for a number of years.

> Our guidance evaluation, and my participation in it, provided me with an opportunity to present results at a provincial level and to be regarded as one of the leaders in the field. This would not have happened without the evaluation and my involvement. I feel recognized as well as more informed about guidance and evaluation issues.

> I think people who go through the process come away richer. They gain useful skills that they can apply.

On the other hand, concerns were expressed about a number of issues related to the evaluation and, in particular, the development and implementation of the resulting action plan. Sample comments about the action plan are:

> It all comes down in the end to the action plan. I don't really know what level of commitment there is to it. Sometimes I think it's like playing a game. Finishing the game even though your heart isn't in it. I don't know if that's the case, but that's my sense of what tends to happen.

> I guess it comes back to the beginning of an evaluation. And you have said this so many times. Don't start unless you're prepared to follow through. There has to be as much emphasis on the results and doing something as there is on the evaluation itself. So many times – and it's like implementation – all of our energy is given to getting started and we don't devote enough energy

to the actual implementation. Evaluations often run out of energy, money, time or commitment to the original goals. Maybe that's because everything takes so long and, with so many changes going on, we've usually started several other things.

There was general agreement that evaluations tend to take on a life of their own. With limited resources, there was a feeling that evaluations took too much time and required labor-intensive involvement. This was especially true compared to the seemingly limited time, resources, and energy devoted to implementing follow-up activities from the action plans. Some illustrative comments from the group discussion follow:

The evaluations take too long. We've got to find ways to streamline the process without diminishing the value of the evaluations. To gather, analyze and turn the data around before it becomes archival material.

I agree. We need to do things smarter and in a less complicated manner. We must do just as good a job, or even better, with fewer resources, in much less time.

Maybe we're too global in our evaluations. We try to do too much, rather than really focus on the most critical aspects of the program. What we tend to do, and it's the nature of the beast, when you have that window of opportunity, you know when it's your turn in the system's way of doing things, there's a temptation to want to do it all. And, as a result, it slows the process down and you may not do anything well.

My experience indicated that evaluations need to be kept very simple, with absolutely clear parameters, and an expectation of turning the evaluation around very quickly.

There was some uncertainty and confusion as to whether the system really valued the evaluation process, especially when the findings indicated significant (as determined by the evaluation team) areas that required improvement.

In my opinion, the system both valued, as a symbol of concern and desired success, our evaluation and did not value it because the recommendations and action plan were not fully implemented . . .

We talk the talk. We talk about the importance of evaluations, but, because we don't always act on the evaluation findings, we often go through the process and there's limited pay off.

Furthermore, evaluation utilization was seen to be easily influenced by changing political and economic circumstances, beyond the control of staff within the system. It appeared that policymakers were consistently overwhelmed by other matters and repeatedly delayed an action plan or proceeded very cautiously, if at all, with it. The following comment provides a glimpse of the external factors such as budget and contract restrictions that can impede the utilization of an evaluations findings:

A noteworthy insight for me happened near the end of the library evaluation. In effect, it was during the development of the action plan and the attempt to bring it forward that I realized that we had made an error in the original formation of the evaluation by trying to incorporate so many different aspects such as materials, plant, program, and personnel. A major reason for not being able to fully implement the library evaluation was a problem with senior administration dealing with the economic and contract implications. They were in a real bind as to what to do. I didn't realize this until near the end of the process, when we were stonewalled.

Although there was general consensus that the protocol and procedures for doing evaluations had progressed significantly, there was also a strong feeling that evaluations were still not integrated into the system's way of doing business. It was suggested that the participatory nature of evaluation is very much limited by structures that are not always supportive of, nor in tune with, using the results of evaluation studies.

Conclusion

The present research study provides specific feedback on the program evaluation model used in this school district. It also reinforces a number of issues identified in the literature on participatory evaluation and evaluation utilization. In particular, this study supports the professional worth of involving primary users in program evaluations. It also demonstrates a relation between primary user involvement and the utilization of evaluation findings.

The characteristics of program evaluations, as posited by Cousins and Earl (1992), were helpful in examining the impact of previous evaluations undertaken in this school district. Noteworthy was the relation between utilization and the nature, amount and quality of communication about the results of the evaluation. Furthermore, the strong influence of the superintendent of program on the evaluation process and, specifically, the development and implementation of resulting action plans linked noticeably with utilization. Shavelson's (1988) comment about trying to understand the mind-frames of policymakers and practitioners is worth considering.

Throughout this study, respondents suggested that evaluations be redesigned so that they could be completed in less time with fewer resources, and yet produce high-quality results. In addition, an organizational culture that values and supports the total evaluation process, and is committed practically to follow through on the action plans, seems to be essential. In this study, a supportive organizational climate related to a number of characteristics of program evaluation, including utilization.

As an initial attempt to come to terms with some of the findings of this research study, the following reflective statements are posited. They provide a basis for further improvement and refinement of the program evaluation model used in this school district.

- Organizational structures and power relationships need to support better partici-patory program evaluation, including improved evaluation utilization. Program evaluation should be integrated into the system's way of doing business.
- It is important to develop a strategy for ensuring that the action plan is devel-oped and implemented.
- The involvement of primary users in the evaluation process results in positive

staff development, a felling of empowerment, and a sense of competence in evaluation issues and procedures.

- Primary users must be more involved in the system and their expertise acquired during the evaluation must be used in follow-up.
- Communication about the evaluation process – at all stages – must be improved and must be of the highest quality.
- The current climate of political, economic and educational change demands prompt and efficient use of time and resources.
- Evaluation must be valued and seen to be valued; this can be demonstrated by acting on the findings of the evaluation.
- Efforts should be made to understand better the perception of and demands on policymakers, so that the design, conduct and use of evaluations can be better planned.

Note

1 It should be noted that the action plan is a decision-making activity and is not part of the formal evaluation process. The evaluation team's responsibility includes interpreting the findings and developing suggested courses of action (recommendations) based on the findings. It is then the policymaker's responsibility to develop and implement an action plan.

References

ALKIN, M.C. (1991) 'Evaluation theory development: II', in McLAUGHLIN, M.W. and PHILLIPS, D.C. *Evaluation and Education: At Quarter Century*, Ninetieth Yearbook of the National Society for the Study of Education (pp. 91–112), Chicago, University of Chicago Press.
BOLMAN, L.G. and DEAL, T.E. (1991) *Reframing Organizations: Artistry, Choice and Leadership*, San Francisco, CA, Jossey-Bass.
COUSINS, J.B. and EARL, L.M. (1992) 'The case for participatory evaluation', *Educational Evaluation and Policy Analysis*, **14**, 4, pp. 397–418.
COUSINS, J.B. and LEITHWOOD, K.A. (1986) 'Current empirical research on evaluation utilization', *Review of Educational Research*, **56**, 3, pp. 331–64.
FULLAN, M. WITH STEIGLEBAUER, S. (1991) *The New Meaning of Educational Change* (2nd ed), New York, Teachers College Press.
GREENE, J.G. (1992) 'Stakeholder interests in program evaluation: How well are they served by collaborative and interpretive perspectives?' Paper presented at the annual meeting of the American Educational Research Association, San Francisco.
GREENE, J.G. (1988) 'Stakeholder participation and utilization in program evaluation', *Evaluation Review*, **12**, pp. 91–116.
HUBERMAN, M. (1990) 'Linkage between researchers and practitioners: A qualitative study', *American Educational Research Journal*, **27**, pp. 363–91.
LAFLEUR, C.D. (1990) 'Program review model', Paper presented at the annual conference of the Canadian Evaluation Society, Toronto.
LEITHWOOD, K.A. (ed) (1987) *Planned Educational Change: A Manual of Curriculum Review, Development and Implementation (CRDI) Concepts and Procedures*, Toronto, OISE Press.
LOVE, A.J. (1991) *Internal Evaluation: Building Organizations From Within*, Newbury Park, CA, Sage.
MAYNE, J. (1992) 'Establishing internal evaluation in an organization', in HUDSON, J., MAYNE

J. & THOMLISON, R., (eds) *Action-oriented Evaluation in Organizations*, Middleton, Ohio, Wall & Emerson.

MURPHY, J. (1991) *Restructuring Schools: Capturing and Assessing the Phenomena*, New York, Teachers College Press.

PUGH, W.C. (1990; October) 'Evaluation utilization and policy formulation: A case analysis of a school district uniform policy', Paper presented at the annual meeting of the American Educational Research Association, Boston.

SCHEIN, E.H. (1991) *Organizational Culture and Leadership*, San Francisco, CA, Jossey-Bass.

SHAVELSON, R.J. (1988) 'Contributions of educational research to policy and practice: Constructing, challenging, changing cognition', *Educational Researcher*, **17**, pp. 4–11; 22.

STOLL, L. and FINK, D. (1992) 'Effecting school change: The Halton approach', *School Effectiveness and School Improvement*, **3**, pp. 19–41.

WEISS, C.H. (1988) 'Evaluation for decisions: Is anybody there? Does anybody care?', *Evaluation Practice*, **9**, pp. 5–19.

Chapter 4

Assessing Program Needs Using Participatory Evaluation: A Comparison of High and Marginal Success Cases

J. Bradley Cousins

Introduction

'Field centres' of the Ontario Institute for Studies in Education (OISE) are located in various regions of Ontario and are designed to help the Institute fulfil its tripartite mandate of graduate instruction, research, and field development, and to aid school districts in their efforts to implement Ontario Ministry of Education and Training policy. Centre faculty are in the unique and fortunate position of being able to offer their field development services *without fee* to school districts within their respective jurisdictions. This arrangement provides a highly suitable context for participatory evaluation activities. As a former member of OISE's complement of field centre faculty located at the Trent Valley Centre in east-central Ontario, I participated in many such projects over the years.

In this chapter, I examine two projects, one considered by me to be highly successful, the other marginally so. Both studies employed a single model of participation, were conducted over a period of about 12–18 months, resulted in the production of a final report co-authored by myself and members of the respective communities of practice, and were completed well before data for the present study were collected. The following sets of questions provided the focus for research.

- What was the impact of the participatory approach to applied research? Were decisions based on the data? Did district staff learn from the data? What effect(s) did participation have on the primary users who collaborated on the project?
- What factors explained variation in impact? Did interaction between researchers and practitioners enhance impact? Did features of the research project predict use of the data? Which organizational features were related to the use of the data?

Author's Note: This research was completed while the author was on faculty at the Ontario Institute for Studies in Education. The research was supported by a grant from the Social Sciences and Humanities Research Council of Canada (Grant # 410–92–0983). The opinions expressed within are those of the author and do not necessarily reflect Council policy. The author thanks Anne Hogaboam-Gray and Jie Mei Li for their participation in the data collection and analysis phases of the project. Also, thanks is expressed to the school district personnel who helped to coordinate the data collection.

The paper begins with a brief description of the cases followed by a summary of the participatory evaluation model employed. The research methods for the present study are then briefly considered and a summary of cross-case findings is presented.

Case Descriptions

Marginal Success Case: Lakeside

Lakeside is a small school district serving a large, predominantly rural region in a distant corner of the field centre's jurisdiction (a $2\frac{1}{2}$ hour drive from the centre office). The district has sixteen elementary and three secondary schools, a student enrolment of about 6,500, and employs about 300 teachers. The board had secured funding from the Ministry of Education and Training to enhance the use of computers in schools and was in the midst of a three-year phase-in procedure. In the first year, four elementary schools and one secondary school served as pilot sites. At each site, resources were made available for the acquisition of hardware (computers and peripherals) and software, but most importantly, for the half-time release of one site coordinator to assist staff in upgrading their computer skills and integrating the technology into the curriculum. District administration planned to shift resources into an additional five schools in each of the second and third years. I was recruited to coordinate a monitoring study designed to inform phase 2 and 3 implementation. A steering committee was formed which consisted of the five phase 1 site coordinators, the supervisory officer, a principal at one of the phase 1 pilot sites, and the central board office computer consultant/curriculum coordinator. The site coordinators worked closely with me on the research.

I met with the steering committee in the autumn of the phase 1 implementation year. We defined the scope of the project, assessed the appropriateness of the conceptual framework, agreed upon the research questions, identified tasks, and assigned responsibilities. We established a workplan for the research team, and proceeded to develop an interview guide. After I had conducted some initial interviews in each of the respective school sites, I conducted an interview training session with the research team. The site coordinators then collected and summarized their interview data and we met once again for the data analysis training session. In total, interviews were carried out with forty-six teachers and school administrators in the pilot schools. In the ensuing weeks, the data was independently coded by the research team members and collectively analyzed, and I prepared a draft of the final report. Each research team member participated in reporting by providing me with a five-page description of their respective pilot site. I edited the descriptions and incorporated them into the main report. I was given feedback on the draft report by the research team and a subsequent meeting was scheduled with the steering committee to discuss the revised report. The final report was about forty pages in length and contained eight recommendations, each having direct bearing on phase 2 and 3 planning and implementation. The entire research process unfolded over a period of about nine months. Subsequently, the full report, complete with draft recommendations, was accepted without change by the steering committee and then disseminated to interested parties within the school district. I was modestly surprised by these events because I knew that the supervisory officer disagreed with at least one of the recommendations.

Through informal contacts with the superintendent after the report had been distributed, I learned that no further monitoring activities had occurred, although phases

> *Following my visits to the schools I immediately reported back to the research team in a memo about my experience. Some respondents interviewed by me had little or no knowledge of the purposes of our project and raised some concerns. I suggested in the memo that the site coordinators spend sufficient time reviewing with interviewees the purposes and intentions of the study.*

> *When it came time to produce the final report, I found the task to be quite straightforward. My participation in data collection and the data analysis session had greatly enhanced my understanding of key variables and processes in the board. I felt confident that my reporting of findings was accurate and was grounded in the consensual understanding of the research team. When I developed and distributed draft recommendations to members of the research team they had some suggestions for fine tuning, but on the whole felt that the set was reasonable and accurately reflected the findings of the study. They were also content with the findings as I had reported them.*
>
> *As we reviewed the draft recommendations some argued to include additional recommendations and fine-tune others on the basis of their interests as site coordinators in the pilot schools. I was careful to argue the need to demonstrate clear linkages to the data including recommendations and came away satisfied that I had achieved this objective.*

2 and 3 of the plan were being implemented. The supervisory officer assured me that the recommendations had been taken seriously and acted on, although our discussions about these specific actions and follow-up activities, in general, were both brief and vague. I did not have a sense from these brief encounters that the impact of the report had been very significant despite a relatively smooth participatory research process with no major setbacks, delays, or obstacles. Given these considerations of impact and process, I concluded that this participatory case was only 'marginally successful.'

High Success Case: Rockland

Rockland is a small school district also located in east-central Ontario. Although closer to the OISE Field Centre the Board office was still about $1\frac{1}{2}$ hours drive. The district has only two secondary schools and seventeen elementary schools, but covers an enormous region that is largely rural and sparsely populated. Rockland employs about 200 teachers and has an average yearly student enrolment of about 5,000.

Chronologically, the Rockland case preceded the Lakeside project by about one year. The board had initiated a pilot program in grade 9 in anticipation of the Ministry's intention to 'destream' grade 9 as part of a province-wide restructuring initiative to ease the transition of adolescents from elementary to secondary school. The provincial initiative, which later became knows as the Transition Years initiative, was designed to better engage students and foster their participation in school life, thereby reducing the rate of early school leaving (dropping out). The Rockland 'multi-level' grade 9 program was designed not to destream, but to combine Ontario's three streams (advanced, general, and basic) into common grade 9 classes. Teachers were recruited for the program on a volunteer basis, although specialty teachers (e.g., music, French) really had little choice. After some informal discussion with a supervisory officer, I volunteered to coordinate a monitoring study of first year implementation activities.

I met with a steering committee that consisted of two superintendents, one principal, one vice-principal, and one district curriculum coordinator. At that meeting many decisions were made about the nature and scope of the study. We decided to collect attitudinal student data from grade 10 students who had just completed the traditional grade 9 program (the control group) and then from grade 9 students who had been in multi-level classes (the treatment group). We also agreed to interview all teachers of grade 9 in the board (N = 33). At my suggestion four teachers, two from each secondary school, were added to the steering committee for our next meeting. A training session on interviewing procedures followed.

Control student data and teacher interview data were collected and interview data were processed and analyzed. As with Lakeside, members of the research team were trained to independently code their interview data and the research team met as a group to integrate findings. Initial results were shared with the steering committee in the spring and a follow-up survey of the teachers was designed and implemented. Treatment group student data were collected at the end of the school year and analyzed by field centre staff over the summer. I wrote a draft final report and sent it to the research team for comment. The draft was then revised and distributed to the rest of the steering committee. We met as a group to discuss the report, identify changes, and plan dissemination and follow-up activities. The report was about sixty-five pages long, including appendices, and made recommendations supported by the findings. The entire research process took about one year to complete.

As with the Lakeside case, I was very pleased with the participatory process at the Rockland Board. The research had gone well, teacher researchers appeared to enjoy the process, report writing was straightforward, the interim and final reports were received enthusiastically by the steering committee, and I had a strong sense that the findings were valid and that the recommendations were well supported. The project also had considerable impact. First, the ministry had moved ahead with its transition years initiatives and announced funding for innovative pilot projects in the province. A proposal from Rockland that drew heavily on data from the needs assessment study was funded. Second, in line with one of the recommendations, one of the research team members was promoted to central office to serve as transition years coordinator. Third, I was invited back to assist in planning further research on the pilot project. This research was coordinated by the recently appointed transition years coordinator and was conducted exclusively by members of the local organization. My role was strictly 'arms-length', although field centre services were offered for the processing and analysis of numerical data. Fourth, in a planning meeting after the report had been released, I inquired about progress in implementing the recommendations from the study. I was favorably impressed by steering committee members' summation of progress with each of the six recommendations. These reasons informed my admittedly subjective perceptions of process and impact, and led me to conclude that the participatory needs assessment experience in Rockland had been highly successful.

In summary, the participatory research model at Lakeside and Rockland were quite similar. In each case I was recruited to coordinate the research but worked in partnership with a steering committee. The research tasks were carried out by myself and teams of teachers not experienced in doing research. The process involved a considerable investment on my part in training the teachers to conduct interviews and analyze data. Final reports were drafted by me and revised by the teacher teams prior to going forward to the steering committee. In both cases the reports were well received by the committee. The results were disseminated within the districts and follow-up activities werè carried out without the researcher's involvement.

Method

Design

The present study is a retrospective interview study of the two cases described above. In each case, about one year had elapsed since the final report was released, allowing ample opportunity for impact to occur, while at the same time permitting respondents to reflect on events that were not temporally distant in memory.

Within each site, all primary users participating in either the research team or the steering committee were selected for interview. In addition, a sample of users (program implementors) *not* involved in carrying out the participatory needs assessment were selected at random from lists of school personnel who had been interviewed during the respective needs assessment processes. At both Lakeside and Rockland, seven 'participants' and fifteen 'non-participants' were interviewed for a total of forty-four interviews. In each case, all research team members were interviewed, although we were unable to interview some steering committee members due to scheduling conflicts.

Parallel interview guides were prepared for the Lakeside and Rockland sites and each adapted to local circumstances and participant and non-participant samples. The guides asked about the participatory process, the study's impact, factors affecting impact, and current status of the program. Private interviews were carried out by three researchers and interview summaries prepared. Procedures for coding interview data were based on those described by Miles and Huberman (1984), and a coding scheme grounded in the conceptual framework (outlined in chapter 1) was applied.[1] The interview data were then sorted and quotations with illustrative value were noted. The cross-case results are reported below.

Findings

What was the Impact of the Participatory Approach?

Decision making Table 4.1 displays data from both the Rockland and Lakeside cases concerning the major sorts of impact that were observed. On balance, instrumental or decision-making outcomes were noted to be stronger for the Rockland case. Perhaps the most significant instrumental use of the data was to inform continuing program implementation activities and, in particular, continued monitoring. The data supported the board's successful bid for transition years pilot project funding (about $120,000 for two years). As part of that funding, one of the research team members was appointed to a central board office consultant/coordinator role and, as one of many tasks, headed the monitoring research for the project. He was called upon to train participants in the

Table 4.1 Impact of the participatory evaluation model: summary of interview data by high and marginal success cases

Type of Impact	High Success: Rockland Supporting Evidence	High Success: Rockland Countervailing Evidence	Marginal Success: Lakeside Supporting Evidence	Marginal Success: Lakeside Countervailing Evidence
Support for discrete decisions	**PPP (strong positive)** • helped generate pilot funding • focus for system planning • continuation with monitoring research • sincere effort to implement recommendations	**N (weak negative)** • unaware of impact • little/poor follow-up • questionable implementation of recommendations	**PP (moderate positive)** • focus for system planning • some follow-up on recommendations	**NN (moderate negative)** • no real follow-up • impact in the system not discernible • change in resource allocation did not benefit phase 1 schools • questionable implementation of recommendations
Educative: program and organizational considerations	**PPP (strong positive)** • knowledge and suspicions confirmed • heightened staff awareness of key issues • enhanced commitment, ownership and motivation • insights into organizational operations and staff concerns • insight from external perspective	**N (weak negative)** • many teachers did not see the report • has not come into consciousness of board members	**P (weak positive)** • knowledge confirmed • enhanced awareness of computers in the system • enhanced computer usage	**N (moderate negative)** • teachers did not really understand project purposes • most unaware of results • no new learning • no useful information for phase 2 or 3 set-up
Educative: technical research skills	**PPP (strong positive)** • good professional development experience • could do coding task again unsupervised • could carry out research from start to finish with technical support • leadership development of participants • found enjoyable	**NN (moderate negative)** • need statistical support • could not coordinate sorting task or pull all research tasks together • would not want to sever link to OISE • reporting task difficulties on subsequent project	**PP (moderate positive)** • able to coordinate and carry out research process with refresher • good professional development experience • leadership development of participants	**NN (moderate negative)** • training insufficient to coordinate subsequent project • reluctant to interview peers • time would have been better spent in schools • did not enjoy coding task

research skills he had acquired through the previous study. According to the new co-ordinator, the prior study gave him 'a base to go on and to do [his] own thing'. The study also provided a focus for system-level planning. The deliberations among ad-ministrators, decision makers, and persons responsible for implementation facilitated the process. As a principal who participated on the steering committee put it,

> . . . we knew where we wanted to go but the study helped us to get there quicker. Having somebody from outside helps us to believe our thinking and results, we probably get there in a quicker and better way.

Several respondents claimed that the administration took the recommendations seriously and made a sincere effort to address each of them. For example, resources were made available for practice-oriented, in-service training; a curriculum coordinator role was created in addition to the transition years coordinator position; activities to enhance exchange among elementary and secondary schools were put in place; and release time was made available for teachers to work together. A recommendation about reducing class size in grade 9 was addressed at the school level and met with varying degrees of success.

Not all evidence was uniform regarding instrumental impact. Some respondents, particularly teachers, were relatively uninformed (or suggested their colleagues were uninformed) about follow-up activities. They also questioned the implementation of the recommendations. For example, in one school, efforts to reduce class size in grade 9 were thwarted by last minute increases in enrolment for the coming school year. This event had the double effect of overloading grade 9 teachers while at the same time causing them to wonder about the school's commitment to the recom-mendation. Further, interactions with teachers from elementary schools and efforts to stimulate teachers' joint work were marginally successful, according to some non-participant respondents.

Similar sorts of impact were observed in the Lakeside site, but with limited breadth and depth. Also, there was substantial countervailing evidence concerning some of the claims made. The most visible outcome of the research was the establishment of a computer advisory group (a committee), which consisted of a representative of the phase 1 site coordinators, central office staff, trustees, and parents. This group report-edly relied on information from the initial report in formulating a system-wide three-year computer implementation plan. However, coverage of other recommendations coming from the report was sporadic and selective. Some effort to step up in-service training activities was apparent but, contrary to a recommendation in the report, novice users did not appear to be given special attention. While the board continued to enjoy success in attaining external funding, support for on-site coordination was restricted to phase 2 and 3 schools. Some progress was reportedly made in computer equipment and software acquisition. Countervailing evidence at Lakeside was considerable. Several research participants and non-participant teachers expressed disappointment with follow-up to the study. As one non-participant teacher suggested,

> [The study] had impact on staff collaboration and in-service. Teachers worked together and spent their lunch time talking with one another. But administra-tive uses [of the computer] depend on the individual teachers. So the impact is very limited and I don't think we are going in the direction of more resources, computer labs, and local experts participating in board-level decision making.

Another commented on the limited quality of the in-service. 'We had in-service alright. But it was such a long time between each workshop that we forgot what we did in the previous one. So, each time we started from square one.' Finally, one of the research participants indicated that resource allocations had changed since the report was released, but that the change reduced the benefit to phase 1 schools, a result that ran counter to the spirit of the report.

Individual and group learning   Rockland yielded stronger evidence than did Lakeside to suggest that individual and group learning had occurred (see table 4.1). While many Rockland respondents commented that the data served to confirm prior knowledge and hunches, some suggested that they served to heighten staffs' and administrations' awareness.

> It also works to raise the awareness of senior administration. For example, the one we just did with grade 7 and 8 students . . . that's valuable information more for flagging the support of senior administration because they can see something tangible and react to that and let the principals know. (*Research team member*)

In addition to confirmation and awareness enhancement for some data from the study provided new insights.

> You got to learn how they felt about very important issues. You learned about the 'hardliners' and the 'oldtimers' and the people who could adjust and who look forward to the challenge. So you might reaffirm some suspicions. And then there are always the surprises you find out too . . . from peoples' responses and students' responses. . . . If I were going back to the study, I'd probably just go back to [the student written comment data]. (*Research team member*)

A superintendent revealed how the data had served to whet his (and probably the organization's) sense of inquiry. In his words,

> . . . also some lines for further research for us to look at. If the kids are this way in grade 8, what are they like later on at the end of grade 12 and OAC? What are the implications for learning? How do you program for kids that go through these kinds of transitions? (*Steering committee member*)

The research process appears to have had given staff pause to reflect on patterns of evidence and to begin to question some deeper assumptions about the teaching and learning process. The availability of 'external eyes' also served to stimulate this sort of response. As a steering committee member put it,

> the technical assistance and the setting up of the study is very important, but there's also been the opportunity to sit down with [the OISE researcher] to focus on what's on hand and the issues . . . get some insight from somebody who is removed from the actual situation, and give us some broad perspectives.

At Lakeside the situation was quite different. There was some acknowledgment of the confirmation of prior knowledge and a suggestion that district staff's awareness of computers had been enhanced. There was also a vague allusion to the enhanced use of computers by teachers. But there was little to suggest that new insights had been provided by the study or that it stimulated a sense of organizational, or even individual inquiry. On the other hand, several respondents remarked on the lack of new insight and the low level of awareness among staff.

> Even before OISE came in, we said to our administrators that we need another technician . . . so they brought OISE in to do this big study and the study revealed that we need a technician. In my opinion we didn't need OISE to do that study from that respect. (*Research team member*)

> Nothing has been done. I've really been quite disappointed in the whole process. There was no follow-up. We spent a lot of time gathering facts and coming together. It looks great on paper, but nobody was able or nobody was willing to make a commitment. As soon as the government funding ran out, there was no attempt even to continue. (*Research team member*)

These comments reveal that some members of the research team were harboring significant levels of resentment regarding their role in the process. There was a definite sense among them that they had been 'used' and that the study had been a waste of valuable time. It is important to know that not all members of the research team were of this view. Nonetheless, even teachers not associated with the study complained of the lack of specific information or follow-up relevant to phase 2 and 3 implementation.

Developing research skills   Staff at both Rockland and Lakeside commented on their development of research skills as a consequence of participation. As noted in table 4.1, however, some concerns were raised.

At Rockland, most participants viewed their involvement in the process as an effective professional development exercise.

> I know for me, it was sort of a learning process . . . it was sort of like going back to university and learning how to do a study. (*Research team member*)

> The professional development for the research team is very worthwhile. It has been shown that their experience has been internalized. Being involved with professionals and setting up the study, you come back with a set of knowledge you didn't have before. It's a practical knowledge, actually going through the process. It has impacts beyond the particular study. (*Steering committee member*)

When asked if research team members could manage a similar process without the technical support provided by OISE, there were varying responses. The research team member who had been promoted to transition years coordinator grounded his response in his own experience; he had taken on the task of coordinating such an effort and was succeeding with it. Another facet of impact regarding participation was the development of leadership potential within the board. Of the four research team members, three had been promoted since the study. The study served to raise their profile within the board as well as to provide them with a tangible addition to their resumé. As a supervisory officer put it,

> Their professionalism is recognized. There is a leadership development component to [the participatory process]. It gives them skills that other people

> don't have. [Teacher X] is an example. He has done a lot of growing and will
> be a marketable person.

On the downside, there was considerable evidence to suggest that the organization remained dependent on the external researcher for technical support. Such support was not restricted to the statistical analysis of data, although this issue was most certainly raised. Some research team members did not feel confident that they could manage the interview data coding task without the direct coordination by the expert. Further, while the research study directly involved participants in almost all phases of the research process, the contribution of the research team to the reporting phase was comparatively light. As a possible consequence, the coordinator of the subsequent research study had some misgivings about his writing skills,

> Writing took a long time to get through. I would start it and then leave it for
> a while. I don't know, maybe that is just myself. Possibly being a little more
> involved in writing the first [study] would have helped. But I don't know how
> comfortable I would have felt writing that first one. I think actually going
> through the process in the capacity that I did was better and then to write this
> one.

Finally, a superintendent remarked that he did not want to sever the link with OISE since the process had been so successful and there was much to be gained concerning the further development of technical skills.

The development of research skills was also an apparent impact in the Lakeside case. Staff viewed the experience as positive and effective from the point of view of professional development. At least some members believed that the process could be repeated, with perhaps some support in the form of a 'refresher' session or consultation. Also, as at Rockland, the participatory experience may have contributed to leadership development. After the final report was released one team member was assigned to a half-time central office role as part of his computer advisory group responsibilities. However, as shown in table 4.1, not all evidence was positive. First, one teacher participant expressed anxiety about interviewing his peers as part of the data collection process. Second, continued close involvement of an external expert was thought to be essential to the success of continuing research projects. According to one of the teacher participants, 'Yes, I think we would have to have somebody who would give us the whole picture. . . . I would think initially we would still need somebody from OISE . . . and from that point we could take over'. Third, for one participant, the development of research skills did not appear to be time well spent in the light of the limited impact the study had.

> In some ways I thought it was helpful in that I learned a little bit more about
> research and interviewing skills, although in retrospect the time would have
> been better used in my own school, teaching teachers and actually doing what
> we were supposed to do [as site coordinator] instead of studying it. We spent
> a good 20 to 25 hours and really for no apparent reason.

This view was supported by at least one other research team member. Finally, another participant found the interview data coding task onerous and 'brutal'.

Summary   Differences between Rockland and Lakeside become apparent, especially in considering the instrumental and conceptual impact of the needs assessment data.

> *From the point of view of the evaluator, the extent and range of impact are gratifying. However, there are also a few surprises. The most vivid example is the dissenting views held by some research team members in Lakeside. In particular, in working through the process, I had privately noted a potential candidate for coordinating research activities after the initial study was complete (research activities that never materialized, I might add). The individual that I had in mind was among the more able and appeared to possess the necessary leadership qualities. Moreover, he worked through the tasks cooperatively and conscientiously. I was very interested indeed to learn that his views of the process and its impact were decidedly pessimistic.*

Differences were less visible regarding the development of research skills among the teacher participants, although at Lakeside, professional development of this sort was not held in high esteem by some, given other commitments and the perceived limited impact of the study. These findings provide insight into the nature and range of consequences of the participatory evaluation model. We now turn to an examination of factors that led to those consequences.

What Factors Explained Variation in Impact?

Table 4.2 summarizes the factors that appeared to be operative within the two sites. The factors are summarized in table 4.2 under the three major components of the evaluation use conceptual framework outlined in chapter 1.

Participation   At Rockland several attributes of the participatory process were identified as having a positive impact. First, the involvement of such a relatively large contingent of local staff on the steering committees and research teams raised the profile of the study and enhanced dissemination activities. In addition to concrete plans for dissemination, participants naturally shared findings with their peers throughout the school district. Second, having teachers interview their peers resulted in a relaxed, trustful environment for the interview data collection. According to one research team member, teachers were willing to be open and honest with their views 'because there was good rapport in the present project and lots of trust'. Third, participation also enhanced the research teams' sensitivity to local values and their ability to get past surface description and closer to the heart of matters at hand. The technical skills brought to the project by the researcher and the training provided were the fourth and fifth aspects of participation that helped. While the former helped to raise the credibility of the research project, thereby enhancing its potential to support decisions and enhance learning, the latter led quite directly to the development of research skills among practitioners. A vice-principal who did not participate in the process reflected on it:

> Technical research skills really make a difference. That skill does not reside within the boards nor the time, I don't think. [The research team] would not have produced as credible or systematic a document . . . [the process] increased the assurances that something would be done because it was done in that professional kind of way.

Table 4.2 Factors influencing impact: summary of interview data by high and marginal success cases

Factor	High Success: Rockland Positive Influence	High Success: Rockland Negative Influence	Marginal Success: Lakeside Positive Influence	Marginal Success: Lakeside Negative Influence
Interactive processes	**PPP (strong positive)** • wide distribution of report • good rapport/trust • provision of technical skills • research training • sensitivity to local values	**N (weak negative)** • limits on dissemination • time away from class/core function	**PP (moderate positive)** • communication enhanced by advisory group • research training • participation in the process	**NN (moderate negative)** • training insufficient • poor communication with teachers • time away from school/core function
Decision or policy setting considerations	**PP (moderate positive)** • support from senior administration • high information needs • strong leadership	**NN (moderate negative)** • limited resources • competing priorities • workload too heavy • inter-departmental and inter-school relations	**P (weak positive)** • endorsement from senior administration • resources from board/ministry	**NNN (strong negative)** • senior administration not sensitive to substantive issues • resources expired, needed badly • study not needed • administration had hidden agenda • variation in teachers' research skills
Evaluation implementation characteristics	**PPP (strong positive)** • report credibility • relevant, usable, authentic • researcher credibility • project scope	**0 (no negative influence)**	**PP (moderate positive)** • report credibility • relevant recommendations • project scope	**0 (no negative influence)**

Another important aspect of the researcher's involvement was leadership: providing the impetus to develop and stick to a workplan. As one of the research team members suggested, 'the collaboration with the OISE staff can help get things started and set down some time lines to get things done. Otherwise, the teachers are so busy with so many things they tend to put things off'. Contrary to the positive aspects of the process, a few respondents believed that follow-up to the report could have been improved and that dissemination was really quite limited. Some also raised concerns about the demands on their time and time away from their core function of teaching. In general, however, such countervailing evidence was not widespread.

At Lakeside, the data was less positive and negative influences were more strongly voiced. Similar patterns emerged regarding the provision of technical skills and training. One research team member reflected on the value of collaborative involvement:

> I found, for me, that [the coding] was difficult the first time round, although
> when we all got together and tried it I found the dialogue very useful . . . without
> that sharing exercise I don't believe the results would have been valid.

Again, the implication here is one of enhancing the potential for use through the mediating effects of the report's credibility. Communication of information from the study was enhanced at Lakeside by the establishment of a formal mechanism to address computer implementation issues, namely the computer advisory group. Part of the group's mandate was to dialogue with teachers regarding the integration of the technology into their program; the research-based knowledge was viewed as being natural to that process.

Dissenting views about the participatory process were quite similar to those voiced at Rockland, but were more intense and more widespread among interview respondents. The chief concern raised was a severe lack of discussion with district teachers about the data. A research team member reported that sharing with teachers was rather limited and typically took the form of a one-way transmission of information: 'I believe at a staff meeting, they were told these were the recommendations . . . it didn't filter down quite as well as it could have.' Another member of the research team was less than enamored with the training process:

> Well, I don't think we were trained at all. [The OISE researcher] did give us
> a little bit of background and some ideas. I have a little bit of experience in
> that, so I didn't find it too difficult. . . . The coding took a bit of work because
> I have never done anything like that before.

He also raised concerns about time away from the school that might have been used to have a more direct impact on potential users of computers. This view was shared by another team member. As mentioned above, both were disappointed with the impact of the study and questioned its need in the first place.

Context for research   Strong administrative support and leadership were two variables that were found to stimulate the use of research information at Rockland (see table 4.2). Efforts to carry out recommendations were viewed by some teachers as sincere, and a superintendent, who was a member of the research steering committee, shared findings with teachers at the school level 'as a way of giving them strokes and showing my support'. Also, the district's high need for information regarding the transition years initiative played a key role. Given the provincial policy agenda at the time, the study was very timely and it heightened the awareness of many teachers about destreaming, in particular, and planned change in general.

> When the study began there was a need for information. We were streamed then. There was no one around to give teachers help on resources and pedagogy for destreamed classes. When we talked about new ideas like class size, we got to voice our opinion and saw something done. It was definitely a good time to start to ask people all about these. (*Non-participant teacher*)

However, several concerns were raised, the most frequently voiced being limited resources, competing priorities, heavy workload, and inter-departmental and inter-school relations. Each was seen to lessen the extent to which the study had an impact within the district. A non-participant vice-principal reflected on the impact of having to retract promises made about the reduction of class size.

> Everything was set up in June, and in September we ended up with 39 more students than we expected. It would have worked if they were all taking the same classes but they were not. This did not go over well with the grade 9 teachers. It has not been a good year in that sense at all.

The administration of the school was working hard to make good on their promise in the next academic year.

Endorsement of the computer project by district senior administration and the provision of resources from the board and the Ministry were two positive forces at Lakeside. However, several respondents recounted a variety of concerns and obstacles that interfered with follow-up to the study. Chief among the concerns were perceptions of an apparent lack of sensitivity of senior administrators to substantive (computers and instruction) issues, that senior administrators were operating according to a hidden agenda, and that the innovation was too heavily resource driven. Regarding the second point, some staff were of the view that the administration was implementing its own plan and that the research study and teacher participation in decision making under the auspices of the computer advisory group were superficial overtures. Surprisingly, one research team member was unaware of the existence of the computer advisory group and insisted that the establishment of such a group would be counter to the administration's *modus operandi*.

> We could fix so many problems if we had a computer committee, it would be so simple to do. We already have asked [the superintendent] to do this and I know it's not going to happen because of the power . . . the decisions are going to be made at the superintendent level and then it's going to be passed down to the computer consultants, and then it's going to be spread out to the technician level . . . it's a mess!

While this respondent was apparently misinformed, the intensity of his concerns speak to the underlying issue of the board's sincerity in adopting a less autocratic policy development process. Several respondents agreed that school-level activities all but ground to a halt as financial (phase-specific) resources expired. Finally, two other concerns noted were, first, that, given its limited impact, the study was really not needed in the first place, and second, that limitations on research team members' skills in conducting research may have hampered the process.

Characteristics of the research   At Rockland, the participatory process acted to enhance the credibility of the report and to make the findings more relevant. Both factors were said to have enhanced the usefulness of the study.

> In terms of the accuracy of the responses, I think it is an essential feature. I don't think we would get the same kind of information if it had been conducted by board personnel solely or even by people outside the board. (*Non-participant vice-principal*)

> The involvement of the local staff with the OISE people is a great idea. It can help the teacher see the whole picture, some areas you can't see otherwise. . . . Prejudice from both sides would be minimized. People tend to look at where the report is from. So local research will get less criticism. (*Non-participant teacher*)

Other factors having positive effects were the scope of the research project, in that it looked at students' and teachers' views, and the credibility of the research team within the board. A supervisory officer remarked that the team was selected with this criterion in mind. At Lakeside, very similar sorts of influences were apparent although not as extensively reported by interview respondents. A non-participant teacher reflected on the study's credibility:

> The fact that I see names there that I recognize, and I know they have been involved with the same kind of things I did . . . I would look at this [report] and know that they went through the same kind of problems and the same kind of assistance that I had. . . . People just come in and take a look at what you are doing and then make recommendations just out of one or two visits. But in our case, these people have been involved in the actual program. I do think [this sort of research process] is excellent.

It is interesting and important to note that no one challenged the credibility of either study.

Summary   Both sites showed positive influences of participation, but at Lakeside these positive effects were at least partially offset by negative ones. Dissenting views were grounded in concerns about senior administration's lack of follow-up and perhaps their lack of commitment to participatory decision making. Some staff were not persuaded by the administration's overt intentions and public expressions of support. For them, lack of follow-up was tantamount to implementing a hidden agenda. On the other hand, administrative support at the Rockland Board was perceived to be sincere and conscientious. Administrators faithfully addressed recommendations and used the data as opportunities to provide staff with positive reinforcement and feedback. Limited resources, competing priorities, and other organizational tensions were found to be deleterious in both cases, but the credibility and relevance to the local context of the research was enhanced by the participatory process in both situations. Claims about compromising the technical integrity of the research by involving local practitioners did not surface.

Conclusions and Implications

That organizations are complex, dynamic entities, and subject to an enormous array of influences is well understood. Given this understanding, it must be assumed that local applied research will be necessarily limited in its impact (Weiss and Bucuvalas, 1980). Participatory evaluation may be one way to enhance the impact of such projects through promoting dialogue and discussion and the development of 'dense interpersonal network', which act to enhance organizational learning (Louis and Simsek, 1991).

The present study provides support for an organizational learning interpretation of the use of applied research at the school and school district levels. The involvement and engagement of practitioners with the research, their deliberations about the meaning of findings, and their active role in diffusing information were all shown to influence favorably the utility of systematic needs assessment, primarily through amplifying the credibility and sharpening the relevance of the research. Findings were used to help inform decisions about innovations and staff development activities, they led to enhanced awareness about planned change and, in some instances, affected positively staff commitment to innovation. The participatory evaluation process was generally a useful professional development experience that, for some, coincided with leadership development opportunities. It also led to continued research activities in one site. But these effects were tempered quite significantly by organizational circumstances and contextual influences. Active, sincere support from central district administration, particularly during the follow-up phase, was found to be a powerful predictor of impact. The absence of such support was shown to lead to suspicion and even contempt, especially among participants in the evaluation process. For teachers who held such views, participation was thought to be a waste of time and energy and a distraction from their primary role and responsibility.

Critics of the participatory model suggest that the practitioner's role in the research process is best restricted to defining the problem for research and interpreting emergent findings, since involvement in research is in many ways incompatible with organizational norms and expectations. Weiss (1991), for example, suggests that involvement of practitioners in technical research activities,

> . . . expects too much both of teachers and researchers. They have different skills, different norms, different time orientations, different reward systems, different ways of dealing with the world. The effort is too costly in time and in its demands for interaction. It also slows the reform to a snail's pace. (p. 13)

Although data from the present study only begins to add to our knowledge about participation, it brings this view into question. Given the proper administrative support, members of the community of practice can become active, eager and effective participants in the process and their participation can lead to significant local payoff. It can, in fact, stimulate the change process rather than slowing it. Moreover, the professional development component of the process can lead to heightened valuing of research and continuation of research activities under conditions of reduced dependency on technical expertise. Sustained activity of this sort holds much promise for promoting organizational learning. But clearly, participation in evaluation in and of itself provides no guarantees. We need to know much more about the organizational conditions that support the participatory model and to develop strategies to ensure that it fits the organizational context.

Note

1 Some of the summaries were independently coded by two researchers and subsequently compared for agreement. The proportion of inter-coder agreement regarding Rockland data was .57 for chunking, .66 for first-order codes (higher order components of the framework), .70 for second-order codes (variables within components), and .46 for causal patterns. While these coefficients are not high, they were thought to be sufficient, given the complexity of the coding scheme and the use of the stringent criterion of exact agreement.

References

Louis, K.S. and Simsek, H. (1991) 'Paradigm shifts and organizational learning: Some theoretical lessons for restructuring schools'. Paper presented at the annual meeting of the University Council for Educational Administration, Baltimore, October.

Miles, M. and Huberman, M. (1984) *Qualitative Data Analysis: A Sourcebook of Methods*, Beverly Hills, Sage.

Weiss, C.H. (1991) 'Reflections on 19th-century experience with knowledge diffusion', *Knowledge: Creation, Diffusion, Utilization*, **13**, 1, pp. 5–16.

Weiss, C.H. and Bucuvalas, M.J. (1980) *Social Science Research and Decision Making*, New York, Columbia University Press.

Chapter 5

Participation in Evaluation of Funded School Improvement: Effects and Supporting Conditions

Linda E. Lee and J. Bradley Cousins

Background

In the spring of 1991, the Walter and Duncan Gordon Charitable Foundation (hereafter called the foundation) launched an initiative designed to support the development and implementation of innovative, school-based projects. After a lengthy research and consultation process, the foundation determined that the most effective way to encourage positive change in secondary education was to support innovation at the school level. The province of Manitoba was targeted as the site for the initial phases of the foundation's program.

In order to apply for funding, school staff members were encouraged to work collaboratively to develop a project or program which would address the needs of identified 'at-risk' student populations. Their proposals were to focus on changes which would affect fundamental aspects of the teaching and learning process. The foundation was interested in supporting changes in classroom methodology and school structure, rather than in establishing computer labs or purchasing other material supports for schools.

Schools received both 'in-person' and financial assistance for the preparation of their proposals. The foundation's Manitoba program coordinator and a designated evaluation consultant (first author) were available to schools. Schools could also receive funding (up to $800.00) to buy teacher release time so that classroom teachers would have the opportunity to be involved in the process of proposal development. It was anticipated that schools would propose projects of three to five years in length, allowing sufficient time for them to embed changes in to their organization and culture. By the autumn of 1992, a total of eight schools had received grant money from the foundation and were at various stages of project implementation.

Authors' Note: This research was supported in part by the Walter and Duncan Gordon Charitable Foundation and the Social Sciences and Humanities Research Council of Canada (Grant # 410–92–0983). The views expressed are those of the authors and do not necessarily reflect the opinions of the funding agencies.

Evaluation Model

A critical component of a school's proposal was an evaluation strategy. Evaluation was built into the development and implementation of each project, the expectation being that those involved in implementing the project would take ownership for its evaluation. Evaluation was to provide useful information for the implementors in order that they could make sensible decisions about the future of their project and, ultimately, about its effectiveness. The evaluation process was to support organizational learning and bolster implementation.

Recognizing that many teachers have neither the technical expertise nor the experience to conceptualize and undertake evaluation, the 'evaluation consultant' was contracted by the foundation to provide the necessary technical support to schools. The role of the consultant included assisting schools in the preparation of their funding proposal – focusing on their objectives and evaluation plan – and supporting schools with evaluation activities once they were successful in obtaining a grant. The evaluation model (which was defined by the foundation's expectations of the schools and of the evaluation consultant) was a participatory one. Partnerships were forged between the school personnel who had program responsibility and the evaluation consultant. The consultant acted as a technical resource person; school team members were their own 'evaluators'.

Through interaction with the evaluation consultant, members of school teams 'learned on the job' the skills necessary to direct their own program evaluation process. While certain technical supports were supplied or purchased by the school (e.g., data entry and statistical analysis of questionnaire data) the school owned and directed the evaluation process as part of its program implementation responsibilities.

Research Questions

The functioning and impact of participatory evaluation in the context of the foundation's Manitoba school-based program forms the basis for this research study. Three questions provided the focus for research:

1   What effects does involvement in participatory evaluation have on schools that are implementing externally funded, school-directed change? To what extent are these effects intended?
2   What are the conditions under which participatory evaluation is feasible in these schools? Are some schools more suitable candidates, and why?
3   What impact does involvement in participatory evaluation have on the evaluation consultant (i.e., the technical resource person)?

Since it was too early in the school improvement process to assess the impact or utilization of evaluation data by the schools, the present study focused on the effects of the participation process. This paper will identify the conditions or factors that support the implementation of participatory evaluation within the context of funded school improvement projects. Programs such as that sponsored by the foundation represent a distinctly 'bottom-up' approach to the problem of planned educational change. The implications for participation in evaluation and the conditions that support such participation remain largely unexamined. Finally, there is little empirical evidence available that addresses the impact of participatory evaluation on the evaluator herself or himself. For many evaluators, this extension of the stakeholder based model is fundamentally different, particularly with regard to the interactive role required in order to meet the demand for research skills development.

Method

The researchers (the authors) had eight potential school sites to consider for inclusion. Four of these sites were chosen because they represented different stages of project implementation. While some had been established for well over one year, others were in their first year of program implementation and evaluation data collection. The researchers also wished to ensure that not all sites were in the same school district.

Members of the project team at each selected site were interviewed, using a semi-structured interview protocol. The interview guide focused primarily on the first two research questions (above) although respondents were also asked about the evaluator's role. A total of twelve interviews of key informants were conducted in November 1992, at the four school sites, six by each of the authors. Following the interviews the researchers independently summarized the responses. These summaries provided the basis of the main findings for the present chapter.

Interview data were supplemented by information contained in the evaluation consultant's log. The consultant's log included the amount of time spent at each funded site, the type of support provided, as well as participant observations concerning the evaluation process and any emerging project implementation issues.

Description of the Sites

The four sites are described in order according to the length of time their projects have been operational. Fictitious names are used.

Monarch Secondary School

Monarch is a large secondary school (by Manitoba standards) with a total student population of approximately 1,200 (grades 7–12). It is situated in a large urban school district that includes many students who are considered at-risk because of conditions such as poverty and transience.

Funded in the first cycle, with project implementation beginning in the fall of 1991, Monarch had a complex project designed to make significant changes in the education of students in the junior high school grades. The project had three distinct strands, which, while having common goals for at-risk students, tended to function as separate initiatives.

A steering committee that was comprised of teachers (and, from time to time, a school administrator) oversaw the project; a task included the coordination of evaluation activities. The teacher designated as project coordinator, who also acted as 'contact' person for foundation communications, chaired the steering committee.

In the first year of operation, the steering committee undertook a variety of data-gathering activities. While some were conducted to document 'baselines' related to the common goals of the project, representatives of each project strand also undertook their own evaluative activities, including, in one instance, classroom action research.

Prairie View School

Prairie View School, located in the same district as Monarch, serves a younger population. While the project focused on junior high school ('middle years') students, the school operates from nursery to grade 8. There were approximately 550 students, of whom 150 are in the 7th and 8th grades.

The school submitted a proposal in the first cycle; while the proposal's promise was recognized, it was returned to the school for further development. The resubmission in the second cycle was successful and the school was granted funding to begin its project in January 1992. Prairie View's project concerned both curriculum adaptation and changes in school organization. The proposal for the project was developed collaboratively by a large group of teachers. Its implementation impacted on the entire middle years section of the school and had ramifications for the younger grades as well.

While the vice-principal acted as the original contact person, the project had an active steering committee of teachers, one of whom was subsequently designated as the contact person and acted as project coordinator. A subcommittee of the steering committee was struck to coordinate the evaluation activities. The teacher who accepted the leadership role for evaluation activities was the same person who assumed the project coordinator position.

Gabriel Dumont Junior High School

Gabriel Dumont has over 900 students and is in close proximity to its senior high school partner. It is located in a school district which includes both new and established suburbs. The school serves a newer housing development which includes a large number of recent immigrants to Canada. The school district has a reputation for valuing educational research and teacher participation in the research process. Concurrently, it was embarking on a high school restructuring study.

Gabriel Dumont received project funding in the third cycle and officially began implementation in the fall of 1992. However, this site had received a development grant as a result of its conceptually compelling submission in the second cycle. The core goal or purpose of the project is 'to make big small', creating a school environment that better suits the needs of all students. Because of the ambitious nature of the school's 'school change' project, it was felt that further details on the implementation and evaluation plan were needed before full funding could be approved.

The project was envisioned as a school improvement project, under whose 'umbrella' various working groups would concentrate on separate, but connected, initiatives. A management team (including administrators and representatives from all the working groups) oversaw the project. A project manager (who was the original force in the development of the initiative) was responsible for many administrative aspects of the project. He had a small amount of scheduled release time, most of which was provided through the school district's 'study leave' program.

A designated subcommittee of the management team was responsible for the project-wide evaluation activities. Like Monarch Secondary School, the various working groups incorporated specific evaluation activities into their implementation plans.

Cuthbert Grant Collegiate

Situated in the same district as Gabriel Dumont, Cuthbert Grant Collegiate is a senior high school of approximately 800 students (grades 9–12). The school program includes a French immersion stream, as well as the regular English program. It draws students from a better established area of the school district than does Dumont. Cuthbert Grant is directly involved in the district's high school 'restructuring' initiative.

The school applied for funding in the first cycle, but, because of internal factors, chose to wait until the third cycle to resubmit its application. The school was funded for project start-up in the fall of 1992. Their project focused on changes in the high school that will benefit students not only who are at 'high' risk, but also those who 'drift' through high school. Curriculum adaptation and the implementation of new instructional approaches represent the major thrusts.

Summary of Findings

Monarch Secondary School

The evaluation consultant worked extensively with this site during its first year of project operation, providing assistance with instrument design, technical data support, assistance with interpretation of results, and consultation on how to present data to other teachers on the staff. Approximately forty hours was spent on consultation and activities related directly to evaluation at this site.

The evaluation consultant's log also shows that, in addition to evaluation-related activities, eleven hours were spent on general consultative and support activities (e.g., helping the steering committee solve problems and develop strategies to surmount implementation barriers). It should be noted that the school's proposal that was funded in the first cycle was constructed in a short period of time; some meetings were held during the summer break in order to meet the August 30th application deadline.

While working through the evaluation process with this team, it was necessary to deal with other issues, such as the time and workload pressures felt by team members. Consequently, meetings and consultation time spent on 'evaluation activities' often included some discussion of other issues. A recurring theme in discussion at steering committee meetings was how to link the strands of the project and, at the same time, involve other staff.

The interviews commenced with a question on the purpose of evaluation. In response, the project coordinator at Monarch stated that evaluation should 'bring a purpose to our own population', thus providing clear information as to 'what the truth is here'. The same sentiment was articulated by the principal when he described evaluation as 'taking the pulse of existing and current situations.' Both had concerns that, without a systematic evaluation process, teachers 'fall back on instincts' that may not prove to give an accurate assessment of their situation: 'If you don't get concrete data, you are just using your intuition.'

The two other teachers viewed evaluation in a more personal sense, relating it to the achievement of their own program goals and objectives.

> It makes me look at the goals and objectives with respect to my program and makes me take a serious look to make sure I do reach them and how I reach them, the process of how I got there, and what I will do in the future.

> *The project team requested that the evaluation consultant be part of their presentation to staff. Background on the project, as well as data from both staff and student surveys, were included. Following the mini in-service, one member of the project team reported, 'we really had positive feedback from staff. For the first time other people really seemed to understand what we were trying to do.'*

Evaluation, as a means of assessing achievement, was confirmed by the other teacher, who noted that over the next few years 'we will look and see if there are differences in the kids who went through this program and the kids who didn't'.

Because this site was one in which a project had been functioning for one year, team members had the most experience in collecting both 'baseline' data and some initial responses from students regarding some of the new initiatives. Therefore, the interviews provided an opportunity to obtain reactions on the utilization of evaluation information. There was general agreement among those interviewed that they had used the evaluation information as intended, either to illuminate the school situation or to reflect on their own programs. While the teachers were particularly focused on their own project strands, there was recognition that sharing the evaluation information with other staff helps to build commitment to the project. They had shared some results in bulletins distributed to other staff and had scheduled a presentation to all staff in an upcoming 'mini in-service' session.

The time and energy demands of the project (including the evaluation component) were noted by all those interviewed. While they believed that the assistance of the evaluation consultant had helped with these pressures, the lack of time remained a factor. The administrator mentioned the problem of the teachers 'spreading themselves too thin', with the 'possibility of exhaustion' not too far away. As one teacher reported, 'We didn't really have time from our timetables to implement this as much as I would have liked. I still teach full time. . . .' The other two expressed the same sentiment through comments which indicated that, without the assistance of the outside consultant, the pressures of time would likely have meant that the evaluation piece would have been neglected, 'We would never have gotten to all that stuff [data collection] . . . it would just be so time consuming. . . . I'm busy with the day-to-day stuff.' The project coordinator echoed this, 'Evaluation wouldn't have happened; it just wouldn't have happened. I know it wouldn't. We don't feel we have the expertise and we don't have the time.'

Prairie View School

The evaluation consultant worked with the school team in developing its evaluation plan. The bulk of this planning or development was done at the time the proposal was being redrafted. Consequently, minimal time had to be spent clarifying the intended evaluation after the school received its grant.

The evaluation consultant also assisted the school's evaluation subcommittee with instrument design (the student questionnaire), technical data support, and, to a minor extent, with interpretation of resulting data. The school's evaluation subcommittee has undertaken the dissemination and discussion of evaluative information collected to date. The school has also set up, on its own, a system for tracking indicators, such as student attendance. A staff survey was planned but had not, at the time of the interviews, been constructed.

When interviewed, the person who had taken on coordinating responsibilities at Prairie View School emphasized the importance of evaluation in helping the school focus on the long term. He noted, at the individual level, that it helps you to know 'what is working', as well as 'what needs to be changed'. He viewed the formalized collection of data from staff and students as important, in that

> . . . when I ask you a question directly you may give me one response, but on an evaluation form you give a different type of response. Maybe you get to issues you would not normally.

The administrator at the school focused on the importance of reflecting on project objectives 'to see what we have achieved . . . the degree to which objectives are achieved or they are not'. The idea of evaluation helping staff to ascertain whether they are 'on track' was also expressed by the two other teachers who were interviewed.

> The evaluation is an acknowledgment of what's working and what's not. Although the paperwork that goes with it is not highly prized, it is important to document the large changes.

The administrator also emphasized the importance of keeping everyone 'on board' through sharing the information collected, because 'enthusiasm is contagious'. Consequently, information from the student survey was shared with all staff (including those in the early years section of the school). This was very deliberately, as one of the teachers mentioned, 'a caution': we 'don't want something which is elitist' or the feeling that 'people think we are in a different camp'.

While there was some discrepancy as to whether results had been disseminated to parents or whether this was about to happen, the intention to use evaluation information to raise project awareness in the community was present. The school had been visited by numerous people from other districts, but interest within the school's own district was not evident at the time.

Again, the issue of time was raised during the interviews. The teacher who was most directly involved in the actual evaluation activities spoke of this when he reflected on the technical assistance provided by the evaluation consultant in questionnaire design which 'was great because we did not have the time. If there was absolutely no funding for [evaluation] and we had to do it ourselves, then it would be a problem. It would be very time consuming'. The administrator also commented on the value of support in instrument design. But, the support of the evaluation consultant was seen to flow into the more general area of support as well. In a couple of instances there was a lack of clarity or distinction between the Manitoba program coordinator's and the evaluation consultant's activities.

> *The next contact with the school occurred within one month of the interview. The visit from the evaluation consultant as part of the present research study appeared to motivate the school to follow-up on some evaluation issues which had been put aside when other implementation activities had taken priority.*

Gabriel Dumont Junior High School

The evaluation consultant worked with the management team, the evaluation sub-committee, and the various working groups to develop evaluation plans. At the time of the present study, instrument development was just beginning. Not unlike Monarch Secondary School, Gabriel Dumont used the evaluation consultant as a 'sounding board' on implementation and evaluation issues. Much of this occurred during the redevelopment of their application for funding.

The two people interviewed at Dumont were both involved in the project from its initial conceptualization. The project coordinator saw the purpose of the evaluation as helping staff 'learn about change' and reflect on their program as it progressed: 'Anyone who is inquisitive would have a variety of reasons for [wanting to do] that'. The other person viewed the purpose of evaluation to 'show that you are doing what you set out to do . . . which things worked. And, to have a basis to help you improve'. As with the other sites, anticipated dependence on the evaluator was substantial:

> I have a fairly large concern that it is going to be difficult to find the time to do it. I think that [the evaluation consultant's] involvement is going to be fairly major. (*Project coordinator*)

The coordinator elaborated on the evaluation consultant's role and commented on the importance of developing the ongoing contact.

> What I like . . . apart from the fact that we need an external resource to [assist with data analysis] . . . is that she is quite familiar with those of us involved in the project and she has been to the school a number of times, so that she will be able to, in conjunction with us, categorize and analyze with a picture of what is really happening here . . . [I would be uncomfortable if it was someone] who did not have a direct sense of what is going on in the school.

Besides 'both time and expertise', the project manager also viewed the evaluation consultant as providing 'emotional' support and 'guidance'. The need to have technical and time-saving assistance was confirmed by the other interviewee, who said, 'I hope it's not just me and the project manager' in response to a question about data collection responsibilities.

Dissemination of evaluation information to all staff at Dumont was considered critical. The project coordinator expressed his desire to use dissemination as a way to stimulate staff engagement in the project.

> . . . not to preach to the converted but reinforcement is good. . . . There is a big staff here. There are some people who are not involved and some people who are really keeping their distance. It would be nice if this could sort of broaden the base.

The project manager concurred: 'It would be ideal for all the teachers in the school to be curious and interested . . . and I would like teachers to share that with their students'.

The time issue was emphasized strongly by both people at this site. The project manager described his already extensive time commitment.

> Much has been done in the area of evaluation since these interviews. Most
> important perhaps is the project manager's commitment to involve staff in the
> discussion of 'what this all means'. Various dissemination methods are being
> used to share information from baseline surveys with both staff and students.
> Discussion as to how to facilitate information flow – regarding both implemen-
> tation and evaluation activities – often appears on the management team's agenda.

This [project management role] could easily be a full-time job for me. I absolutely refuse to let my job totally take over my family life. Literally, the only
time I have to do a lot of this stuff is Sunday nights and almost every Monday, with the exception of a couple, I have come to work Monday morning
with 1 to 2 hours' sleep. And that affects . . . you know.

The other teacher expressed concern about the project manager and others on the
school's management team, because of the number of tasks in which they were directly
involved. While he saw 'lots of important things starting to happen here', he recognized
the 'danger of people being overworked and then pulling out'.

Cuthbert Grant Collegiate

At the time of data collection, the evaluation consultant had been primarily in contact
with the project coordinator (a school counsellor) and the school principal. Discussions
had centered on the framework for their evaluation plan. The administrator saw the
purposes of the evaluation and the project as a whole as being synonymous. The process
was viewed as continuous improvement, with a strong emphasis on reflective practice,
'Everything you do changes the way you look at other things. I guess evaluation is a
way of documenting [what you are doing] along the way.' The commitment to evaluation
appeared to be strong with the project coordinator as well.

> Everything in schools should be evaluated somehow, sometime. Whether we
> have the money or not we should be evaluating new programs. Maybe the
> money motivates us to get started a little sooner and keeps us on a timetable,
> so we don't say, 'Well, we'll get around to evaluating it sooner or later.'

While the project coordinator tended to see himself and the administrator as 'spear-
heading' both the project and the evaluation, he hoped that ownership of evaluation
activities would be spread more widely among staff. If people are not widely involved
'their enthusiasm will fizzle . . . and the whole point of the foundation is to see some
school-wide changes'.

The administrator had no doubts that the school's project committee would be
involved in carrying out various aspects of the evaluation. Given previous experiences
with research activities, and their current involvement in the district's restructuring
process, the administrator recognized that certain technical aspects could easily be
contracted out. He felt that the predominant aspect of the evaluation consultant's role
was not the 'number crunching', but

> *The supervisory officer's department has indeed taken an interest and has requested copies of some of the evaluation information which has been collected. The anticipated links between the project goals and the district's wider restructuring initiative are being strengthened as the school district attempts to garner learnings from this school's experience.*

. . . the guidance of her saying, 'No, it can be simpler than that' and her perspective is very much one of 'what documentation and data can be assembled and flow naturally out of what you are doing actually?'

Looking to the future, the administrator saw the writing of results and reports as a positive process, one that would really establish the credibility of the research.

I think the value of doing the research is struggling with the data and trying to figure out what it does mean. I see that as a positive force. . . . There is a tendency to disregard research done in other situations. [We think] 'that may be true somewhere else, but it is not true here'.

The project coordinator was more concerned about the technical aspects, although he too felt the main use of the consultant to date had been in 'bouncing ideas . . . [evaluation] is not an area where I have any background . . . and we don't have the time and the energy'.

The sharing of evaluation information with all staff was again viewed as important in order to avoid having the project team perceived as 'elitist'. Also, the project coordinator felt the evaluation information could be used for 'good sales in the community'. He commented that the supervisory officer's department would be 'very interested' in the evaluation results.

Discussion

Involvement in a participatory evaluation linked to an externally funded, 'bottom-up', school change project affects the attitudes and actions of teacher participants. Those interviewed in project schools generally had a clear idea of why evaluation was important and how they could use it to their advantage. They were positive about its benefits, both for themselves and for its potential to impact on others. Evaluation was viewed as a tool which could foster enthusiasm and encourage wider staff participation in school improvement activities. A commitment to evaluation as part of the process of innovation was evidenced in the attitudes of those interviewed. Reported actions – particularly in the more established sites – indicate that once data are collected they are indeed shared with other staff. There is an excitement in discovering 'what the truth is here'. While it is too soon to assess long-term effectiveness or utilization, those interviewed felt very strongly about the importance of disseminating and sharing information, as well as continuing to use information in the process of self-reflection and program improvement.

The potentially negative effect of being the owner of your evaluation is that, despite the assistance provided by the evaluation consultant and all the best intentions of not making evaluation another 'add-on', it does take time. Teachers implementing change within their school already find they are overworked. They participate in a variety of committees, encourage increased teacher involvement, interact with their administration on project implementation issues, and, in addition, they retain the bulk of their teaching responsibilities. (None of the evaluation plans had any significant amount of release time built in for the project coordinator to coordinate the evaluation activities on site.) Time is the commodity in short supply. Evaluation quickly becomes one more drain on this scarce resource.

All sites, however, shared a condition which appears to promote success in the participatory model. Key team members at all sites are people who want to see change and are willing to work to make it happen. The fact that they were successful in a demanding grant application process (three of the sites received funding only after resubmitting) speaks to this commitment and enthusiasm. They are people who see a value in evaluation as a part of the change process. They want an 'objective' view of their current reality and want to be able to have a perspective on how this reality has changed over time.

While the sites, by their nature, all share this feature, other conditions differ. The schools that were not funded on their first application had the opportunity to plan their project implementation in more detail. In these cases, the schools had a clearer plan for implementation. With the stress of project start-up diminished, evaluation can more easily fall into place. The amount of evaluation consultant time needed at this stage also decreases. The value placed on research by the district may also be a condition which fosters success in a participatory model. At one site, time had been given by the district to help support the project manager role, while at the other site in the same district, resources were already in place to support research for a high school restructuring thrust compatible with the school's project goals. The two schools in the other district knew that their evaluation efforts would be valued by their senior administration.

While doing a participatory evaluation impacts on the school team, it has demonstrable effects on the role of the evaluation consultant as well. Participatory evaluation is time consuming by nature. Working through the evaluation process and supporting the learning inherent in the participatory model requires more time than pursuing or using a model where the technical evaluation person acts as 'outside evaluator'. On a continuum from the consultant as external judge, to the consultant functioning as a stakeholder, to the consultant working in a participatory model, the amount of time spent by the consultant in the school increases. The consultant in the participatory model is not simply a technical resource, nor even an 'evaluation coach'. The consultant's role also includes acting as 'sounding board' and 'counsellor' when the process of implementation encounters its unavoidable difficulties. While the foundation's Manitoba program coordinator assumes a support role, the consultant is the person likely to be on site because of the evaluation activities.

With evaluation built into the implementation of the project it is only natural – and probably appropriate – that implementation problems dwell in the domain of evaluation. However, some of this time can be reduced if schools begin implementation with a clear, comprehensive, and mutually agreed-upon plan of action. Given the close working relationship between school team and evaluation consultant, it sometimes becomes difficult for the evaluation consultant to maintain a clear view of each project. Participatory evaluation is seductive. Interestingly, in the interviews conducted for this research

> *As the number of schools funded by the foundation has grown to sixteen, maintaining a 'multiplicity of contacts' with all funded sites has become more of a challenge for the evaluation consultant. Those schools which are further along the implementation continuum, including those discussed in this research, have had, by necessity, to assume more responsibility for their project's evaluation. While regular contact still occurs, greater demands on the consultant's time may have helped to force increased school level ownership.*

the evaluation consultant – in the role of interviewer – found out some 'new' things from project team members. Asking questions from a different perspective allowed the evaluation consultant to uncover issues which, ironically, may hold significant implications for project implementation and evaluation.

Teachers in Manitoba schools generally have little experience in developing evaluation plans or conducting evaluation activities. Therefore, working with them as a technical resource person can be frustrating as well as time consuming. In this case, the evaluation consultant had previously supported school personnel, both when she was employed with the provincial department of education and, subsequently, with a large school district. Her expectations regarding the evaluation expertise of teachers were grounded in previous experience. However, in the case of the foundation initiative, the strong motivation of the project participants and their high level of commitment and ownership of their projects made the process a rewarding one. Clearly, when school personnel are involved in the evaluation of projects which are of their own making, resistance, apathy and 'other priorities' are not in evidence.

Time spent by the evaluation consultant with school personnel was not just face-to-face contact. Telephone 'checks' regarding both evaluation and implementation issues were frequent (and, difficult to log in terms of total time spent with each school). This 'multiplicity of contacts' helped to build and maintain a close relationship between school staff and the evaluation consultant. Surprises concerning the evaluation process or misinterpretations of the consultant's suggestions, were rare.

Conclusions and Suggestions for Practice and Research

Despite the early stage of project implementation at the four school sites, some conclusions can be made regarding school and consultant involvement in a participatory evaluation.

The evaluation demands inherent in the foundation's Manitoba school-based program virtually force funded schools to accept a participatory evaluation model (although schools certainly have the option to forgo evaluation assistance, but to date none have found that option attractive). From the four school sites, which are the focus of this research, it can be concluded that there are positive effects. School team members have developed (or enhanced) their understanding of evaluation and their commitment to its inclusion in their school change process. In the early stages, they are using the evaluation information for its intended purposes. They are eager and willing to initiate baseline data collection and plan for evaluation activities to come. It is likely that this eagerness is an extension of the ownership and enthusiasm they hold for the larger school improvement project. However, involvement in evaluation activities also has the effect of increasing the time and workload pressures on the primary participants. Consideration needs to be given not only to keeping evaluation activities within a realistic scope, but also to clarifying for which technical activities project team members can relinquish responsibility. Well-defined role expectations need to be articulated and continuously reinforced by the evaluation consultant. Time for the project coordinator – and perhaps for other key team members as well – is required if teachers are to avoid burn-out in a participatory evaluation model.

Pressures on both the schools and the evaluation consultant are reduced if schools begin implementation with a clear and detailed plan. It can be concluded that where the foundation's feedback on an initial application forced further planning, the conditions for participatory evaluation were improved. This requirement is one that external funding agencies can ensure is in place when funding new projects. Schools may also prove more suitable candidates for participatory evaluation if their district is known to value research and practice self-reflection. While this may not be a necessary condition, it is surely a helpful one.

If the evaluation consultant can force a means of stepping outside the process, this may be helpful at strategic points. As part of participatory evaluation, the technical person can be drawn into the team's perspective. While this may be advantageous in gaining the team's trust and commitment to evaluation, the consultant and the team then also assume that the consultant knows all the important details. This may not be so. Also, if the evaluation consultant is to encourage formative evaluation, modelling this process may indeed prove a useful teaching method.

Several implications for continued research emerge from the present data. First, replicating the present study as the projects mature will add to the learning to be gleaned. The impact of the evaluation may be assessed more deeply at a later stage, and by the inclusion of other staff and stakeholder groups in the sample. Has the evaluation information had any impact other than on those immediately involved in the project? Did it contribute to organizational learning? Did it foster site-level project decision making? Preliminary evidence from the Manitoba evaluation projects suggests that impact is likely to be significant, but further study is required.

Second, the present study adds to knowledge about the conditions supporting the participatory evaluation model in schools; but many questions remain. As projects mature, are staff responsible for evaluation likely to be viewed as elitist by peers? What will be the effect of negative data? Will dependency on the external consultant regarding evaluation issues change and, if so, in which direction? From a different point of view, the conditions inherent in the current situation are somewhat forced by the requirements of the funding agency. Further research is needed about participation in circumstances where such requirements are not in evidence. Of particular interest are projects which are also decidedly bottom-up. On the one hand, the propensity for staff to systematically self-reflect is likely to be greater; but on the other, the lack of external pressure may diminish the perceived importance of the evaluation function in view of competing demands for staff time, especially concerning the school improvement process.

Finally, the role of the evaluation consultant in the Manitoba case may have been somewhat anomalous in the current circumstances, given her prior experience of working within these school districts on evaluation problems. The data suggests that a relatively comfortable arrangement can be worked out. But these data offer little insight for evaluators who are new to the participatory model. What sorts of interpersonal and pedagogical skills are required in order to be effective in the evaluator/consultant role? What are the implications for technical quality of direct, versus consultative, participation? Do the time frames of practitioners fit those of the evaluators and, if not, can they be reconciled? Speculative answers to these questions based on the present data look promising, but there is a significant need to accumulate relevant data through further systematic inquiry.

Chapter 6

Involving Practitioners in Evaluation Studies: How Viable is Collaborative Evaluation in Schools?

Jean A. King

Introduction

The notion of involving practitioners in a school-based research* process is not new. At the turn of the century, John Dewey gave teachers and students direct roles in ongoing inquiry, and the progressive tradition, with newfound support from the teacher researcher movement (Stenhouse, 1975), has continued to encourage that practice in schools. Action research, named by social psychologist Kurt Lewin in the late 1940s, brought together university-based researchers with community individuals to engage in collaborative problem solving about some of the most difficult issues of the day. The related rise of educational action research in the 1950s (Corey, 1953; Taba and Noel, 1957) pointed to the potential of research collaboration to effect meaningful change in schools. However, a number of factors – for example, the lack of time for such work in the traditional school day; methodological challenges from the research community; and the development of a federally-funded Research, Development, and Diffusion (RD&D) model following the launch of Sputnik – led, until recently, to the decline of collaborative research in the United States (King and Lonnquist, 1992).[1] The currently burgeoning literature on teacher research (e.g., Kincheloe, 1991; Cochran-Smith and Lytle, 1993) and educational action research (e.g., Holly and Whitehead, 1984) points to the re-emergence of this process as a means of professional development, school improvement, and, some would claim (e.g., McTaggart, 1991), long-term social change.

In contrast, the field of program evaluation, developed in part to meet the evaluation needs of the federally funded RD&D model, has traditionally assigned school-based educational practitioners a different role. Stereotypically, they are first the data sources and last the potential recipients of the products of evaluation. Whether or not anyone uses these products – and what it might take to get someone to do so – has been a topic of discussion in the evaluation use literature for well over a decade (see Alkin, Daillak and White, 1979; King and Pechman, 1982; Patton, 1986).

---

* The conceptual distinction between the terms *research* and *evaluation* is important, and many would label the processes that I am discussing here evaluation. However, throughout the paper, I use the two terms interchangeably, in part because 'action research' appropriately includes the word *research*, and in part because I am taking linguistic liberty for the sake of variety in my language.

Fairly early on in the field, the notion of responsive evaluation (Stake, 1975) suggested the importance of responding to the information needs of people participating in evaluation studies, an approach extended in the stakeholder model to include virtually all possible participants (Worthen and Sanders, 1987). Patton's utilization-focused approach (1986) created an evaluation process that was based on the questions of those who would use the results; an ongoing and interactive collaboration between evaluator and practitioner. Participatory evaluation (Cousins and Earl, 1992) made this collaboration explicit. It is:

> . . . applied social research that involves a partnership between trained evaluation personnel and practice-based decision makers, organization members with program responsibility, or people with a vital interest in the program. (pp. 399–400)

Over time, successful participatory evaluation seeks to transform schools into learning organizations, building their research capacity to go it alone without an outside evaluation collaborator: 'We see participatory evaluation as a powerful learning system designed to foster local applied research and thereby enhance social discourse about relevant organizational issues' (Cousins and Earl, 1992, p. 401).

The purpose of this paper is to discuss the related concepts of participatory evaluation and practitioner-centered action research (King and Lonnquist, 1992), first conceptually and then through three brief case descriptions: two of participatory evaluations and one of a collaborative action research effort. Personal lessons learned from these approaches will be presented, followed by a discussion of implications for further development of this work.

A Comparison of Collaborative Evaluation/Research Approaches

Table 6.1 compares four evaluation/research approaches that involve practitioners. Two approaches, the stakeholder model and participatory evaluation, are explicated in Cousins and Earl (1992). The remaining two approaches, traditional- and practitioner-centered action research, are presented in King and Lonnquist (1992). Definitions suggest that these approaches share two defining characteristics: they actively involve practitioners in the research process; and they study existing programs *in situ*. With the exception of practitioner-centered action research, their differences are more of degree than kind:

- Practitioner involvement in the *stakeholder approach*, although important, may be fairly minimal. In a stakeholder evaluation, evaluators purposefully involve people who have a stake in the program – as administrators, policy makers, clients, service deliverers, etc. – and work throughout the process to insure that, to the extent possible, the needs and interests of multiple audiences receive attention.
- In *traditional action research*, a small number of practitioners are involved, providing input to researchers (typically university based), making suggestions, facilitating data collection, and so on. Practitioners play an active role, but outside researchers insure the validity of a research process that is designed to generate social science data while simultaneously addressing real problems.[2]

Table 6.1 Comparison of approaches to collaborative evaluation/research

Characteristic	Stakeholder	Traditional Action Research	Participatory Evaluation	Practitioner-Centered Action Research
Who's in charge of the study?	Evaluator as principal investigator	Researcher/evaluator, with input from practitioner	Evaluator, with assistance of practitioner/student at first	Practitioners, with assistance of research consultants
What practitioners are involved in the study?	Large number of stakeholders; anyone with a stake in the program	Small number of those who actively engage in the study; people who are interested or helpful	Small number of primary users	Action researchers
How do practitioners participate?	Consultative role; give information on context, information needs	Active role; ask questions, give input, help analyze, etc.	Active role; engage in 'nuts and bolts' of evaluation process	Active role; control the research process
What time frame?	Length of study	Length of study	Length of study or ongoing	Ongoing research cycle; organizational learning
What involvement in theory development?	[If any] Develop program theory	Create traditional social science theory	Develop program theory (theories-in-action, mental models)	[If any] Develop practical theory or critical theory

- The role of practitioners in *participatory evaluation* is also active. In fact, a small number of people who will become the primary users of evaluation information engage in the very 'nuts and bolts' of the process. In contrast to traditional action research, participatory evaluation has long-term implications for the practitioners it involves. Over time, the evaluator teaches site collaborators sufficient research skills to develop learning within the organization. In that sense, the goal of a participatory evaluator is eventually to put him or herself out of work when the research capacity of the organization is self-sustaining.

- The important difference in *practitioner-centered action research* is that the researcher/evaluator no longer is in charge of the evaluation process. Instead, site-based practitioners themselves engage in a process through which they frame their own questions, develop their own designs, collect and analyze data, reflect, and then begin the collaborative cycle again.[3] Outside facilitators can join in the process, but only to provide expertise as 'critical friends' and peers, not as controlling superiors. In practitioner-centered action research, it is more important to answer the right question, however messy the methodology, than to answer the wrong question extremely well. Issues of utility and feasibility sometimes demand trade-offs in technical accuracy.

These four approaches each give program practitioners a role to play in an evaluative process. I would argue that the concept of organizational learning upon which Cousins and Earl (1992) base their theoretical justification for participatory evaluation at best is exactly what can take place over time in practitioner-centered action research. But what exactly is the role of evaluator in these collaborative approaches?

Like Molière's *bourgeois gentilhomme*, who proudly realized that he had been speaking prose all his life, I was rather pleased recently to realize that I have engaged in participatory evaluation virtually my entire career. Having identified my *modus operandi*, I became interested in reflecting on my practice across three studies, each of which challenged me to learn.

Three Program Examples: CPIP, OEL, and CARP[4]

Extending over the past fifteen years, my involvement in collaborative evaluation approaches has included three projects that provided heartfelt lessons. The first two are examples of what I would now call the initial stages of participatory evaluation. Although it was a one-shot effort, program coordinators in the Curriculum Process Improvement Program (CPIP) evaluation played an active role in framing questions, analyzing data, and suggesting recommendations. In the Office of Educational Leadership (OEL) study, a network of site representatives worked collaboratively with the evaluation team to conduct a two-year study, with the expectation of long-term commitment to the evaluation process. In both cases, the demise of the programs summarily executed the development of organizational learning, except in an extremely negative lesson about the long-term prospects of major change efforts in large bureaucratic organizations. The third case is a recent project involving practitioner-centered action research in which teachers conducted their own studies with facilitation from university-based critical friends.

CPIP

The Curriculum Process Improvement Program (CPIP) was an attempt to place a learning for mastery (LFM) approach (Bloom, Hastings and Madaus, 1971) into the grade 7–12 curriculum of a large city school district. CPIP was an expensive program. Benjamin Bloom himself gave the keynote address during a highly visible program launching in the late 1970s. Program brochures labelled CPIP a 'self-paced mastery program which provides all students with the opportunity to experience their fullest educational potential'. It was, over time, to 'give the community renewed faith in the capability of graduating students to function effectively in their chosen careers'. And so, unit by unit, CPIP tests were created in various subjects. Centralized computer scoring would provide rapid feedback to teachers and students, as well as create a district record for accountability purposes. Structurally, a group of teachers was released from classroom responsibilities to serve as district CPIP trainers, and all secondary teachers were eventually cycled through a two-week training period. District administrators proudly prepared transparencies, articles, and audiotapes proclaiming their hopes for the success of CPIP. In the words of the then superintendent: 'Frankly, I do not see CPIP as a gamble at all. The program as developed so far makes sense educationally, and we hope it will achieve its anticipated results.'

But as is often the case when hopes are proclaimed in public before a program is well in place, the CPIP implementation ran into major snags. While the trainers were extremely enthusiastic about the LFM process, those they trained were often less committed. Some questioned the viability of a mastery learning approach in their content area. Others resented the amount of work required to keep the program going with over 150 students a day, even assuming the computer support worked smoothly, which, from the beginning, it did not. Teachers who dutifully submitted their CPIP computer sheets often waited weeks for the scores to return, and, by then, the effectiveness of the feedback was limited at best. Stacks of user-unfriendly test results sat on teachers' desks across the district, and word quickly got out that this was a program in trouble. Despite major expenditures for staff development and computer support, CPIP was not working. This is not to say that some teachers did not support the program. For example, virtually all were pleased to receive additional CPIP instructional materials, although these often arrived far into the school year.

Within three years, the superintendent who created CPIP left the district and another was named who immediately hired a go-getting deputy superintendent for curriculum to shape things up in that area. In an era of tightening budgets, CPIP's price tag made it an extremely visible target for cuts. The well-known problems related to computerized scoring and classroom implementation provided little evidence to support continuation, and rumors circulated that the deputy had set his sights on CPIP. However, because he was new and did not want to appear unfair, the deputy superintendent commissioned the district evaluation office to conduct a full-scale CPIP evaluation study. The evaluation director, well aware of CPIP realities, was committed to an inclusive process that would create useful information about the program and its outcomes, regardless of its eventual fate. Knowing the professional commitment of the staff developers, she proposed a participatory effort through which their concerns would be joined with those of the deputy superintendent; I served on the team and helped facilitate discussions. However, the deputy superintendent refused to collaborate, telling the director that the evaluation was *her* job and questioning why his involvement was even desired.

Suffice it to say that the evaluation was ill-fated from the beginning. People across the district saw the writing on the wall, so the incentives for participation were few. As one of the people facilitating the process (and at the same time trying to understand it), I lived amidst the frustration and fears of people who saw their hard work threatened. Nevertheless, some CPIP trainers did collaborate over the course of the year, brain-storming issues, deciding on questions and methods, and discussing data. Their hope was that their good efforts could somehow be salvaged and that the program would continue in some form. Meanwhile, classroom teachers dutifully completed question-naires, documenting their frustration with the program, which still was not working well.

The CPIP bombshell was dropped shortly after the evaluation director informally presented the initial results of the study to the deputy superintendent. During the budget planning for the following year, CPIP funding was noticeably absent, and, when ques-tioned, the deputy cited the evaluation outcomes as the rationale for the cut. As the final evaluation report bluntly stated: 'The Curriculum Process Improvement Program is not scheduled to be continued because of the relatively small number of teachers involved and benefiting from the program.' The CPIP staff developers were devastated. Their involvement in the evaluation had done nothing to save their central office positions, and most were reassigned to secondary classrooms. Remnants of CPIP lived on in some of these classrooms, but seemingly no one in the central administration used the data that detailed what had been learned from this massive experiment in LFM to make decisions about a new secondary curriculum.[5]

OEL

The Office of Educational Leadership (OEL) existed in the Minnesota Department of Education for two years (1989–91), funded by the state legislature to build the foun-dation for the radical transformation of schooling in Minnesota. Enabling legislation directed the OEL to develop a two-year research and development project to determine the effectiveness of an outcome-based system of education, and develop it they did. The four-person OEL staff set about to do nothing less than redesign the process of K-12 education at ten volunteer project sites, the winners of an OEL grant competition, who were funded with a grant of $50,000 a year for two years. In September 1989, the ten sites, comprised of seventeen districts and five educational consortiums and represent-ing rural, suburban, and inner city communities, began what OEL staff believed and told them would be a long-term change effort (ten years plus) to which the legislature was committed.

In March 1990, the OEL contracted with the Center for Applied Research and Educational Improvement (CAREI) in the College of Education, University of Minne-sota, to develop a collaborative research process, led and facilitated by me, that would model the organizational learning that schools of the future might use. This process was based on the assumption that collaborative problem-solving involving *all* OEL par-ticipants at some level would facilitate meaningful transformation at the project sites. This was participatory evaluation writ large, with the expectation that, over time, sites truly would take on their own research. Initial research planning included over fifty individuals, representing each of the ten sites, CAREI, the Minnesota Department of Education, and the College of Education at the University of Minnesota; we did not, however, invite legislators or their aides. Michael Quinn Patton facilitated a two-day planning session in April 1990, which resulted in guiding principles for our collaborative research,[6] baseline data questions, and a list of appropriate methods. Much to our pleasure and amazement, we left with virtual consensus both on a participatory evaluation process and on the questions the group wanted answered.

If that was the momentary good news, the longer term bad news became immediately apparent. It was mid-April, and year 1 baseline data, including classroom observation data, had to be collected before school ended in June. Knowing how the school year winds down, this actually gave us about four weeks to gain entrance at ten sites across the state, which were actually thirty-seven or thirty-nine different schools, depending on how you counted them. Given the timing, our on-site collaborators were unable to assist in data collection or analysis, beyond setting schedules and making arrangements.

In retrospect, the frenzy of the data collection was reminiscent of piranhas feeding on a hapless beast. Fifteen graduate students descended on project sites with a fairly long list of data requirements. While the list had been developed collaboratively in the planning session, people at the sites were often unaware of what their colleagues had agreed to, and, as the end-of-the-year crunch set in, they were sometimes frustrated by the demands of this state-funded, university-personed evaluation process. Some CAREI staff added to the problems. One research assistant inadvertently offended a key figure at one site, who basically cut off data collection for the year. Another research assistant, in the throes of a serious illness (we learned later), exhibited strange behavior that made people who interacted with her question the evaluation process. Nevertheless, the team managed somehow to collect all the needed information and then set about writing the thirty-nine short case studies summarized in Volume II of the OEL Phase I Evaluation Report. Cases were reviewed at the sites and led, by the end of the year, to a report in which we and our OEL colleagues took great pride.

Determined never again to put ourselves in such a frantic position, we convinced the OEL Director to create a group of site representatives for ongoing discussion and project monitoring. The OEL network, with representatives from OEL, CAREI, and each site, began meeting in September 1990, with an expectation, at least on my part, that over time these network participants would become fairly sophisticated coordinators and users of research data. An early decision of the group was that a short survey of people involved in the OEL effort would provide useful information for the legislative session beginning in January. That was done and, with the cooperation of people at the sites, completed with less stress than the preceding year. The network discussed and reflected on initial analyses, then used the data they found helpful at their individual sites. The group then planned more extensive work for the spring, including a core study across sites and the option of voluntary site-specific studies.

With fewer and more reliable research assistants, a more reasonable time-line, and continuing interaction with our on-site collaborators, the Phase II data collection – individual interviews with administrators and/or opinion leaders; group interviews with site leaders, teachers, parents, and students; and a survey of all administrators and instructional staff across all sites – was completed in a timely manner. We were truly confident that the participatory evaluation process was succeeding. Certain principals, central office administrators, and even some classroom teachers were helping frame questions, administer surveys, and make collective sense of the information at network meetings. These individuals had become our colleagues, and the process of watching the OEL effort grow was invigorating. The notion that the network would truly lead the ongoing evaluation efforts began to make sense.

We should not have been so sanguine. While we did our work, the recession hit

Minnesota, dropping state revenues drastically. The legislative promoters of outcome-based education and the OEL left the legislature, leaving the OEL director politically vulnerable. Changes in the Department of Education made the OEL a virtual step-child, and rumors began circulating across sites that funding trouble was brewing. The ten-year development process we had taken for granted suddenly vanished, and there was talk, to our dismay, that after two years of intense effort, the OEL would not be reauthorized. Mazzoni, Freeman and Stewart (1992) document in detail the fate of the OEL, including the one and only clear impact of the fruits of our evaluation labor. The sole remaining legislator who had been head of an education committee when the OEL was first created commented to a group of OEL site representatives that the Phase I report was a 'piece of ____' because it included no standardized achievement scores. This was one reason given for recommending the program's elimination.

It is important to note that an explicit outcome of the April 1990 planning session was the group's consensus that it would be wrong to include test scores in the early evaluation of the OEL transformation process. To do so would send an inappropriate signal to school sites that our study represented evaluation business as usual. If we are serious about transformation, the argument went, then we also need to transform the evaluation process. In retrospect, we all questioned our seeming naivete and the wisdom of our collective decision. With the dissolution of the OEL office, both the change effort and the evaluation process ended.

CARP

The Minnesota Collaborative Action Research Project (CARP) is an umbrella that encompasses a number of practitioner research activities fostered by CAREI. I will discuss here the practitioner-centered action research we studied for two years (1991–93)[7] through which teams of teachers at two elementary schools in outer-ring suburbs collaborated on an important change issue in their buildings. An assumption underlying the research was that by involving teachers in a participatory research process, they could make sense of change as it occurred and simultaneously make adjustments suggested by the data collected.

At one site, a kindergarten centre, the team began the first year by studying the effects of mainstreaming on special needs children in their classes. They studied children who were 'double programmed' – that is, children who spent half a day in a district special education program and half a day mainstreamed in their classes – examining what happened to these children during kindergarten and planning for a smooth transition to first grade. During the course of their work, the action researchers innocently ran up against district special education politics related to pull-out versus inclusionary programming and learned political lessons that went well beyond their classrooms. Certain special education teachers feared that they would lose their jobs if policies were changed, and this unavoidably created tension for the action research effort that was focusing in part on how to effectively mainstream children served in separate classes. Nevertheless, the teacher researchers concluded year 1 with data they believed would help individual children when they left the centre, as well as improve continuing practice with new children. They also believed that the district central office understood their concerns since they presented the results of the research at district-level meetings involving high-level administrators.

From one perspective, their action research in the second year was less successful.

Given their initial success, the four teachers involved in year 1 decided to split into two two-person teams, one to look at transition issues for special needs children and the other to study another special population: children needing English as a second language (ESL) instruction. However, other matters for the most part overwhelmed the two person studies. Because of the first-year success, two of the teachers were appointed to a district-wide transition committee, and this commitment reduced their out-of-class time available for reflection and continued study. One of the teachers became pregnant and went on leave to have her baby during the year; another later became pregnant with twins. In addition, planning for the building of a first grade wing at the centre involved the teachers in numerous meetings they simply could not miss, and action research became secondary to other activities. If year 2's action research was in some ways a failure, from another perspective the teachers reported learning a lot about the process during the second year, for example, that two-person teams lacked the depth needed to counter inevitable time conflicts during the school year, and that other teachers and administrators gave great credence to local teacher-collected data.

The action researchers at the other site studied multi-age grouping (MAG). In year 1, the teachers conducted what they called their 'MAG experiment'. The team developed ten one-hour lessons on the theme of the egg to integrate children from two or three grade levels in innovative, MAG activities. To their surprise and pleasure, twelve other teachers agreed to participate by sharing children and teaching the lessons to mixed age groups (combinations of kindergarten through third grade). Data collected (student questionnaires and anecdotal records) confirmed the teachers' sense that the results of the experiment were mixed. While the innovative lessons were often fun, the multi-age interactions were limited, owing to the once a week structure of the activities. The children just did not have time to develop relationships and group process skills. However, the results encouraged the teacher researchers to become more fully committed both to the notion of multi-age grouping and to working as a close-knit team. Fortunately, a new principal supported their proposal in the second year to have two, first grade classes and a second grade class involved in a year-long, multi-age experience.

In year 2, then, they studied their continuing efforts to create interactions across age levels, especially through a common 'family time' involving all children, and through sharing students during reading classes that applied a whole language approach. Some data were encouraging. Family time was a positive coming together where different students could share thoughts and presentations with the entire group. The whole language process created positive environments in the three classrooms and extensive interactions among students who, after a year's working together, knew each other well. But the action research also pointed to concerns. For example, shifting children for reading instruction proved complicated and led to embarrassing situations for the home-base teachers when parents called for information they did not have readily at hand. Over the course of the summer, the teachers revised their plans in light of what their study had shown them and planned, also, for continuing their action research effort.

Our role as evaluators/researchers in this practitioner-centered process was an ongoing learning experience. Unlike the other two cases where the evaluation process was clearly my responsibility, as an action research collaborator my job was to facilitate the teachers' ongoing research. Knowing how busy they were and understanding that they had lives outside of school, this was at times both frustrating and discouraging. Our staff set up meetings, bought the snacks (not a trivial detail), took notes on who was doing what, and, in the words of more than one researcher, served as 'cheerleaders' for the process. We rendered technical assistance, but unobtrusively, and we tried to intervene positively when problems arose. For example, when teachers at one site were concerned about being allowed to participate in an important meeting during school hours, we cleared their involvement through the central office. One thing was clear: after our first year together, the second-year teams were far more independent, and our role as outside consultants diminished considerably. But was this a success? In one case, other professional and personal matters diminished the action research process, and, at the end of the year, the teachers decided (in their words) to 'take a break' from such efforts. In the other case, the practice of action research was integrated into the teachers' work, and is now, they report, an ongoing part of their practice.

Lessons Learned from Collaborative Evaluation/Research Studies to Date

Tatters and bruises are not necessarily signs that someone has learned something. Unreflective people can have the same experience many times, while others can analyze a single experience to grow and develop. I hope I fall in the latter category. The three studies described previously created dynamic classrooms[8] for my evaluation practice, and reflection on this work points to four lessons: the importance of people's wanting to participate; the power of political context; the necessity of continuing support; and the need for common meaning between distinct worlds of practice.

Volunteers Needed

To paraphrase an old saw, you can lead a person to evaluation, but you cannot make him or her participate. The power of the human factor has long since been accepted in the evaluation literature (e.g., Patton *et al.*, 1978), but the special power of people to affect collaborative studies both positively and negatively cannot be overstated. My evaluation experience documents three types of individuals in schools. Fortunately, there is one group of individuals eager to join forces with evaluators in collaborative efforts. These individuals become primary users and potential creators of evaluation information.

A second group are those who, for various reasons, might be willing, but are unable to engage in meaningful collaboration. Some reasons are obvious. For example, in the action research study, one teacher was unable to collaborate for health reasons: halfway through the first year, she became pregnant and required extensive bed rest. Another with small children had little time for projects that extended beyond the work day. In the second year of the study, a principal wanted to be supportive, but, given the demands of district and building activities, could only participate on an occasional basis. Other reasons making people unable to collaborate are less obvious. Control issues seem important. In the OEL study, for example, one of the state department collaborators early on became concerned that the research agenda was slipping from her fingers and, verbal support to the contrary, that the translation of the language of collaboration into action had simply gone too far. A tense confrontation resolved the issue at least temporarily, but the evaluation team, blindsided once, never again fully trusted that individual.

A third category of people are those who choose not to participate. In the CPIP study, for example, the deputy superintendent who commissioned the evaluation wanted only the results; he had a clear sense of what his ultimate decision would be even before one piece of data was collected. He was neither interested in collaborating nor willing to interact with those conducting or affected by the study. Given his status in the district, he could opt to do what he wanted. The OEL project also included people who chose not to engage. Six of the ten sites elected not to develop a site-specific evaluation, and some did not actively participate in the network meetings that determined the course of the study. Clandinin and Connelly (1992) note that *requiring* teachers to become emancipated is itself a form of domination, and collaborative approaches simply cannot empower people who are not willing to be empowered.

Collaboration is not just a set of skills to be taught. The process demands a commitment that some people are unable or unwilling to make, and evaluators must accept these individuals' choices. Practitioners must also acknowledge that not all evaluators will choose to engage in highly participatory practice. Even though current best practice includes some form of meaningful interaction between evaluator and primary user, the extent of that interaction over the course of the study may be minimal. Mandating that people – whether practitioners or evaluators – participate in an interactive evaluation process for which they have no time or with which they are uncomfortable seems an unlikely way to insure its success.

The Political Context

My experience has taught me that the collaborative evaluation process is fragile, with virtually continuous opportunities for failure. Prime among the potential causes of failure are the politics of evaluation settings, which can destroy a collaboration in a single thoughtless comment. Failure to acknowledge this fact is to risk setting people up for extreme frustration. Each of the studies described provides an easy, if sad, example of the truth of this claim.

- In the CPIP evaluation, certain training coordinators willingly worked with the research and development evaluator, hoping that positive documentation would both justify the program's value and enable at least some of them to keep central office staff development positions. When the duty superintendent eliminated the program with seemingly little attention paid to the evaluation data, the coordinators and the evaluation staff felt betrayed. The district evaluation head wondered, in retrospect, if the collaboration had been worth the upset it unavoidably created.
- One of the most frustrating moments of the OEL study was when we learned that the legislator mentioned earlier cited our study, which purposefully contained no standardized achievement scores at the end of the first year, as one of the reasons for cutting the program. Mazzoni *et al.* (1992) suggest that this individual had his own reasons for wanting the program eliminated, but for school district collaborators the attack on the research suggested an egregious error on our part. Their efforts to provide existing test scores to the legislator were rejected in a face-to-face meeting that insulted many and left them furious.
- Building-level politics have played an interesting role in our action research efforts. The teacher researchers report feeling like 'elite lepers', rebuffed, on the one hand, because others see them as the chosen few who garner special favors from the administration, yet ostracized, on the other hand, because they

appear overly enthusiastic about school improvement and professional development. At one site, for example, to continue the action research process is to risk
the disfavor of an experienced faculty who view the researchers as overly
committed and idealistic do-gooders. As outsider facilitators, we cannot protect
our research collaborators, but we can at least engage them in reflective dialogue and a professional community. At the end of last year, one teacher said,
'We were validated as professionals for our own observations'; this made us
feel validated as well.

The point to be emphasized here is that sometimes – and not surprisingly – the
politics of a situation can overwhelm even the best of collaborative intentions. Whether
or not to proceed with a participatory process is not a decision to be made lightly.
My experience suggests that it is better *not* to begin if you can see that politics will
unavoidably limit the likelihood of a successful collaboration. For example, the CPIP
task given the evaluation unit was clearly a hatchet job; asking people to participate
in the demise of their own program did not, in the end, make them feel better about
its elimination. A second example comes from the OEL study. Through the fault of a
bureaucratic delay in funding and owing to political demands for accountability, its first
year carried an impossible time-line; the planning could not begin until early April. This
meant that we collected data in May and even as late as June; predictably the worst
months to ask teachers, students, or administrators to reflect quietly on their experiences. School-based people blamed university collaborators for their lack of sensitivity
to the facts of school life, and in retrospect we might have built a stronger project had
we convinced our state department collaborators to wait until the fall.[9]

The first two lessons suggest necessary conditions for collaborative evaluation:
finding people who want to participate and a political setting that makes participation
viable. Assume that you have led willing practitioners to the evaluation project, ready
to jump in. Assume also that the politics surrounding the project make the project
possible. The third and fourth lessons speak to what the evaluator must do to increase
the ongoing research connection.

Building Support and Trust

My experience suggests that even willing collaborators will limit or drop their involvement if they do not feel supported during the study or they do not trust the people
involved. Evaluators who collaborate with practitioners need to pay considerable attention to motivating and supporting their involvement from beginning to end, and trust
building must be ongoing. In part this can be done structurally. By making regular
connections into a structural part of the evaluation process and two-way communication
an ongoing reality, evaluators can create necessary venues for discussion and reflection,
both on the content of the study and on the collaborative process itself. Informal connections should also be included systematically so that different individuals have a
number of possibilities for expressing their concerns.

Structure is important, but support and trust building is also a matter of belief.
Evaluators must project an attitude of true interest in practitioners' concerns, respect for
the challenging world of school practice, and a continuing openness. No problem is too
big or small to be discussed, and, to the extent possible, it is the evaluator's job to
resolve glitches when they arise. One of the bigger challenges for me personally comes

from the fact that, as a collaborative evaluator, I never get to whine and be small-minded, even when people are systematically undermining a carefully wrought study. With each person added – whether evaluator or practitioner – the trust-building process begins anew. As the mother of the process, I must be the person calmly above such pettiness, working tirelessly to make it succeed. But wearing a constant smile can be tiring. Reaching a higher level of trust, where I can truly express my feelings and opinions about the evaluation process, has been relatively rare. Consider the following examples:

- Providing support to site-based collaborators was a problem throughout the OEL study. In the first year, there was an impossible time-line and simply too many of them and not enough of us to do more than field complaints. In the second year, the planning network created a smaller group, but it met only occasionally and not everyone attended every meeting. Connection with state department colleagues was better, but because the staff had literally taken on the task of transforming education at the project sites (along with teacher education in the state), they had virtually no time to discuss evaluation issues until there was an external pressure or minor crisis that required resolution. Although we believe we had good working relations with virtually all the sites, the extreme lack of trust evidenced by the confrontation at the state department described earlier suggests the degree to which our overall collaboration failed.

- CARP provides several counter-examples to this, cases where our ongoing research connection has resulted in a growing and viable partnership (as well as, I would add, personal friendships). At one site, for example, a team of teachers referred to us as 'friendly nags' because whenever we called to schedule a meeting, they felt that they had to have something new to report and this motivated them to take the next step in their study. To the initial surprise of another group, we met teachers at their school at 7:15 in the morning, in the afternoon, or whenever they were available, trying to fit the action research into the limited time slots they had available. The CARP group as a whole chuckled at our 'meeting and eating' together, but over the course of two years, the feeling of support and trust generated by what Huberman (1990) would call this reciprocal engagement motivated us all. When we needed questionnaires completed at each school site on fairly short notice, our collaborators did not blink an eye; they willingly took the surveys, administered them, and got them back to us.

Creating Shared Meaning

Even the existence of support and trust is not sufficient to insure an effective collaborative process. In addition, collaborative evaluation efforts demand that practitioners and evaluators truly speak the same language in order to make collective sense of the evaluation process and its outcomes. For some, this requires changing the common belief (and, in many places, the virtual reality) that practitioners and evaluators live in distinct worlds. For teachers and school administrators, the evaluation process may seem irrelevant, time consuming, and overly quantified. As Jones (1989, p. 51) notes, its results may have the 'cutting edge of sponge' in the eyes of practitioners. For their part, evaluators may be concerned with the immediacy of daily practice and the messiness of trying to study it. I continue to be surprised when school people think I'm selling collaborative evaluation and action research for my own benefit, that is, that somehow it is of value to me as an educator, but not to them. In part this stems from a tradition that places researchers and evaluators above school-based personnel on some grand hierarchy of education, although the growth of teacher research suggests that this may be changing.

In my evaluation experience, people have placed me in three distinct roles. Some want me to be their hired hand, disappearing after being given an assignment and reappearing at some point with a useful analysis; or at least a report to file somewhere. A related role is that of the outside researcher, the dispassionate 'scientist' who lends credibility to the evaluation process and its results, often in contentious situations. 'She's from the university', people whisper even when I leave my lab coat at home. The third role I am asked to play – and the one I actively cultivate in my practice – is that of critical friend. This notion, taken from the action research literature, suggests an objective participant in an ongoing discussion of what is happening in schools: in short, a true collaborator in long-term program improvement. The roles of internal evaluators and the notions of organization development, developmental evaluation (Stockdill, Duhon-Sells, Olsen and Patton, 1992), and perhaps even the emancipatory evaluation that was the theme of the 1993 meeting of the American Evaluation Association, suggest that this is not unusual. For people seeking someone to fill the first two roles, however, acceptance of the third may require some active explanation and instruction over time, if, and only if, they are willing to learn.

How is the notion of shared meaning created in practice? The studies provide examples of how we have worked to create the common ground of mutually acceptable, shared meanings with our site-based colleagues. We work to develop and maintain primary users.

- Throughout the two-year collaboration, the OEL study sought to create a shared world by documenting the situation in which the schools found themselves: forced to implement top-down, intrusive mandates; inhabited by challenging students different from those of earlier years; assailed by parents who assume the schools are either 'not broken' or in need of major reform; and running hard just to stay barely in place (King and Bosma, 1991; King, Bosma and Binko, 1992). Some school-based participants reported pleasure when the first-year report passed their litmus test by including negative information about the project. State department staff were predictably less pleased!
- In addition, our team struggled with site-specific tensions (e.g., issues related to two communities' long-term racism and hostility towards 'outsiders') and sought to infuse evaluation information back from whence it came. The shared meaning in one case was welcomed; district staff included rather negative OEL community data in a grant proposal for funds related to improving diversity. In the other case, evaluation participants agreed that while racism was, indeed, a problem affecting the school, it was an open secret that could not be made part of the evaluation record.
- Our involvement in action research provides the most visible examples of a merging of worlds as the cycle of planning, acting, observing, and reflecting, places teachers directly in the practice of evaluation. The teacher researchers became the immediate beneficiaries and users of the information they gener- ated, and they often reported their surprise at the relative straightforwardness

of the process. In the words of one of the teachers, 'Action research helped us to focus on the problem and bring awareness to the entire building staff. It provided a framework or a process to work through; to come to some under-standing of and some solutions to these problems.'

As is often the case with lessons learned through experience, the four that I discuss here are not surprising. I could perhaps have created the list after reading the tenets of good evaluation practice. But that is also the reason they are important. If we are serious about nurturing practitioner involvement in evaluation studies, I would argue that we must pay direct attention to potential participants, likely political contexts, the develop-ment of ongoing support and trust, and the creation of shared meaning.

Summary and Conclusion

Are collaborative evaluation approaches viable in school settings? I would answer an enthusiastic 'maybe.' In this paper, I began by comparing four conceptual approaches, each of which involves school-based practitioners. I then described three cases that used a participatory process, followed by the lessons I learned from those experiences. In two of the cases (CPIP and OEL), the evaluation process was unable to counteract the powerful political setting within which the programs operated. This is not entirely a fault of the process, but at one level the outcomes were nevertheless damaging to those who agreed to participate. While we all learned from each other and the events, in both cases people might have been reluctant to commit quickly to a similar research involvement.

To date, few existing school organizations engage in organizational learning of the type Cousins and Earl (1992) discuss. We need research evidence that this process is worth the effort, and, based on my ongoing study and reflection as an evaluation practitioner, I have hope that the developing practice of practitioner-centered action research may provide us such evidence. The four lessons I cited are all applied in an action research effort: only volunteers take part in the process since they must study themselves and take charge of research activities; action research takes place in a known context, and, while you may still have political challenges, the probability of being blind-sided is greatly decreased; support and trust are characteristics of the pro-fessional community fostered by action research; and the process itself brings research to life in the school setting, thus merging the worlds of research and practice. Numerous questions remain, relating, for example, to the training necessary for such efforts, the role of theory development in action research, and the effect of such research on teacher behavior and student learning. From my perspective, however, the prospects for contin-ued development of collaborative evaluation approaches at this point look bright.

Notes

1　Contrary to common belief, action research did not, however, disappear. As Noffke (1990) documents, action research work continued in a number of fields.
2　The concept of participatory action research as practiced in the field of organization development in business, industry, and agriculture (e.g., Whyte *et al.*, 1989; Whyte, 1991) uses the process of traditional action research.

3   I am speaking here primarily of what critical and emancipatory action research theorists (e.g., McTaggart, 1991; Kincheloe, 1991) would call practical action research. Emancipatory action research, developed from the perspective of critical theory, uses a broader frame for its work.
4   Certain details related to the cases have been altered to conceal the identity of specific individuals or sites. The basic content has not, however, been changed.
5   As a poignant commentary on the situation, the deputy superintendent left the district in a year and a half, saying that the district politics made his job unworkable. The CPIP trainers reflected that they might have still had their program and jobs had he not been hired.
6   The guiding principles, revised in September 1990, were as follows: the research process must respect the uniqueness of the learning sites; it must be supportive of learning without being a burden to learning sites; it must involve, receive input from, and be sensitive to multiple levels of diverse stakeholders; it must include multiple and 'people-sensitive' methods; it must foster communication and understanding of the ongoing change process; research outcomes must be useful within and across learning sites; and they must provide tangible feedback on student success and solid, usable data about what is good for learners (King, Schleisman and Binko, 1991).
7   This work is funded, in part, by the Center on the Organization and Restructuring of Schools, supported by the US Department of Education, Office of Educational Research and Improvement (Grant No. R117Q00005-91) and by the Wisconsin Center for Educational Research, School of Education, University of Wisconsin-Madison. The opinions expressed are those of the author and do not necessarily reflect the views of the supporting agencies.
8   Actually, the image of fiery crucibles immediately sprang to mind!
9   Ultimately, of course, this would have made no difference in the program's demise.

References

ALKIN, M.C., DAILLAK, R. and WHITE, P. (1979) *Using Evaluation: Does Evaluation Make a Difference?* Beverly Hills, CA, Sage.
BLOOM, B.S., HASTINGS, J.T. and MADAUS, G.F. (1971) *Handbook on Formative and Summative Evaluation of Student Learning*, New York, McGraw-Hill.
CLANDININ, D.J. and CONNELLY, F.M. (1992) 'Teacher as curriculum maker', in JACKSON, P.W. (ed) *Handbook of Research on Curriculum*, New York: Macmillan, pp. 362–401.
COCHRAN-SMITH, M. and LYTLE, S.L. (1993) *Inside/outside: Teacher Research and Knowledge*, New York, Teachers College Press.
COREY, S. (1953) *Action Research to Improve School Practices*, New York, Teachers College, Columbia University.
COUSINS, J.B. and EARL, L.M. (1992) 'The case for participatory evaluation', *Educational Evaluation and Policy Analysis*, **14**, 4, pp. 397–418.
HOLLY, P. and WHITEHEAD, D. (eds) (1984) *Action Research in Schools: Getting it into Perspective* (CARN Bulletin No. 6), Cambridge: Cambridge University Press.
HUBERMAN, M. (1990) 'Linkage between researchers and practitioners: A qualitative study', *American Educational Research Journal*, **27**, pp. 363–91.
JONES, B. (1989) 'In conversation with myself: Becoming an action researcher', in LOMAX, P. (ed) *The Management of Change: Increasing School Effectiveness and Facilitating Staff Development through Action Research*, Philadelphia, Multilingual Matters.
KINCHELOE, J. (1991) *Teachers as Researchers: Qualitative Inquiry as a Path to Empowerment*, London, Falmer Press.
KING, J.A. and BOSMA, J. (1991, April) 'After one year: implementation issues for ten transformational R&D sites.' Paper presented at the Annual Meeting of the American Educational Research Association, Chicago, IL.

KING, J.A., BOSMA, J. and BINKO, J. (1992, March) 'After two years: A study of educational transformation in ten Minnesota sites.' Paper presented at the Annual Meeting of the American Educational Research Association, San Francisco, CA.

KING, J.A. and LONNQUIST, M.P. (1992) *A Review of Writing on Action Research*, Minneapolis, MN: Center for Applied Research and Educational Improvement.

KING, J.A. and PECHMAN, E.M. (1982) 'The process of evaluation use in local school settings (Final report of NIE Grant No. 81–0900).' New Orleans, LA, Orleans Parish Schools.

KING, J.A., SCHLEISMAN, K.E. and BINKO, J. (1991, March) 'Collaboration: Partnerships for transformation.' Paper presented at the Annual Meeting of the American Educational Research Association, Chicago, IL.

MAZZONI, T., FREEMAN, C. and STEWART, D. (1992) 'State policymaking and outcome-based education: A Minnesota case study.' Unpublished manuscript, University of Minnesota, Minneapolis.

McTAGGART, R. (1991) *A Brief History of Action Research*, Geelong, Victoria, Australia, Deakin University Press.

NOFFKE, S.E. (1990) 'Action research: A multidimensional analysis.' Unpublished doctoral dissertation, University of Wisconsin, Madison.

PATTON, M.Q. (1986) *Utilization-focused Evaluation* (2nd ed), Newbury Park, CA, Sage.

PATTON, M.Q., GRIMES, P.S., GUTHRIE, K.M., BRENNAN, N.J., FRENCH, B.D. and BLYTH, D.A. (1978) 'In search of impact: An analysis of the utilization of federal health evaluation research', in PATTON, M.Q. (1986) *Utilization-focused Evaluation* (2nd ed), Newbury Park, CA, Sage, pp. 30–7.

STAKE, R.E. (1975) *Evaluating the Arts in Education: A Responsive Approach*, Columbus, OH, Charles E. Merrill.

STENHOUSE, L. (1975) *An Introduction to Curriculum Research and Development*, London, Heinemann Educational Books.

STOCKDILL, S.H., DUHON-SELLS, R.M., OLSON, R.A. and PATTON, M.Q. (1992, Spring), 'Voices in the design and evaluation of a multicultural education program: A developmental approach', *New Directions for Program Evaluation*, **53**, pp. 17–33.

TABA, H. and NOEL, E. (1957) *Action Research: A Case Study*, Washington, DC, Association for Supervision and Curriculum Development.

WHYTE, W.F. (ed) (1991) *Participatory Action Research*, Newbury Park, CA, Sage.

WHYTE, W.F., GREENWOOD, D. and LAZES, P. (1989) 'Participatory action research: Through practice to science in social research', *American Behavioral Scientist*, **32**, 5, pp. 513–52.

WORTHEN, B.R. and SANDERS, J.R. (1987) *Educational Evaluation: Alternative Approaches and Practical Guidelines*, New York, Longman.

Chapter 7

The Many Modes of Participatory Evaluation

Michael Huberman

Introduction

For a good fifty years, the educational research and evaluation community has tried to find procedures that have local legitimacy, technical robustness, and the capacity to move a 'client' public along a recommended trajectory. No one has succeeded cleanly, but several communities, including the community represented in this set of papers, are still at it. It is, in fact, a tall order. How to provide crucial evaluative information unequivocally? How to make certain that this information is understood and actually used in sensible ways? How to marshal this data in order to consolidate or reorient the implementation of new measures?

Some of the answers are contained in two cognate fields: evaluation utilization and knowledge utilization. Alkin (1991) has reviewed some of the key variables in the evaluation field, such as the quality of the evaluation, its local credibility, its relevance, the means and amount of communication about the evaluation results, the agreement between findings and expectations, and the timeliness of the findings. In the knowledge utilization field, Huberman (1993) has homed in on 'dissemination competence', and 'quality of dissemination products'. The first set includes targeted products, interpersonal modes of disseminating information, follow-up, multiple channels of dissemination and reinforcement of users. The quality of dissemination products category includes a focus on malleable or 'alterable' factors, the contextualization of findings and the operationalization of key findings. These factors then determine whether users will invest time and resources in the data and whether they will act on the information, even if it differs from their own assumptions.

As it happens, these two communities – evaluators and dissemination specialists – have come together, conceptually speaking. For example, many of the variables just mentioned are identical or reconcilable. There has not, however, been as much feverish work on two of the directions taken here. First, the objective in each of the forgoing chapters has been to achieve some measure of *'organizational learning'*. This is a slippery measure, and I am one of several who is wary of it.

The guiding – and plausible – premise behind organizational learning is that knowledge is socially constructed, and that these social symbol systems can become salient and operative in a given organization. Changes in understanding, perceptions and interpretations are then indicators of shifts in reflective frameworks. These changes, logically enough, occur more frequently when there is a dense interpersonal network for sharing and discussing information (Cousins and Earl, 1992; Louis and Simsek, 1991).

This is not the place to argue over the shift from an individual-level construct (learning) to an organizational one. It is, however, a good place to point out the rationale behind these papers. If more and more trustworthy evaluative data can find its way into a school system, they could run along the wires of interpersonal networks, then find their way into the deliberative mechanisms that school systems use to make sense of who they are and what they need to do. The objective, then, is to create mechanisms for evaluation that have a better 'hit' ratio than conventional measures. In many respects the formulas used in these papers are original attempts to do just this.

Participatory Evaluation – and its Predecessors

This takes us to the second direction. In one way or another, all the papers have to do with 'participatory evaluation'. The key here – and I shall return to it at the end – is this: whether or not research (or evaluation) findings find their way into practitioner organizations depends on the number, variety and mutuality of contacts between researchers and practitioners (Huberman, 1990, p. 364). Citing this finding, Cousins and Earl (1992) cite other studies, including an influential one by Jennifer Greene (1987). Here multiple opportunities for discussions and reflection, along with the analysis of substantive program issues, were coupled with active, ongoing assimilation of information. Personal contacts were also important. The key skills for evaluators were those of knowing how to listen, how to be responsive and technical competence. The 'magic formula', if there is one, involves intensive social interaction, real engagement by school people, and follow-up and involvement on the evaluator's end of things.

Participatory evaluation is a noble but elusive construct. It seems to recur every thirty years in a new rhetorical guise, but it presents the same tough conceptual and practical problems. With the recent onset of critical theory, and the influence of J. Habermas, it is even more salient these days.

As Jean King notes in chapter 6, there have been several 'traditions' of participatory research. All entail the exchange of information between researcher and local actor such that the latter appropriates the information and acts on it. As King notes, John Dewey and his colleagues at the turn of the century gave direct roles to teachers and students in ongoing inquiry.

The classic incarnation comes from Kurt Lewin, and the invention of action research in the 1940s (for a good compendium, see Wheelan *et al.*, 1990). Here, it was essentially the researchers who set the agenda and engineered the social processing activity in such a way as to set changes in perception and behavior within the group of actors. Educational action research, as King notes, rose to prominence in the 1950s (Corey, 1953; Taba and Noel, 1957), but declined in the ensuing decades. Here, under the guidance and technical support of researchers, local actors underwent a process of reflection, investigation, action, interpretation, and, if possible, durable change.

A 'softer version' of action research comes in the form of 'stakeholder' research. Typically, this involves interactions between researchers, who carry out the brunt of scientific work, and a set of presumably active professionals, who help to refine research questions, have a role in interpreting the data and carry the results into their – and sometimes others' – organization(s). I will be arguing later that, given the conditions the authors had to work under, the papers appearing in this volume are more instances of stakeholder research than of any other species.

Next on the continuum from researcher-dominated to teacher-managed modes of research comes the kind of work pioneered at the University of East Anglia by L. Stenhouse and known in North America as 'teacher research'. This is work conducted solely by teachers who, via their own tools of data collection and analysis (logs, observations, work products, reflective memos, annotated diaries) answer the questions they themselves have posed (Cochran-Smith and Lytle, 1990). This need not, however, lead to changes at the classroom or school level. One version of teacher research, however, does follow the classic action research cycle. Teachers frame their questions, develop their own designs, collect and analyze their data, interpret their meaning, then undergo the same cycle. Jean King calls this variation 'practical action research'.

Finally, at the other extreme, we have action research back in the guise of critical theory, with the objective of bringing local staff to an 'emancipatory' understanding of the forces that surround them. In other words, this is, unabashedly, a conflict model. With or without the researcher, the objective is to analyze pedagogical and organizational practices in order to transform them. In some instances, there are hints of this 'drift' in the papers under review, almost as in a sorcerer's apprentice scenario: by bringing evaluative data directly to teachers, the evaluator or primary researchers raised local consciousness beyond what was expected. Since the primary researcher was typically a senior administrator (central office administrator, principal, program coordinator), we had a surreal situation, with the hierarchical chiefs firing up their subordinates in directions they would have preferred to ride away from.

What Version of Participatory Evaluation do We Have Here?

This turns out to be a hard question to answer. At the outset, I came to the conclusion that Cousins, Earl and their colleagues had invented a new species of participatory evaluation. I am still there. It is, however, a curious version, and I have my doubts as to its intrinsic viability and likely generalizability. To argue that point more tightly, let us have a close-up look at the set of papers.

Participatory evaluation, considered generically, involves social research applied through a 'partnership' between trained evaluation personnel and practice-based professionals. As Cousins and Earl (1992) put it, the objective is to transform schools or school systems into learning organizations, building their research capacity to go it alone, without the continuing aid of an outside evaluator. On the way there, the professionals working with an evaluator are not consultants, as in the stakeholder model, but are fully fledged participants, with joint responsibility. This satisfies the need for responsiveness, while still maintaining sufficient rigor, argue Cousins and Earl.

Maybe so. Before going on, however, we need to digest this paragraph. For one thing, as we know well through a plethora of empirical studies, these 'partnerships' are made, not born. They take time, almost the time of friendship. For the majority of teachers, for example, the role of an evaluator is perceptibly set. Listen to Jean King:

> I continue to be surprised when school people think I'm selling collaborative evaluation and action research for my own benefit, i.e., that somehow it's of value to me as an educator, but not to them. (p. 99)

If teachers think this, it's because, in the past at least, they have had good reason to. In effect, the role of external evaluator is fundamentally ambiguous, especially since, in several of these studies, the 'primary users' have not only been people at the locus of action in the schools, but also administrators, principals and program coordinators. Many of this latter group have been 'second-layer stakeholders'. They, in turn, have been apprenticed to research methodology by the evaluator and have collected – and sometimes shared – the data from local sites. When a central office administrator comes in to interview teachers on a sensitive instructional or organizational issue, it puts those teachers on a tightrope, no matter how benevolent each party may be. It also, incidentally, casts some shadows on the trustworthiness of the data that have been gathered, with virtually no opportunity to assess the nature and degree of any resulting bias.

What we have, then, is a particular kind of stakeholder evaluation, but one in which the stakeholders are at two levels: the actual level of conduct of the study (where administrators and program directors collect data on their own enterprises), and the school level where findings are collected, fed back and discussed. There is even something communitarian in this model – provided, of course, that everyone agrees on such a mixture of hierarchical levels and provided that there is shared meaning around the evidence presented. In one case, at least, reported by Jean King, this was refused. To the extent that, say, central office personnel inhabit different planets from classroom teachers, this is a real challenge.

A few more caveats. First, the very process of feeding back data is a delicate business. It is not for nothing that this part of the cycle is entrusted to well-trained professionals. One wrong sentence and you're out. One hint that you don't master the local context, and you're history. Then, too, how to contend with data – summative *or* formative data – that is negative, discouraging, or that works against a continuing program (see King's chapter), and that bring to the surface some rifts that were best left underground? In this same vein, how to contend with the fact that we have here a highly rational – perhaps hyper-rational – procedure for studying and feeding back evaluative data, while we know all too well that inside the classroom or inside the principal's office, there is a good deal of emotional, haphazard, politically sensitive information flying around? Another way to put this is to point out that information that is 'rationally' delivered may not be rationally received. When this happens, its impact is either null or mischievous.

A final issue: who *owns* these data? Who decides what will be fed back or not? Who decides what will be followed up or not? Who identifies the strong findings and sets them apart from the dubious ones? Who deals with responses to formative or summative feedback that are overtly hostile, that contest the findings or the procedures used to generate them? There is too little conflict, perhaps, in the participatory evaluation paradigm laid out here, far less than we find out in the field, and far less than surfaces in evaluative research when the findings reach people whose careers or reputations depend on them. So many open questions for which we need more answers. . . .

A Look at the Individual Studies

In Lorna Earl's chapter (chapter 2), we have an internal evaluation unit working directly on the questions and decisions with which the school administration is contending. Apparently, the relationships between evaluators and managers were positive; Earl even speaks of 'strong bonds' – something slightly unusual in this business. But the principle issue here is strongly evaluative: was the school improvement connected to a curriculum development project actually being implemented? And, if so, which factors facilitated or impeded program execution? How might further implementation be directed?

On the face of it, these are questions for which administrators need answers. They are not necessarily pertinent questions, say, for teachers who don't like this innovation, or who have used their energies otherwise, or who have transformed the innovation to fit their own purposes. On the other hand – and this is the ambiguity of the approach – senior administrators seldom *ask* teachers how they are getting along, which factors are impeding progress, what might be done at the administrative level and so on. No wonder, then, that a follow-up inquiry showed many teachers favorable to the exercise, grateful for being listened to or involved in 'real educational discussions'. Despite the low response rate on the follow-up questionnaire, most schools reported that they appreciated the 'direction and focus', the 'opportunity to share'. Earl also suggests that the interviewers – the administrators and program coordinators – felt they had derived the greatest benefit. They had, in fact, double-dipped: as researchers collecting data on projects for which they were, in varying degrees, responsible, and as administrators trying to get a major project firmly in place.

This is an example of the uniqueness of the approach. There are stakeholders at two levels, and those closest to the evaluator are doing some of the research themselves as well. In so doing, they are getting useful information and learning new skills as apprentice evaluators. At the same time, they are having to listen carefully to the stakeholders in the trenches, and to do so in a position of near equality. And yet we cannot deny, even in a formative evaluation study such as this one, that a key aim of the project is to see whether teachers are following through in the implementation of a major curriculum development. Whereas, in a typical instance, a professional evaluator would collect this data, we have a key stakeholder group of administrators doing the data gathering. The evidence provided seems to say that the process is a rewarding one. It may also, of course, make a virtue of necessity, when a research centre has two or three trained evaluators covering dozens of schools and hundreds of miles. In that situation, one is obliged to work through intermediaries.

Participatory Evaluation with Focus Groups

This is a felicitous transition to Clay Lafleur's chapter (chapter 3). Lafleur was the sole educational researcher for a school district with 48,000 students and 3,100 teaching staff in ninety-seven schools. He, too, relied on intermediaries, a similar type of 'primary user' as in Earl's study, but including teachers. This team was meant to review nine internal evaluations completed during the past eight years in such areas as in technical education, behavior, grade 4–6 mathematics, library services and grade 7–10 history.

Following the administration of a questionnaire, this team participated in a focus group discussion. All found the experience worthwhile, indicating they had learned more about the inquiry process and the programs under review. Still, they were guarded as to the actual impact of the evaluation, given the implementation of the resulting action plan. One criticism was that the action plan was laid on from 'above'.

One can legitimately ask here: but what did the organization 'learn?' The team of administrators and teachers doubtless learned about evaluation methodology. In the focus group, they probably came to grips with programs they had administered or taught but had not examined for several years. This has always been the forte of evaluation research: a look square in the face, warts and all, at a program that has been taken for granted, despite its limitations. If, however, there is no following on activity, that look square in the face will have been largely gratuitous. Nor can we say that these key factors represent 'organizational learning', unless we take that construct as a collection of individual achievements.

Finally, Lafleur takes up two themes that we shall return to in a moment: the labor intensiveness of evaluation work, and the weakness of evaluations on the political battleground. Lafleur puts it well:

> . . . evaluation utilization was seen to be easily influenced by changing political and economic circumstances, beyond the control of staff within the system. It appeared that policy makers were consistently overwhelmed by other matters and repeatedly delayed or proceeded very cautiously, if at all, with an action plan. (p. 51)

And so it goes. Evaluations take time, and they take time away from other tasks for people who have more than one role. Nor is there any certainty they will result in desirable changes. *That* is a political issue.

Measurable Effects?

In his study of the work of field centres with evaluators servicing a wide geographical area, Cousins (chapter 4) documents a 'marginally successful case' (Lakeside) and a 'highly successful case' (Rockland). In both cases, the process includes a 'steering committee' of administrators who work with the researcher on the less technical aspects of the evaluation. 'Success' appears to be acceptance of the committee's recommendations pursuant to its study, which is a sturdy enough measure, although it is not directly measured here. The summary tables show, for example, that Lakeside's teachers did not really understand the purposes of the project, were generally unaware of the results, reported no new learning and found no useful information in the later phases of the study. Their senior administrator was apparently not sensitive to the substantive issues, had no resources, felt the study wasn't needed and had her own agenda. The corresponding cells on table 4.2 are positive for Rockland: support from the senior administration; high information needs; strong leadership; heightened staff awareness; enhanced commitment; insights into organizational operations and staff concerns; and insight from an external perspective.

The lesson here – and Cousins draws it – is that some contexts are favorable, and others less so, to the implementation of policies they themselves have often approved at the outset. These contexts offer different 'receiving structures' for new data. We can also see here the prodigious role of the 'gate-keeper': the administrator who has other fish to fry and who blocks access to junior staff – and this despite the fact that the steering committee is loaded with administrators.

Finally, we have in this paper the strongest argument yet for the usefulness of the external evaluator who manages to remain neutral. Time-lines are kept. Instruments are context sensitive. Data analysis results in plausible findings. Follow-up mechanisms are established. The field centre is credible. As such, it legitimates recommendations that individual members of the steering committee could not have brought to fruition by themselves. This is the magic of social science well done. It is not, however, an exercise in participatory evaluation, save in the weakest sense, when a team of senior administrators help design, collect, analyze, and diffuse a data set to two school districts. Rather, it is a study run with intermediaries or, as I said earlier, with two layers of stakeholders. Finally, it is a relatively short-lived endeavor, one that is uncertain – despite Cousins' claims to the contrary; he speaks, for example, of the creation of 'dense interpersonal networks' – to result in any durable form of 'organizational learning'.

Still, the two-layered procedure is a promising one. It 'educates' administrators to the research enterprise. It brings them down in the trenches, in a new, initially disorienting role, which is itself conducive to forming new perceptions. It enhances the status of the research centre. Above all, perhaps, it shows administrators that there is *another* relatively powerful and disinterested manner of diagnosing their district's needs and of turning these diagnoses into workable solutions. To participate in such an exercise, then, is a professionalizing experience. Some of this is reflected in Cousins' summarizing remarks.

The Many Roles of Evaluators and Evaluations

In the final paper, written by Lee and Cousins (chapter 5), we have a similar scenario. Here were four project teams conducting what was essentially a self-evaluation of their programs with 'at-risk', secondary-level pupils. The idea, as one principal put it, was that of 'taking the pulse of existing and current situations'. What they learned first, it seems, was that 'taking the pulse' is far more time consuming and arduous than the metaphor implied. There was also a clear sense of the evaluation providing 'another kind' of look, of asking different kinds of questions, of ascertaining whether or not one is 'on track', and of taking a 'long' view as well as a more immediate one.

It is in this piece that a latent issue comes to the fore. The professional evaluator, for Lee and Cousins the 'consultant working in a participatory model', has to put in more time than in other models of program evaluation. Lee is a 'technical resource', a 'sounding board', a 'counsellor', a local aide during implementation, presumably also conflict resolver, catalyst, knowledge linker. On the side, as it were, she designs the instruments, trains the team in interview skills and questionnaire analysis, sets up the data analysis, and shows where the interpretation of the findings is warranted or not. The technician, the pedagogue, the therapist, the advisor – all loaded on to small amounts of one person's job. It would be impossible to generalize the model. It would also be impossible to construe, at least in these cases, a 'participatory evaluation' in which a professional evaluator did not play the role of *deus ex machina*.

Finally, I would suggest to Lee and Cousins, who are so attuned to the 'commitment' of the team members, that this may matter less than the *time-out* afforded by the project. Evaluators offer a precious commodity to administrators and teachers caught up in the daily bustle of their work: a time-out to look at their own surround from another perspective, calmly. It is in this sense that the evaluator is essentially an educator rather than a judge. This educator provides a forum – another 'place', both physically and cognitively, to take stock and look both at congenial and discrepant data. Also, as an educator, the best posture is to help local staff do their own learning rather than teach them. In all these papers, this objective appears to be met. These are all powerful learning experiences for individuals, and sometimes for teams. Whether this relatively

Michael Huberman

short experience translates into 'coordinated mental maps' or 'organizational learning' is another issue.

Concluding Remark

There are several ways we can profit from this set of papers. First, they pin down the factors which predict the degree to which evaluations will be imported locally to some effect. This is important case material, and it is better aligned than most case studies tend to be. Next, they give weight to the assumption that the involvement of 'stakeholders' in the design and conduct of a study will increase its chances of its findings being taken seriously. This, in fact, is the heart of the volume: the participation of local personnel is a facilitator, in spite of its cost in time and – a very important factor – its cost in time away from the school or district office. These experiences are also lived as 'professionalizing' by local staff, independently of their institutional impact. From the data presented here, the degree of that impact is mostly uncertain or highly variable. From my perspective, the case for 'organizational learning' is not made convincingly, but is less important than the host of second-order effects mentioned earlier.

Finally, I would argue, as I did in the text alluded to by Cousins and Earl (Huberman, 1990), that the evaluation may matter less than the collaboration established during the evaluation – the 'linkages'. The links between, on the one hand, the research centres and, on the other, the local or provincial school districts, are now far tighter. When a new study is called for, the evaluators will know where to go, and can expect to be well received and helped there. Conversely, when a school district runs into trouble or wants a second opinion, they will know whom to call on. The tighter the links among these units, the more they can 'service' one another, and the more research or another form of disciplined inquiry will have its place in the school district. From that vantage point, the experience of an 'adventure' in 'participatory evaluation' will have been more ephemeral, less important, than the creation of more enduring linkages between a center of inquiry and a set of schools trying to create their own internal centers of inquiry with a little help from their friends.

References

ALKIN, M. (1991) 'Educational theory development: II', in McLAUGHLIN, M. and PHILLIPS, D. (eds) *Evaluation and Education: At Quarter Century*, Ninetieth Yearbook of the National Society for the Study of Education. Chicago, University of Chicago Press, pp. 91–112.

COCHRAN-SMITH, M. and LYTLE, S. (1990) 'Research on teaching and teacher research: The issues that divide', *Educational Researcher*, **19**, 2, pp. 2–11.

COREY, S. (1953) *Action Research to Improve School Practices*, New York, Teachers College, Columbia University.

COUSINS, J.B. and EARL, L. (1992) 'The case for participatory evaluation', *Educational Evaluation and Policy Analysis*, **14**, 4, pp. 397–418.

GREENE, J. (1987) 'Stakeholder participation in evaluation design. Is it worth the effort?', *Evaluation and Program Planning*, **10**, pp. 375–94.

HUBERMAN, M. (1990) 'Linkage between researchers and practitioners: A qualitative study', *American Educational Research Journal*, **27**, 2, pp. 363–91.

HUBERMAN, M. (1993) 'Linking the practitioner and researcher communities for school improvement', *School Effectiveness and School Improvement*, **4**, 1, pp. 1–16.

LOUIS, K.S. and SIMSEK, H. (1991; November) 'Paradigm shifts and organizational learning: Some theoretical lessons for restructuring schools.' Paper presented at the annual meeting of the University Council for Educational Administration, Baltimore.

TABA, H. and NOEL, E. (1957) *Action Research: A Case Study*, Washington, DC, Association for Supervision and Curriculum Development.

WHEELEN, S., PEPITONE, E. and ABT, V. (eds) (1990) *Advances in Field Theory*, Newbury Park, Sage.

Part 3

Educational Participatory Evaluation: Variations in Form

In the early stages of compiling the collection we were fortuitous in stumbling across two additional studies that we thought might add substantially to our knowledge about participatory evaluation. In retrospect we were right. The first is a narrative case study presented by Lyn Shulha and Bob Wilson that focuses on a protracted, systematic effort to develop a school–university partnership that would produce some truly exciting collaborative research and development of innovative approaches to classroom assessment in elementary schools. While not wanting to give away the ending, we can tell you that some unexpected twists and turns take shape as this all important phase for any collaborative project unfolds.

Finally, Donna Mertens and her colleagues Terry Berkeley and Susan Lopez share with us their experiences and insights gained in working on a collaborative project with educators from a culture that is decidedly distinct from our own. They take us from Washington DC to Egypt for a look at the evaluation of a significant special education initiative underwritten by interests from two nations. Along the way, they highlight several interesting events that one might expect in an international project of this sort. They end up with some sound advice for folks who may find themselves working on similar projects.

Chapter 8

Inviting Collaboration: Insights into Researcher–School Community Partnerships

Lyn M. Shulha and Robert J. Wilson

Introduction

Because program evaluation is rooted in the search for accountability, a central criterion for judging its success has been the degree to which the results have been used for instructional purposes by clients. Perhaps because this criterion has not often been shown to be met, and perhaps, more fundamentally, because of developments in program evaluation theory, new purposes for evaluation have been suggested. These include such goals as improving curricula and programs (Cronbach, 1963; Stufflebeam, 1983); engaging stakeholders in reflection and decision making (Guba and Lincoln, 1989; Patton, 1986; Stake, 1983; Stufflebeam, 1969); shaping the development of policy (Grob, 1992; Weiss, 1988); and, most recently, facilitating organizational learning through researcher–practitioner linkages (Cousins and Earl, 1992; House, in Alkin, 1990).

Some of these newer purposes suggest a larger role for collaboration and partnership among the many participants involved in programs and their evaluations. Collaboration, however, can mean different things to those engaged in the practice. With no documentation on how this process differs from traditional practice, or how its own variations differ, there is a danger that the concept itself will be lost in ambiguity.

Collaboration in this Study

Robert Wilson is a professor of measurement and evaluation in the Faculty of Education, Queen's University. He and colleagues (Wilson, 1992a; Wilson 1992b; Wilson, 1990; Wilson and Rees, 1990) have investigated how the assessment of student achievement proceeds in classrooms and schools. One of the emerging conclusions from this work is that teachers assess in the way they do largely as a result of having to fulfill the policies and procedures in their school concerning reporting. Merely removing these policies, however, is not seen as sufficient to change student evaluation practice because the practice of documenting student achievement is likely to have become integrated into the whole fabric of classroom life.

In our view, if real progress is to be made in understanding assessment practices, teachers need to become collaborators in developing that understanding. A first step in allowing that understanding to grow would be to have a school abandon the traditional reporting policies that requires teachers to produce grades. In this context, teachers could indicate whether or not they want to change their current practices and, if they so desire, could suggest changes they would like to make. The role of university researchers would be to document the desired changes; provide expertise related to the adequacy of those changes; help the teachers implement what they had determined was useful; and monitor the whole process.

From a research perspective, engaging teachers as collaborators rather than as subjects or implementors of reform requires a different type of research plan. The first step in the collaborative process involves coming to some shared understanding of what the research (and teachers' participation in it) might entail.

The Invitation

The 'invitation' was designed as a pre-reform evaluation process whose purpose was to help Robert Wilson (co-author) and the members of a single school community determine the feasibility of collaborative research. A decision to collaborate would be based, in part, on the degree of fit that could be established between the goals of the research and the context of the school.

From a program evaluation perspective, there was a strong rationale for investing resources in such an invitation. First, it would be possible to investigate the capacity of the school to generate the conditions already known to predict successful educational restructuring and reform:

(a) the opportunity for evolutionary planning;
(b) the availability of teacher release time;
(c) the presence of political and physical resources;
(d) a commitment to vision building (Louis and Miles, 1990);
(e) the capacity of the organization to restructure (Fullan, 1991);
(f) the expression of teacher 'will' (McLaughlin, 1987); and
(g) the ability of those initiating the project to acquire a holistic conception of the system being influenced (Sarason, 1990; Weiss, 1993).

It was predicted that these conditions would also describe a collaborative context.

A second argument for conducting pre-reform evaluation lay in its potential to generate, in some detail, a new kind of data for evaluating the outcomes of collaboration, should it proceed. In settings where change is mandated and implemented through traditional bureaucratic structures, policy makers have a working premise: successful implementation of a proposed reform will lead to desirable outcomes. When actual outcomes do not match the expected ones, it is common to hold the implementors responsible for the discrepancy. In schools, for example, teachers often shoulder the blame for ineffective reform, and this point was not lost on the teachers of the school involved in this study (hereafter called Central School):

> Teachers feel that they are responsible for . . . implementing what others want in the classroom, and yet, [we] are the first ones to be blamed when students aren't successful at more fundamental things. (*Field notes: December 16 1991*)

Teacher practice is not independent of school structure and culture. The practice of system-wide, top-down policy change rarely takes this complex interaction into account. Senior administrators will often predict system-wide outcomes when implementing such policies despite considerable evidence. That schools become very adept at preserving the status quo of organizational life in the face of reform (Clark and Astuto, 1988; Cuban, 1988; Fullan, 1991; McLaughlin, 1987; Sarason, 1990). Should the invitation establish that collaborative research was desirable, it was projected that the outcomes would be influenced as much by organizational behavior as by individual teacher behavior.

It was anticipated that the university personnel and the school community would need approximately four months to prepare for a decision about the appropriateness of collaboration. This seemed a reasonable investment of time, given that a decision to go forward would commit the participants to an additional two-year relationship. This time line was also consistent with the optimal planning time for innovation offered by Louis and Miles (1990).

Wilson's work was non-funded research. The invitation was a non-contracted evaluation. These conditions helped to give credibility to the claim that the invitation was not a strategy to promote collaboration, but an investigative process to promote learning about the meaning of collaboration. No assumption was made about the degree of fit between the proposed research project and the school community. No assumption was made about the readiness or ability of the school to participate. There was a vested interest in the integrity of the evaluation process but not in any specific outcome.

Establishing a Context for the Invitation

It was June 1991 when we first discussed the possibility of employing collaborative research as a way to extend Wilson's investigation of assessment and reporting practices. To participate in such a process, Wilson needed assurance of four conditions:

1   The school community could endorse a policy of non-graded reporting.
2   Current assessment practices in the school could benefit from collaborative research once the requirement to produce graded report cards was removed.
3   Teachers would be willing to share their experiences and concerns about assessment and reporting once the new policy was in place.
4   The organizational structure and operating procedures in the school could support the conditions negotiated between the researcher (or Wilson) and teachers for collaborative research.

In October 1991, we had our first contact with Central School. At that time, Central was a junior kindergarten to grade 8 school of approximately 530 middle- and upper-middle class students. The twenty-three regular classroom teachers, three specialty teachers (core French, core English, and a planning time teacher), two teacher-librarians, one special education resource teacher and two administrators (principal and vice-principal) were educating students in both English and French. The availability of French Immersion at this school meant that many students were bussed to Central. Most junior and intermediate students were taught in portable classrooms, located behind the school, in what was known as 'cottage country'. During 1991–1992, the staff managed to support twenty-five different school activities (including Reach for the Top, read-a-thon, science fair, school show, parent appreciation tea), thirteen house league activities, eight school athletic teams and numerous individual class trips.

Initially, Wilson was contacted by the administrators of Central School. Their request was that he facilitate a professional activity day for teachers, focusing on assessment and reporting. This contact paved the way for two subsequent meetings involving the principal, vice-principal, Wilson and Lyn Shulha (co-author). These discussions produced a general agreement that Wilson's research agenda matched the administration's long-term goals for assessment and reporting, and that joint research between teachers and university researchers might be desirable for the school community (*Interview transcript: November 8 1991*).

Wilson's plan was to collaborate with teachers within the context of school life. However, teachers are employees of a larger political system. For this reason, it was essential that a school board formally authorize the intentions of the research and approve any conditions of the research that might impinge on system policy. Specifically, all levels of administration would need to approve the potential change in school reporting policy, and be willing to invest teachers with the authority to make the ultimate decision about collaboration. Wilson and Shulha worked directly with the school principal. He, in turn, negotiated approval for the research from senior school board administrators: the curriculum coordinator, the superintendent of curriculum and instruction, and the administration council. Early senior administrative support for the proposed research project was likely grounded in its compatibility with the board's own review of assessment and reporting policies: Central School was one of eight schools already experimenting with alternative reporting formats as part of a board pilot project.

On November 25 1991, following a half day of professional activities that highlighted current dilemmas in assessment and reporting, Wilson asked teachers to consider the possibility of collaborative research. Shulha's role at that meeting was to propose the invitation. Here, for the first time, teachers, along with Wilson, were publicly identified as primary users (Alkin, 1991), both in the proposed collaboration and in the pre-reform evaluation.

The interest shown by teachers following this meeting was enough to launch the invitation. As the evaluator, Shulha would assist the primary users in developing a deep understanding of the premises and intentions underlying the proposed research and the fit that might exist between the research and the school's organizational structure and culture.

The Design and Methods of the Evaluation

A Focus on Primary Users

There was no doubt that any change in the assessment and reporting practices resulting from collaboration would have significant impact on both the school community (administrators, teachers, students, parents) and the school system (central administration and other elementary schools). In a traditional stakeholder design, the invitation would have attempted broad consultation with all of these parties as a way of sampling the domain of questions that might exist about the research. Instead, the invitation focused on teachers and Wilson, and was extended to other stakeholders only when these primary users identified the need to do so.

One obvious reason for this approach was the central role played by teachers and Wilson in the proposed research. A second reason was the assumption that, within the school community, teachers would have the most stringent criteria for determining the appropriateness of collaboration. It was predicted that teachers' pragmatic concerns about collaboration would provide the most insightful information about the organizational complexity of the school and how it might impact on the proposed collaborative research project. Making teachers primary participants and primary decision makers for the school community was a design decision requested by Shulha and Wilson and endorsed by the school principal (*Interview: November 8 1992*). It did not take long for teachers to experience their status as primary participants.

> The principal and vice-principal are not putting pressure on us in any way. There haven't really been any comments from them. You had to wonder at the beginning, when they accepted you coming in, that maybe they were really sold on this. But they haven't said anything since then. This is going to make it possible for us to really decide. They're really saying, 'This is your baby.' (*First focus group interview: February 7 1992*)

Fullan (1991) argued that a certain degree of administrative pressure *and* support are essential during change, and that a principal detached from the change process jeopardizes its success. While it was always intended that the administrators be active participants in the collaborative research, not involving them as regular participants in focus group interviews was a calculated decision. It was essential that the invitation provide a context where teachers could risk expressing their misgivings about possible changes in policy and practice. Analysis of these misgivings (stated during focus group interviews) would lead to the identification of information and assurances that would need to be woven into the evaluation of the fit between the research and the school community. 'Teacher-only' focus groups were designed to ensure that the agenda of the invitation was anchored in teacher needs. This would, in turn, substantiate our claim that teachers were to be the primary decision makers in determining the fate of collaboration. It was a decision that would be revisited.

Figure 8.1 presents a methodological log of the invitation process. The process began with Wilson and the clarification of his intentions for the collaborative project. It proceeded with three distinct rounds of data collection. Each round involved Shulha visiting classrooms, spending informal talk time in the staffroom and the office, and having regular information meetings with Wilson. Each round culminated in a focus group interview with the teachers who had been visited, as well as others invited by their colleagues. This method resulted in the formal participation of eight to ten teachers during each round of data collection, with some teachers involved for a second time during the third-round focus group.

It was a challenge to have teachers participate in shaping the direction of the evaluation and the analysis of information without being overburdened in the process. Teachers were asked to consult with parents, students and colleagues and to incorporate discussions about the proposed research into informal professional talk. They were also encouraged to feed ideas or concerns into the focus group interviews or back to Shulha directly.

It was teachers' concern about parental support for non-graded reporting that led to a formalized open meeting between parents and Wilson early in the invitation process. Teachers took on the responsibility of assistant moderator during all focus groups. In this role, they monitored the contributions of their colleagues, assuring participation; kept interpretive notes on the questions that arose; and provided a verbal summary of the discussion. Shulha then took the tapes and summaries and produced an information

Date 1991		September	October	November	December
1			First meeting with VP at the school Oct 9	Host a meeting with principal and VP Nov 8	
15		Shulha & Wilson review theoretical frameworks and methods for both studies. Determine the role of focus group interviews.		Principal receives school board support for the project	First visit to a classroom, grade 5/6 Dec 16
30				PA Day, Presentation at the school Nov 25	

Date 1992		January	February	March	April
1			Staff Bulletin #1 -Update, Feb 4 Open parents meeting Feb 4 First focus group interview Feb 7 **End of 1st Round** Summary of parents' meeting Staff Bulletin #2 Feb 17	2 x 2nd Round teacher visits Mar 3 Second focus group interview Mar 6 **End of 2nd Round** Teacher phone interview, Mar 11 Summary of FG Mar 12	Open Q & A meeting for staff Apr 3 Teacher visit Apr 6 Third focus group interview Apr 10 Summary and analysis of focus group III, Staff Bulletin #5
15		Teacher visits Jan 8 (x1) Jan 13 (x2) Jan 20 (x2) Jan 27 (x2) Administrator interviews Jan 13 Jan 27	Summary and analysis of focus group I, Staff Bulletin #3 Feb 18 6 x 2nd round teacher visits Feb 17, Feb 20, Feb 24, Feb 27	Meeting with administration – Mar 25 Summary and analysis of focus group II, Staff Bulletin #4 Mar 26	Apr 22 **End of 3rd Round Wilson extends his invitation to collaborative research Apr. 13**
30					

Figure 8.1 Sequence for the invitation to collaborative research (*debriefings and interviews with Wilson occurred weekly)

bulletin for Wilson and the rest of the staff. Outstanding concerns and responses to this bulletin shaped the next iteration of data collection.

The Invitation as Investigative Evaluation

The invitation was designed to elaborate on, rather than judge, the values and practices of Wilson and the teachers of Central School. While some preordained decisions were made about the use of participant observation, interviews and focus groups, much of the design was recursively sequential, in that, 'What to do next is determined on the basis of the results of what is currently done' (Smith, 1992, p. 7).

In practice, the classroom visit scheduling process began with three volunteers who, in turn, arranged for the evaluator to meet other teachers who furthered the process by recruiting still others wanting to know more about the invitation and the proposed collaborative project. The observation and interview protocols for classroom visits evolved out of weekly debriefings with Wilson and were structured to help him develop a profile of current practices and dispositions toward reporting without grades. The visits, in turn, raised questions about Wilson's intentions, the support of administrators and the backing of parents. After meeting with a teacher in his or her classroom, Shulha interviewed Wilson, and sometimes the principal, to clarify their needs and roles in relation to the teacher's concerns. Collectively, this information formed the basis for focus group interviews. These methods made it possible for Shulha to work continuously with Wilson and twenty-three of the twenty-nine full-time teachers at Central School.

True to investigative designs, the invitation had the quality of being alternately exploratory and confirmatory (Smith, 1992). As one set of questions was answered, another set arose. For example, teachers asked to hear about each others' experiences during reporting. This led to a discussion of the different reporting demands faced by those working in French Immersion, in core programs and in split grades. Teachers discovered that for some, reporting meant producing reports in students' first language on a self-contained community of twenty-six students (or fewer). Other teachers had a similar context for reporting, but were working in English as a second language. This necessitated completing written reports earlier so they could be edited by an administrator or a colleague before being sent out. Then there were teachers working in split grades and producing reports for fifty to sixty students. Some of these teachers met frequently with their morning or afternoon counterpart in the weeks prior to report cards being sent out, in an attempt to produce a more integrated summary of student growth and achievement. The two teachers in core English and French were expected to produce, over the year, anecdotal and graded reports on all students in their program. (Core French enrollment that year was 138 students.) This responsibility, it was acknowledged, was particularly problematic when a core teacher was both a beginning teacher and new to the school.

After looking at the discrepancies of reporting responsibilities, teachers asked the evaluator to help clarify the constraints the school organization would place on the number and timing of reports during a collaborative research project. This was done in a joint meeting which included Wilson and the principal.

> *Shulha to the principal*: . . . Then the question becomes, does someone [with 144 or 138 student contacts] need to report in the same way, at the same time as someone [with 17 students]? . . . This again is an area in which you have the authority to make decisions. . . .
>
> *Principal*: I have no problem with that. I can even see reports for a division going out at a certain time and reports from another division going out at a [different] time. There's nothing to say that they all have to be done [at once].
>
> *Wilson*: So that's not part of the rules and regulations under which you operate?
>
> *Principal*: The only bottom line is . . . the end of June those report cards will go out. That's the standard reporting time.
>
> (*Interview: March 25 1992*)

The need to involve parents at the outset was a perception that was shared between the researchers and the school administrators.

Wilson: *Will you have any difficulty at the school level with people coming to you and saying, 'This all well and good what the teachers are telling us, but I want to know where my kid is, like I'd really like some kind of number.'*

Principal: *We will have some difficulty with that. . . . That's why I want parents involved in what's on going . . . you see that's part of our job. Changing parents' mind sets from what school was when they were there, how they got a result . . . actually . . . one of our grade 8 teachers [has] been through thirty-two interviews and she thought she had two negative comments regarding the [anecdotal] report card because they would have preferred marks. All the other comments were highly supportive of the new reporting system.*

Wilson: *You Know, that's really interesting! . . . I'm beginning to think . . . that 'the parents won't like it' is akin to 'I don't have time.' It's one of those automatic reflex reactions that people make that you really need to get underneath a little more.*

(Principal, vice-principal, Wilson & Shulha. Transcript: November 8 1991, p. 8)

'What if' scenarios were also played out as part of the design, at least conceptually. What if parents are not willing to give up grades? It was this scenario, posed by the teachers, that brought Wilson and the school administration together with parents to discuss the proposed research. The discussion at this mid-morning meeting attracted over thirty parents (three times the number that usually attended Parent Advisory Committee meetings).

During the meeting, parents expressed anxiety over the possibility of abandoning grades altogether. But, with time and encouragement, they began to clarify what they were looking for from a reporting procedure: 'I'd like to know . . . this is what should be learned halfway through the year and we're now halfway through the curriculum and this is what your child is doing. I want to know how I can help.' Some parents offered alternatives to graded reporting: 'Student reports could look like job appraisals, where certain goals are targeted and everyone talks about what their responsibilities and strategies are for meeting these goals. Good performance becomes more of a shared responsibility' (*Parents meeting field notes: February 4 1992*). On this day, Wilson was able to assure the parents present that their needs would continue to play a central role in discussions and decision making during collaborative research.

In retrospect, the timing of this morning meeting was ideal only in assuring parent participation. Teachers, confined to their daily routine, learned about the meeting's tone and parents' general endorsement of collaboration only by talking to those in attendance and by reading the evaluator's account of the discussion. At the time, this was sufficient to revitalize teachers' participation in the invitation. Later, it became evident that a wiser course of action would have been to call the meeting outside of school hours, or at least to arrange teacher representation at the meeting. Both of these options could have been negotiated by Shulha through the school administration.

A second 'what if' scenario played itself out during the wrap-up of the invitation. What if there is a change of personnel at the senior administrative level? After the collaboration had been authorized by teachers, news came from the board office that the curriculum coordinator responsible for the board's pilot project in reporting was leaving his position to return to an elementary school principalship. At Wilson's request, a meeting between the evaluator and the coordinator was scheduled to confirm the support of the senior administration for the research, and to clarify the conditions under which the project had been approved. The discussion verified the role of teachers in determining reporting practices and the requirement to produce, in each of the two years of the project, the standard June report card for each student in the school.

> [The curriculum coordinator] asks what we are going to be doing with our project. I explain that we don't have a [reporting] strategy that we will be imposing on the school, and that teachers will be asked to share what their needs and concerns are when they are freed up from doing the standard graded reports. . . . [He] points out that our project is philosophically in line with the pilot but also has special board clearance to act outside of the pilot guidelines. (*Interview field notes: May 6 1992*)

The coordinator also stated during this meeting that while he was going back into a school the board reporting pilot would remain under his jurisdiction and that he, through Central School's principal, would continue to be our contact with the superintendent of curriculum and instruction.

The Decision to Collaborate

It had taken six weeks of negotiation with the school principal and the school board's senior administration to establish a context for pre-reform evaluation. The invitation itself had extended over another fifteen weeks. Teachers participating in the final focus group confirmed that a decision rule was in place about the degree of support needed to accept Wilson's invitation to collaborative research. They also negotiated with the administration to have regular school time available for the final teacher meeting and vote. A contact person was selected to inform Shulha of their decision. On April 13 1992, Wilson wrote a letter to the staff confirming the parameters of the collaborative project as they had been negotiated. These were that

1   Teachers and Wilson would collaborate to investigate the kinds of assessment practices that emerge when there are no demands to report student growth and achievement using marks or grades.
2   During the first year of the collaborative project, a group of ten teacher volunteers would abandon graded reporting to reflect on the type of assessment practices that are most appropriate for measuring, recording and reporting student growth and achievement.
3   It would be the responsibility of Wilson to provide support and resources for this activity.

4   During the second year of the project all teachers would adopt non-graded reporting using resources available from Wilson and the volunteer group.

In this same letter, teachers were encouraged to think of a 'no' vote as a legitimate professional decision. The letter concluded with Wilson extending a formal invitation to the teachers of Central School to join him in collaborative research in student assessment and non-graded reporting.

On May 1 1992, twenty-one of the twenty-four teachers returning to Central School for the 1992–93 school year voted to collaborate with Wilson in research on teachers' assessment and reporting practices. The strength of this vote exceeded the minimum support level of 80 per cent that teachers had set for themselves. At the end of June 1992, the staff put together a volunteer group that reflected the interests of all divisions, both English and French Immersion programs, men and women, classroom and resource teachers as well as those new to the profession and those with considerable experience. The pilot group numbered eleven, rather than ten, with approval of the principal who gave assurances that this number could be supported with release time.

The Results of Pre-reform Evaluation

The Presence of Predictors of Successful Reform

At the June meeting of the volunteer group, there was a sense of anticipation about the collaborative project. Assessment and reporting had been established by the school community (teachers and administrators) as a 'growth by design' priority for the 1992–93 school year. The principal had committed himself to deflecting other professional development projects from the school (as far as his formal authority would allow) and had negotiated with the senior administration to use board-designated professional activity days for activities related to the project.

> *Principal*: We have PA (professional activity) days that are tied in. I have no difficulty with even arranging, say, an overnight workshop. If they have a PA day on a Friday, OK, I'll send them to a particular spot Thursday night and they stay over the next day and they have the whole PA day the next day.
> *Wilson*: Great! Super!
> *Vice-principal*: . . . PA days are becoming more . . . independent and school-based, as opposed to centrally operated. And it's my understanding that, even on designated system days, other than the one designated Federation day, schools can write a letter and opt to have it as an 'in-school' thing, as opposed to having their staff participate with the system.
> *Principal*: Right! Oh ya, that's no problem. But, as I say, in June I can tell you what our PA days are going to be and plan around that.
> (*Interview: November 8 1991*)

There was evidence from the focus group interviews that teachers had formulated a vision of what working within the research project might be like.

> Maybe it's time not to take for granted what's been laid down for us (here's the form, fill it out) but to evaluate it and determine the way we would like

to see reporting done. . . . Some of our marking could be collaborative with parents. A lot of students' project work and essay work may be done at home, so why not have the parents make a comment on the work that was done at home? . . . All the teachers who are involved with a child may have to get together and conference on the child. (*Focus group interview summary: February`18 1992*)

While voluntary participation and candid talk indicated teachers' interest in vision building, there was early evidence that the invitation had failed to produce a truly collective vision of collaborative research. During the final classroom observation session of the invitation, Shulha encountered a teacher who could not articulate any of the goals of the collaborative research project – but was still interested in being told what they were.

The availability of time to devote to the project was one of the key issues of the invitation. Teachers were concerned about time in two different ways: (a) Would participating in the collaborative project give them additional workload? and (b) Would new student assessment and reporting practices require more time to complete? Protecting teachers' time during collaboration was addressed during the invitation's final meeting between Wilson and the administration.

Shulha: [This issue] came up in my first interview, and came up again, and again, and again! It's the business of time. What teachers are telling us . . . is that they don't want this project to be another thing that they have to do.
Wilson: . . . assuming we go ahead with this, one of the things we make sure we contribute to is that whatever we advocate or encourage or display for teachers will be in replacement for something they presently do. That is, we'll make a commitment to them that we will not ask them to spend more time doing evaluation activities than they presently do. If we come in and say, 'Here's a neat way to collect data about "X"', at the same time, we would say, 'and the thing that you can replace for that is what you presently do, called "Y". . . . This will not take more time than you are presently doing'.
Principal: [Some will] be saying, 'Well, this is going to eventually work into after-school workshops and things like that.' I think in order to allay some of their fears, if it's a go, and we're going to do this, we have to sit down and look at the coming school year and say, 'Here are professional activity days. Can we work them into some of the things you're going to do and let the staff know that this is going to be a major emphasis for us this year?' I'm not going to drop this down on top of them. I have to deflect other things that are going to come in, or incorporate them into what we're doing . . . and the board is aware of that. They know this is going to be a major growth strand for this school.
(*Interview field notes: March 25 1992*)

Once again, the commitments made by Wilson and the principal were summarized and distributed to teachers as part of the negotiated conditions for collaboration.

During the invitation, the principal of Central School accommodated all requests to have teachers released from class time to participate in focus groups. This was interpreted by both the university researchers and the teachers as a willingness on his part to restructure the operation of the school and allocate resources to the project. It was in March that further evidence of this apparent flexibility was documented: this time in the areas of leadership and policy making.

> *Shulha*: The issues [teachers have been raising are] directly related to your roles and responsibilities. In most cases, as administrators, you have the formal authority to mandate. . . . To what extent would [participation in collaborative research] require a change or rethinking of your use of this formal authority?
>
> *Principal*: Maybe I can put that into focus for you. . . . Report cards for instance. . . . What I want to go out is a report card that is effective for the teachers, so that they're reporting on what's proper, and that it's understandable to parents. So, the people that are designing those report cards are teachers and parents, not me. . . . I could draw up a design at any time and say, 'There you go. Report on it!' And teachers would do it and parents would read it. But it's not that the report card should be effective for me, it's for the teachers . . .
>
> *Wilson*: That's very nice to hear. . . . How much standardization do you need as administrators? It's that kind of authority that we're talking about.
>
> *Principal*: I don't need to have standardization. . . . I can even see reports for a division going out at a certain time and reports from another division going out at a certain [different] time. There's nothing that says they all have to be done [at once]. . . . The only bottom line is . . . the end of June, those report cards will go out.
>
> (*Interview field notes: March 25 1992*)

Teachers understood the importance of having a strong will to engage in the project. This understanding was reflected in their decision rules about the viability of the project. First, they established that only returning teachers had a stake in the future of the project. Then they established the 80 per cent rule. The teachers felt that, without this degree of support, transition to the second year of the project would be very difficult.

> It was agreed that those who volunteer at the beginning would have a responsibility to keep others up to date with what they are learning during the first year. But, they cannot also be responsible for convincing others that working with [Wilson] would be worthwhile. A large majority of staff needs to believe this before anyone volunteers for the project at all. (*Focus group interview summary: April 10 1992*)

Had Wilson and the teachers acquired a holistic conception of the system being influenced by the invitation? Because they were able to negotiate some restructuring of the organizational context in the invitation, both the university researchers and the teachers approached collaboration optimistically, believing that, at least conceptually, the school could incorporate the goals of the research into its structural and cultural identity.

Organizational Growth

Schools, to the extent that they are open systems, are subject to a variety of political pressures and mandates. Between December 1991 and May 1992, the invitation to collaborative research was only one of many stimuli influencing the organizational activities of Central School. While Shulha was encouraging teachers to consider the implications of collaborative research in assessment and reporting, teachers were also being required to:

(a) design and implement a new anecdotal reporting system consistent with the policy underpinning the board pilot project;
(b) survey parents about interviews and reports;
(c) indicate a personal professional development priority from a list of options provided by the board office;
(d) consider professional training in a computer program that would make it less onerous for them to produce formal report cards; and
(e) maintain a high degree of commitment to the normal duties of teaching and extracurricular activities.

Given this context, isolation of the effects of the invitation on the school's structure and culture was unlikely. It did seem reasonable, however, to attempt an analysis of organizational growth during the invitation period.

Expanded ideas about the teacher's role in school reform   Teachers talked about how the invitation and the proposed research represented a new approach to change the way things were decided on in the school. Many experienced teachers told stories of anxiety and frustration in having to implement reforms such as French Immersion and Whole Language. Becoming a pilot school for the school board's reporting project was another example of how little influence teachers felt they had in determining policy: 'In the board pilot, we [had] one staff meeting to give our input, and then the administrators [made] the decision' (*Focus group interview summary: March 6 1992*). Teachers reported that having a 'voice' in change meant, historically, being able to express an opinion about the proposed reform. This, they argued, was not the same as shaping school policy. The idea of being involved in the construction of reform appeared to have great appeal.

> Again, group members pointed out to each other that the [collaborative] project seems to offer teachers more than just input into a process. There seems to be an opportunity for 'empowerment in the decision making process'. More specifically, they expressed confidence in being policy makers. Teachers felt validated because this new role had been supported by their principal. (*Focus group interview field notes: April 10 1992*)

Enhanced appreciation of the value of collegial interaction   Teachers talked a great deal about the value of exchanging ideas, specifically ideas about evaluation: '[I learned] that we can . . . vent our frustrations by talking together. I feel we are all saying the same things, we just had to learn from each other. By being open, honest and direct, we can learn a lot from one another. I liked the feeling that you are not alone in your ideas about evaluation' (*Teacher survey: June 22 1992*).

The principal confirmed that teacher behavior both during and after the invitation reflected a new regard for what teachers could contribute to and learn from each other.

> I've seen some sharing go on between teachers about how they evaluate their program, and look at their program. . . . So [the invitation] opened a lot of

doors just in the last year to [get] people talking about things. . . . I've seen people . . . take on leadership roles in some of the activities that have happened here. They didn't do this before. It's given people an opportunity to express themselves and be recognized for what they do, and show a side of their expertise that maybe hadn't been available before. Maybe that's because I've kept my nose out of it and let them know that I respect their decision. . . . I'm going to get some people who are going to recognize they are professionals, and who are not just doing a reporting because the board or the principal says they have to do that. (*Year-end interview: June 22 1992*)

Structured sharing and low stakes observation had emerged as two strategies that could promote collegial interaction, reflection and professional growth. Yet, there was no evidence to suggest they would be integrated into mainstream professional life. Teachers' daily experience of school would remain fundamentally unchanged, with the exception of modifications that had been specifically negotiated for the volunteer group, in support of collaboration.

Researcher Learning

Wilson had always referred to teachers as collaborators. Still, the early research design referred to the volunteers as a 'sample'. During the invitation, Wilson was sensitized to individual qualities of potential volunteers, recognizing the likelihood that they would share only a few group characteristics. He concluded that the research data collected in the first year would be richer if he approached collaboration as a series of case studies, with the group itself representing only one of the cases.

The original design also called for the volunteer group alone to engage in reform during the first year. The rest of the staff would be considered the 'control' group. This design feature was considered by most teachers to be problematic. Their concern was that the research would differentiate their staff and create an 'in group' of collaborators. Wilson abandoned the need for an alternative group of non-participants during the first year. Instead, he agreed to make any information and material generated by the volunteer group available to everyone.

Evaluator Learning

As the evaluator, Shulha also reflected on the experience. The purpose of the invitation was to map Wilson's research project onto the school community and allow the primary users to establish a degree of fit. A review of the methodological log revealed that this mapping process had been predominantly a conceptual one: that is, it primarily involved the exchange of information and ideas.

What had not been designed into the invitation was the meaning of the project in practice. Teachers had not actually experienced what it would be like to work with Wilson and generate, collaboratively, new learnings about assessment and reporting. Even though many teachers had seen their classrooms described, they had not been formally challenged by either Shulha or Wilson to do more than reflect on how their current assessment practices might fit into a research project that eliminated graded reporting. It would be important to test out the strength and utility of these conceptual, shared meanings during collaboration.

Another learning stemmed from the question that the invitation eventually posed to teachers. It had never been the intention of the invitation to promote collaboration. For this reason, in the final bulletin, teachers were encouraged to consider a vote against collaboration as a valid professional option. It was acknowledged that teachers must prioritize the many opportunities that become available to them and that, 'A no [vote] is a professional judgment about the relative importance of this project to you, your students and the parents of your school community' (*Focus group interview: April 13 1992*).

Teachers understood that if they voted in favor of collaboration they would be risking change. Still, there was promise of an opportunity to play a large role in shaping, over two years, the assessment and reporting practices of the school. A 'no' vote, however, could not be interpreted as simply a rejection of collaboration. Without the collaborative project, the school would continue to be under the auspices of the board pilot project in reporting – a process considered by some to be an imposition rather than a meaningful addition to their professional life. Because the consequences of a 'no' vote had never been clarified, interpreting the strength of the 'yes' vote was problematic.

Collaboration in Practice

From Glitch to Gridlock

Following an opening day assembly in September 1992, Wilson invited the volunteer group to consider an off-site workshop as a way to begin the research project. While the volunteer group worked on assessment, the remainder of the staff would participate in a board-wide PA day. Less than two weeks before the workshop, the research team, now a collective of teachers and university researchers, was informed by the principal that all teachers would be required to attend the board-wide PA day on environmental issues.

It was significant that only the university researchers were prepared to challenge this edict. Wilson drew the principal's attention to assurances made that activities related to the research project would have priority for the volunteer group. The principal reminded us of a warning he had given us during the invitation; that the senior administration did have the authority to impose policy on the school at any time and that he and the teachers were bound by such policy decisions.

> *Principal*: The one thing I don't want you to avoid, though, is the fact that the board is there as well. We have permission from our administrative council to go ahead with this project. That's solid. But they are still a very strong political entity that can do things to us.
> (*Interview: March 25 1992*)

The principal did agree to plead our case with senior administration. He was unsuccessful. The explanation given was that the superintendent of curriculum and instruction was unaware of any special arrangements that had been made between the previous curriculum coordinator and Central School about attendance at board-sponsored professional activities. The teachers' response to the cancelled workshop was interesting. While they were disappointed, they were also reticent. The general feeling was that nothing could be done to change the ruling and that, in some ways, it was not a surprising turn of events. The principal suggested, as an alternative, that we meet with volunteers, possibly in two smaller groups, during times when he could guarantee their release.

The university researchers decided to treat this incident as data about the complexity of school life. An alternative beginning to the collaborative project was designed. During September and October, Wilson and Shulha visited the volunteers' classrooms as a way of generating discussion and responding to immediate concerns about assessing growth and achievement. These visits were followed by meetings with the group (two meetings attended by half the teachers on November 17 1992) to plan both a direction in reporting and the type of professional activities that would support this direction. The principal, as promised, arranged for supply teacher coverage so that five teachers at a time could be released. Both meetings took place on the same day, so that all the volunteers were engaged in planning the future of the research.

Because fall teacher–parent interviews had just concluded, teachers were eager to talk about their interview experiences: how they might be improved, as well as how they produced anxieties in both parents and teachers. The talk then centered on the January reporting period. Teachers' expectations – that they would be required to produce the standard board report card – caught the university researchers off guard. The conditions of the project as they had been negotiated with the principal and the senior administration during the invitation were reviewed.

> *Shulha*: I think we should clarify something. . . . The only requirement we have is to have one written report in June.
> *Teacher 1*: That's the legal one?
> *Shulha*: The board requires a June report . . .
> *Teacher 2*: And not January?
> *Shulha*: . . . do you want to do one in January? (The group laughs.)
> *Wilson*: That's my understanding, too. We, as a group, because of the nature of our project, can decide however we want to do it. We could do that as a group and say we all together want to [report in a certain way], or we could decide that Jill likes to do it this way [and] Kevin wants to do it that way. . . . That was our understanding. I know in June there has to be some written documentation because that's important for records . . .
> *Teacher 3*: So, it's conceivable that in January we could have a parent interview instead of having a report. . . . I have a hunch that a lot of parents would like to see something written. I could be wrong.
> *Wilson*: It's also possible to say that, because I think parents would want to see that [written report], that's what I'm willing to provide. But, the choice is still yours. . . . Really, what we're talking about here is, what would be a good way to report to parents? . . . then we can talk about how you . . . collect information in your classroom in order to facilitate that.
> (*First group meeting: November 17 1992*)

Teachers began to discuss reporting options ranging from no formal reporting in January to continuous reporting on their students right up to the June report. By the end of both group discussions, eight of the nine classroom teachers had indicated that, given an option, they would prefer to report to parents in January, possibly using a form of interview with an accompanying written summary to be signed by parents. One primary teacher felt strongly about the need to send home the official anecdotal written report card. The university researchers supported this need and agreed that this type of reporting should be an option for January. Plans were made to have two teachers work with the administration to prepare the parents of students in eight classrooms for a second round of interviews. The research team was to develop some professional activities to help teachers learn more about interview formats and the kinds of information and activities that could be useful during interviews.

With these decisions in place, teachers returned to their classrooms and the university researchers met with the principal to report on the intentions. At this time, the principal informed Wilson and Shulha that senior administration was expecting all teachers, including those in the research project, to produce the standard division reports in January. The principal listened to Wilson's protest, agreed to investigate the origin of this expectation and to try to renegotiate some flexibility for the volunteer group. To support this effort, Shulha agreed to put together a document that tracked the agreements that had been forged between Wilson and the board administrators during the invitation.

The Story of Separation

Wilson saw the senior administration's stipulation that volunteers in the research project produce a January report card as an erosion of one of the cornerstones of the research design. When the principal was not able to resolve what appeared to Wilson to be reneging on previously negotiated conditions for the research, Shulha wrote to both the principal and Wilson, and sent copies of her memo to the teachers in the volunteer group (December 1 1992). This memo described the ambiguities that had arisen in implementing the research project and proposed a joint attempt to clarify, with senior administrators, the intentions of the volunteer group. It was argued that written approval for the conditions negotiated during the invitation would be essential for the long-term success of collaboration. In the meantime, the research would need to be suspended.

The school's response to this memo was a great surprise. Shulha was told by the principal during a phone conversation that teachers were generally uneasy with the reporting agenda that the university researchers had imposed on them. He explained that the board's primary division report cards were already anecdotal and that by using these reports Central School felt it was making significant steps towards their agreement to move to non-graded reporting. Since neither he nor the teachers could see any real justification for the imposition of interviews on the volunteer group, he would not argue for an exemption of the volunteer group from the required board-wide January report card (*Phone interview field notes: December 1992*).

This position was supported, the principal explained, by results of a questionnaire he had sent home to parents following the fall parent–teacher interviews. Parents, he reported, while pleased with the interview process, had requested a January report card. While the principal acknowledged that a low return rate and the types of questions he used might have affected the validity of the results, he continued to argue that his responsibility was to attend to the needs of parents and provide them with the reporting mechanism they requested. Wilson asked that one more attempt be made to save the project. On January 20 1993, Shulha drafted a 'memo of intent'. While directed at senior administrators in the board, it was intended to help the school community and Wilson review the shared meanings that were in place at the end of the invitation process. The president of the Parents' Advisory Group, the principal and the research

> Wilson: *I want to make clear that, it is not essential for our research for anybody to change anything that they're presently doing. It is important that we remove the report card as the traditional way of doing it, meaning those teachers that have to report that As = 80–100. But, if they still want to go on and measure things the way they've always done and keep their mark books or whatever that they did under that system, we are not going to insist in any way that they alter that. But we're certainly going to provide lots of opportunities to see alternative ways of doing it.*
> (Principal, vice-principal, Wilson & Shulha. Interview: November 8 1991, p. 6)

team were asked to sign the memo as evidence of their commitment to collaborative research.

Shulha then visited the school and met with the principal. On Wilson's behalf, efforts were made to assure him that the university researchers had no agenda to implement interviews as a reporting mechanism, even though they supported teachers' interests and had promised to help teachers develop interviewing skills. They also clarified that a major responsibility of the collaborative research team was to discover the actual needs of parents and to reflect these needs in the reporting process. On January 29 1993, the evaluator received a phone call from the principal of Central School asking that Wilson be informed that the teachers had declined his invitation to collaborate in the research project on assessment and reporting.

Discussion

All participants created stories to explain the collapse of the collaborative research project. Early stories were likely to have been influenced by the stress involved in terminating a relationship that had been ongoing for over a year, and by the natural tendency to ascribe blame when there is a perceived failure. The pressure for stability in school life no doubt contributed to the need for the school community to close off the project and contact with the university researchers. Given the importance of teachers and the administration continuing to work together, it is understandable that their stories would become, at least partially, a joint narrative. The university researchers – with the advantage of time, a data trail, and the stories of the school community – have constructed different understandings of both the invitation and of the attempts at collaboration.

The Administration's Story

The principal's account of the breakdown focused on three perceived weaknesses in the university researchers' work: Shulha and Wilson had misinterpreted the administration's commitment; they were not sensitive to the needs of parents; and they did not know how to work with teachers.

The principal argued that it had always been his understanding that existing reporting policies would need to be honored and that only the format for the interim reports was open for change. The mandate to produce January report cards, therefore, should not have been either a surprise or a stumbling block.

> From my point of view, as a local administrator, my original concern was to improve the assessment and evaluation practices to make them a little bit more broad based and to remove the emphasis of marks. It caught me by surprise when you said, 'We want to do away with a report card.' That wasn't what I was originally looking at . . . what I wanted to do was to move the emphasis from an A, B, C; or 80, 85, 90; or G, VG, so that parents could actually read the report card and get a clear view of how the child is functioning in class. [The report card would look at] not just the achievement but their effort, behavior, and socialization skills. I didn't see having to remove the report card but as having to do that. (*Final Interview: February 15 1993*)

From the principal's perspective, Wilson and Shulha had shown a real disregard for the needs of parents. The evidence the principal used to support this claim was the insistence that eight teachers be allowed to pursue interviewing as a means of reporting to their students' parents, despite some evidence that parents generally were anticipating a January report card. It was the obligation of the principal, he argued, to honor parents' requests. Exempting the volunteer group from the January report card would be an abdication of his responsibility.

The principal then indicated that teachers had grown skeptical about the true agenda and the commitment of the researchers. Teachers had told him that reporting with interviews was the agenda of the university researchers and not something they had requested themselves. Teachers, he said, were committed to anecdotal reporting but saw no need to give up written report cards. Also, he had not seen the university researchers provide any worthwhile resources to teachers since the beginning of the project, except for 'a couple of pieces of paper' (final interview field notes: February 15 1993). Teachers, he explained during a closing interview, were 'just like kids' in their need to be given concrete resources, models and targets. If the researchers had been more directive with teachers, given them more concrete things to hang on to, they would have been more open to doing what the researchers and school administrators had initially hoped for (*Final interview field notes: February 15 1993*).

The Teachers' Story

The teachers' story was one of disappointment: the university researchers had not been teaching and they had not been learning. As experts, the researchers had failed within the first four months of the project to transmit the knowledge and skills that would help teachers do a better job of assessing and reporting. The teachers had allowed the researchers into their classrooms and spent time talking with them about assessment and reporting, but had not received anything but a few sample observation and recording instruments in return. They had given far more than they had received from us. As well, the university researchers had not orchestrated the learning very well. Having two weeks or more go by without contact with the researchers made it difficult for teachers to stay enthused about the project. There had been no consistent push by the researchers to keep the project rolling at a reasonable pace.

Teacher 1: Both of you have a lot of knowledge. We were hoping to get some of that knowledge so we could put it to use. We're educators so we're always wanting to be fed new ideas and that's the way the majority of us are. . . . (*Final interview: February 22 1993*)

Possibly their greatest frustration was that the university researchers had failed in their responsibility to clarify what the volunteer teachers would be allowed to do. The teachers discussed how they were not free agents in decision making. They explained that it is the administration's role to determine what the school requires and that teachers, role is to put these things in place. The university researchers should have communicated better with all levels of the administration about what was permissible within the project, and not wasted teachers' time exploring alternatives that were not feasible.

Finally, there was disappointment in the sensitivity of the university researchers. If Shulha and Wilson had truly understood the crush and complexity of school life they would have realized that teachers are always required to adjust their classroom life to the needs of parents and administrators. A good teacher is one who has the flexibility to meet external expectations and still accomplish what is important with students in the classroom. Collaboration between the researchers and the teachers could have continued if the researchers had just accepted the administrators' decision to use the January report card.

The University Researchers' Story

The events between September 1992 (the beginning of the collaborative project) and January 1993 exposed three discontinuities between the idea of collaboration as it was negotiated conceptually, and what happened in practice.

First, during the invitation, teachers talked a great deal about wanting the authority to influence the policies and procedures that would directly affect their professional life. In practice, teachers appeared caught between the policies of the board and the school administration, on one hand, and what they perceived to be the agenda of the university researchers on the other. Encouragement to think of reporting possibilities was subsequently reported to the principal as pressure to do something different from what was expected of them. Enthusiasm for January interviews, whatever its source, quickly evaporated in the face of administrative expectations.

Teacher 1: . . . when we talked in [November], we talked about just having plain interviews and how some people could just do plain interviews.
Shulha: And some people could do a report [card].
Teacher 1: But then it came down from above that everyone was doing a report [card] and there was no choice given. . . . OK, in the group I was with, I said I would prefer to do interviews. I was under the impression that I could do interviews. But then I was told, report cards are due: anecdotal report cards. I didn't go in and speak with the administration and say, 'Hey I want to do interviews' . . . so, that never happened I guess. So, I just went ahead and did the anecdotal report.
(*Final interview: February 1993*)

It is possible that the dilemma for teachers was not how to begin shaping the assessment and reporting procedures within their school, but where to place their loyalty. There was little to be gained from a confrontation with their principal, especially when there was no easily accessible support for their tentative first steps. Any confrontation would certainly have been a big risk and disruptive to the operation of the school since it would have challenged the cultural norm that 'teachers put into practice the policies of administrators'.

Second, before and during the invitation, there was much talk about flexibility with regard to the types and timing of reporting. In practice, no variation from what was already being sanctioned by the board's reporting pilot project proved to be acceptable. The argument to stay the same was built, in part, on the language of reporting. References during the invitation to 'non-graded reporting' were interpreted so stringently during collaboration that Wilson was eventually accused of promising the school an anecdotal report card format (and the assessment tools to support it) and not delivering on this promise.

Finally, the principal saw himself as a responsive educator, one who put a great deal of energy into attending to the needs of parents, students and teachers, and one who would be responsive to the outcomes of collaboration. In practice, there was evidence that this principal carried a strong professional agenda and that once the agenda was set little deterred him from what he judged to be in the best interests of his school community. It was likely that the invitation had served his needs very well.

> Well, I saw it evolve from a very selfish point of view. I had some staff here who I was very unhappy with. I guess they had a very narrow view about evaluation and what that meant. Also, I had parents who had a very narrow view. Their views of evaluation were that evaluation be 'a mark' and an A or a B or a C did not jibe with my philosophy of the goals of education. The evaluation procedure didn't involve any input from parents or anything like that.
>
> The project we have and the [invitation] has . . . given an opportunity for us to clarify some of the things that happen in evaluation: that it's not just a mark, not just a test. We do look at overall growth of students. That's what I really wanted to get across to parents; that our role is not anymore the role of a strictly academic institution. And [teachers] have to get that role across to teachers. Parents now understand better that kids don't progress at the same rate. They can't all do grade one. You sat at the [parent] meeting where I told them, 'I cannot tell you what grade 1 is!' That's what I want to see happening.
>
> The initiative to me was to change some teachers' views and that's happened as a result of things we've done: the [board] report card pilot, you being in the school and looking at those things, and [me] demanding that certain things have to be done in an evaluation procedure. I just see people recognizing that better. And that's what I wanted to see happen. (*Principal, year-end interview: June 25 1992*)

With much of his agenda attended to during the invitation, there was little motivation for the principal to risk engaging in the process that might cause him to lose some control over determining the school's structure or policies, even if these processes had been negotiated as the cornerstones of collaboration. The glue that enabled the principal to hold his agenda together turned out to be the parents. They were viewed as uninformed gatekeepers of traditional practice when their needs conflicted with his initiatives, and as primary stakeholders in the educational enterprise when their needs reinforced his agenda.

Collaboration as Learning: School as Classroom

For Wilson, the purpose of collaborating with Central School was to learn about teachers' assessment and reporting practices when these are unconstrained by traditional reporting policies. Collaboration meant 'joint intellectual effort' (American Heritage Dictionary, 1982); an opportunity for interactive learning. For the school community, collaboration with researchers meant a willingness to provide information about their school life in exchange for expert guidance in the conduct of school assessment.

It was only in revisiting the data in the light of the final outcome that a discrepancy became evident between how learning and leadership were conceptualized during the invitation and how they were actualized during collaboration. The observations and activities of the invitation led the university researchers to believe that the school community was also interested in an active, process-based approach to learning about assessment and reporting. Classroom visits had revealed varying degrees of student participation in the planning and achieving of learning outcomes. One classroom in particular had featured a teacher as guide and mentor. In this environment, students were active inquirers and problem solvers, reliant on each other, as much as on the authority of the designated leader to progress and assess the quality of their learning (*Observation field notes: January 20 1992*). Even in classrooms where more traditional models of teaching and learning occurred, teachers talked about wanting to work towards alternative models.

Collaboration in practice contradicted what we had thought we had learned. As learners, teachers tended to be passive and reactive, judging the quality of their learning on the basis of the amount of content that was covered during contact with the university researchers. Learning was viewed as a commodity more than a process.

Leadership in this bureaucratic school structure was placed squarely on the shoulders of the principal. In return, the larger system gave this person the authority to be directive when enacting a professional agenda or solving organizational problems. The principal of Central School felt comfortable working within this structure.

> Using marks is a cop out. I don't want to see a list of math test marks. When I see $^4/_{10}$ I want to ask, what reteaching did you do? What kind of instruction followed this? . . . I may sound very rigid on this but, there's a lot of transfers available if you don't like this. I'm pushing it because I think it's right for kids. (*Principal interview: January 20 1992, p. 1*). . . . When I came here, I had the sense that the Parents Association ran the school. . . . They had a network that would mobilize anytime something happened in the school they didn't like, and then they would show up and demand things. I had to break the network. I had to tell them that we'll run things from here with your input and support. (*Interview: January 20 1992*)

It is likely that differing enactments of learning and leadership caused the university researchers and the school community to view the events of collaboration differently. For example, in November 1992, the researchers interpreted the mandating of the January report card as a provisional imposition of a system-wide expectation likely to be reversed by a rational appeal from the entire research team and the principal. Reference to the negotiated conditions of the collaborative project would be a substantial part of the school's case. The school community, conversely, viewed the same statement regarding reporting as an edict and one that required acquiescence. Their task was to honor the requirement; such demands were in the natural order of things. The decision regarding the volunteer group's participation in the September professional activity day foreshadowed which of these views was more apt to prevail.

The university researchers saw the spaces between formal contacts as time necessary to integrate the new learnings being generated. Reflection on each visit contributed to a more fully developed notion of what the project was becoming. The school community saw the same spaces as downtime – periods where no activity was required or expected. In this scenario, Wilson and Shulha were significant only when present and only for what they could provide. When they were present, they appeared simply to satisfy their own needs. Not surprisingly then, the school community felt used and abandoned by the same behaviors that the university researchers saw as essential for collaborative learning (*Final interviews, field notes: February 22 1993*).

Conclusions

Understanding Collaboration

In this case study, it was after collaboration was attempted and failed that two assumptions carried by both Shulha and Wilson were re-examined: firstly, that the purpose of collaboration is to generate new knowledge; and, secondly, that collaboration requires the active engagement of all participants both in intellectual and practical activities of learning. These assumptions had been the cornerstones of our behavior and their importance was central to understanding our experiences with the school community. The complexity of attempts to enact collaboration as learning is best captured by the metaphor 'school as classroom'.

The significance of this metaphor is that it had different connotations for the school community and for the university researchers. Wilson and Shulha anticipated working with a school that was metaphorically equivalent to an active-learning, process-based classroom. Within this conceptual framework, learners are generative, self-reliant and interested in creating and controlling the outcomes of the learning process. In practice, these teachers as learners tended to be receivers of knowledge. Learning was a commodity and judgments about the significance of learning were based on the amount of information and material accumulated during each contact with the content experts.

Wilson and Shulha had also envisioned a learning environment where leadership would be shared. Collaboration from this perspective includes conferencing about how the learning might best proceed and negotiating outcomes that attend to the diverse needs of individuals within the learning community. The experience of collaboration indicated that teachers expected leadership from those vested with formal authority. When the university researchers did not prescribe strategies that would lead teachers toward more effective assessment practices they were perceived as abdicating their responsibility. The principal, on the other hand, did exemplify appropriate leadership by continuing to implement his administrative agenda. It was understood by the teachers that the needs of the principal and the larger system he represented would always take precedence over any needs they might have. Within this school as classroom then, leadership could only be temporarily delegated to teachers as learners and this could occur only when teachers' needs were consistent with established norms or the administrative plan of how the school should operate.

In our view, it was this mismatch of meanings associated with the nature of learning and leadership, as these are established within the school-as-classroom, that best explains the eventual breakdown of the collaborative research project.

The Invitation and Collaboration Revisited

In proposing participatory evaluation[1] in educational settings, Cousins and Earl (1992) challenged evaluators to learn more about the intended and unintended effects of 'participation/linkages' (p. 408). The invitation demonstrated the appeal that a rational, participatory decision-making model has for educational professionals; the attempt at collaboration revealed the complex nature of socially constructed meaning and organizational learning.

As promised, the invitation did engage the Central School community and the university researchers in a joint analysis of the implications of collaboration, both for individuals and for the school as an organization. Wilson made fundamental changes in the proposed research design, from one conceived of originally as quasi-experimental to one that more closely approximated a series of case studies. Also, teachers, the administration, and the university researchers were able to negotiate a set of conditions and implementation strategies for collaboration that took into account factors known to predict real change. The invitation concluded with a commitment to establish a partnership designed to generate new knowledge about student assessment.

In practice, however, the volumes of field notes and interview data that tracked the evolution of this partnership had little influence on the way collaboration played itself out. The paper trail generated by the invitation represented espoused theory (what we all thought we could do) rather than knowledge generated through action. The conditions and agreements negotiated throughout the invitation – products of rational cognitive processes – were no match for the roles and obligations summoned by the perpetual and pervasive business of schooling. The shared meaning of collaboration and its implications for individual behavior had remained untested within the context of ongoing organizational life. In the framework of the school-as-classroom metaphor, this organization turned out to be teacher-directed. The invitation had provided few opportunities for the learners – researchers as well as teachers and administrators – to assess the feasibility of alternative learning or leadership styles. Neither had there been opportunities for the school to test out its promised autonomy within the larger political structure. Without these opportunities, and the trust that develops out of shared experience, collaboration was something akin to a leap of faith.

Note

1 'By participatory evaluation we mean applied social research that involves a partnership between trained evaluation personnel and practice-based decision makers. . . .' (Cousins and Earl, 1992, p. 399)

References

ALKIN, M.C. (1990) *Debates on Evaluation*, Newbury Park, CA, Sage.
ALKIN, M.C. (1991) 'Evaluation theory development: II', in MCLAUGHLIN, M.W. and PHILLIPS,

D.C. (eds) *Evaluation and Education: At Quarter Century*, Ninetieth yearbook of the National Society for the Study of Education, Chicago, II, University of Chicago Press, pp. 91–112.

AMERICAN HERITAGE DICTIONARY (1985) Boston, MA, Houghton Mifflin Co.

CLARK, D.L. and ASTUTO, T.A. (1988) 'Paradoxical choice options in organizations', in GRIFFITHS, D.E., STOUT, R.T. and FORSYTH, P.B. (eds) *Leaders for America's Schools*, Berkeley, CA, McCutchan Publishing, pp. 112–130.

COUSINS, J.B. and EARL, L.M. (1992) 'The case for participatory evaluation,' *Educational and Policy Analyses*, **14**, 4, pp. 397–418.

CRONBACH, L.J. (1963) *Educational Psychology* (2nd edn) New York, Harcourt Brace & World.

CUBAN, L. (1988) 'A fundamental puzzle in school reform', *Phi Delta Kappan*, **70**, 5, pp. 341–44.

FULLAN, M. (1991) *The New Meaning of Educational Change*, New York, Teachers College Press.

GROB, G. (1992) 'How policy is made and how evaluators can affect its agricultural price policies', *Evaluation Practice*, **13**, 3, pp. 175–83.

GUBA, E. and LINCOLN, Y. (1989) *Fourth Generation Evaluation*, Newbury Park, CA, Sage Publications.

LOUIS, K.S. and MILES, M.B. (1990) *Reforming the Urban High School*, New York, Teachers College Press.

MCLAUGHLIN, M.W. (1987) 'Learning from experience: Lessons from policy implementation', *Educational Evaluation and Policy Analysis*, **7**, 2, pp. 171–78.

PATTON, M.Q. (1986) *Utilization-focused Evaluation* (2nd edn) Newbury Park, Sage Publications.

SARASON, S. (1990) *The Predictable Failure of Educational Reform*, San Francisco, CA, Jossey-Bass Inc.

SMITH, N.L. (1992) 'Aspects of investigative inquiry in evaluation', in SMITH, N.L. (ed) *New Directions for Program Evaluation: Vol. 56. Varieties of Investigative Evaluation*, San Francisco, Jossey-Bass, pp. 3–13.

STAKE, R.E. (1983) 'Program evaluation, particularly responsive evaluation', in MADAUS, G.F., SCRIVEN, M. and STUFFLEBEAM, D.L. (eds) *Evaluation Models: Viewpoints on Educational and Human Services Evaluation*, Boston, Kluwer-Nijhoff.

STUFFLEBEAM, D.L. (1969) 'Evaluation as enlightenment for decision making', in BEATTY, W.H. and WALCOTT, A.B. (eds) *Improving Educational Assessment and an Inventory of Measures of Affective Behavior*, Washington, DC, Association for Supervision and Curriculum Development.

STUFFLEBEAM, D.L. (1983) 'The CIPP evaluation model for program evaluation', in MADAUS, G.F., SCRIVEN, M. and STUFFLEBEAM, D.L. (eds) *Evaluation Models: Viewpoints on Educational and Human Services Evaluation*, Boston, Kluwer-Nijhoff.

WEISS, C.H. (1988) 'Evaluation for decisions: Is anybody there? Does anybody care?', *Evaluation Practice*, **9**, 1, pp. 5–19.

WEISS, C.H. (1993) 'Where politics and evaluation research meet', *Evaluation Practice*, **14**, 1, pp. 93–106.

WILSON, R.J. (1990) 'Classroom practices in evaluating student achievement', *The Alberta Journal of Educational Research*, **26**, 1, pp. 4–17.

WILSON, R.J. (1992a) 'Evaluating student achievement: Perception and reality', *The Canadian School Executive*, **11**, 10, pp. 13–16.

WILSON, R.J. (1992b) 'The context of classroom procedures in the evaluating of students', in BATESON, D.L. (ed) *Classroom Testing in Canada*, Vancouver Center for Applied Studies in Evaluation, University of British Columbia.

WILSON, R.J. and REES, R. (1990) 'The ecology of assessment: Evaluation within educational settings', *Canadian Journal of Education*, **15**, 3, pp. 215–28.

Chapter 9

Using Participatory Evaluation in an International Context

*Donna M. Mertens, Terry R. Berkeley and
Susan D. Lopez*

Introduction

Cousins and Earl (1992) proposed a participatory model of program evaluation that they defined as 'applied social research that involves a partnership between trained evaluation personnel *and* practice-based decision-makers, organization members with program responsibility, or people with a vital interest in the program' (pp. 399–400). They identified three characteristics of participatory evaluation: (a) involvement of a relatively small number of stakeholders (primary users); (b) involvement of the primary users in problem formulation, instrument design or selection, data collection, analysis, interpretation, recommendations, and reporting; and (c) an interactive and coordinating role for the evaluator, with a broad understanding of technical support, training, and quality control, while recognizing that conducting the evaluation is a joint responsibility of some of the primary users. Cousins and Earl also noted that local context provides an important basis in determining the exact form of the participatory evaluation.

Participatory evaluation approaches can be used to assess projects and to empower people. Brunner and Guzman (1989), for example, argued that participatory evaluation can be useful in international contexts because of the need to identify factors that contribute to and hinder the successful implementation of a project; and to relate those factors to the specific place in which the project is located. To identify these factors, they posited that it is necessary to design and to implement the evaluation with members of the relevant society (or organization), while professional evaluators act as facilitators of the evaluation process, and, importantly, we contend, as educators about program evaluation.

In this chapter, we discuss the application of a participatory model to the evaluation of a special education training project in Egypt, with a special emphasis on those factors that facilitated and inhibited the empowerment of primary users in an international context. The struggle to involve primary users in a meaningful way is applicable

Authors' Note: This work was sponsored, in part, through an agreement among the United States Agency for International Development, the Ministry of Education of the Arab Republic of Egypt, and Gallaudet University. The opinions expressed in this paper do not necessarily reflect the position, policy, or endorsement of the funding agency, the United States Agency for International Development (Cooperative Agreement No. 263-0139-A-00-1206-00), the Ministry of Education of the Arab Republic of Egypt, or Gallaudet University.

in any participatory evaluation, domestic or international. However, the international setting of this project helped us to highlight the unique issues and variations involved in applying a participatory approach when there is a multiplicity of intervening cultural and political traditions in the place in which one works.

We provide a brief description of the special education system in Egypt and the framework that guided the development of the project and the evolving challenges of the evaluation, so that the context of the participatory model is more fully understood. For us, we needed to work toward understanding these dynamics. We were Westerners offering our expertise for the first time in an Arab culture. We wanted those from the host culture to use in their schools what we outsiders offered in the training.[1]

Context

In September 1991, a cooperative agreement (the Egyptian Training Project) was begun by Gallaudet University, the Ministry of Education of the Arab Republic of Egypt (MOE), and the United States Agency for International Development/Egypt (US AID). The purposes of the agreement were to provide training, equipment, and consultation in order to assist in improving the provision of education and other human services to Egyptian students with disabilities (i.e., students who were blind, deaf, or mentally retarded).

In Egypt, approximately 16,000 students with disabilities are served in twenty-three of the nation's twenty-five governates (regions). The students are served in 110 separate schools for students with disabilities. It has been estimated, conservatively, by Ministry of Education officials that 15 per cent to 20 per cent of all students with disabilities in Egypt are provided with special education. The students enrolled in special education programs receive those services in 1,500 classrooms, and they are served by 1,600 teachers.

The great majority of educational services for students who are deaf or mentally retarded have a vocational orientation. However, 40 per cent of the students who are blind receive academic programming and many students from this group enter universities at the completion of their secondary schooling. Additionally, services for very young children with disabilities are now being started due to recent progressive changes in Egyptian policy to provide up to two years of pre-school special education for children who are 4 and 5 years old. In terms of age coverage, then, with the exception of students who are blind who attend school until they complete preparatory (secondary) training, students who are deaf or have mental retardation go to school until they are 14 years of age, or until they are 16 years of age if a petition is approved by the national director of special education.

Special education in Egypt, like non-special education, suffers from a limited infrastructure: too few buildings, classrooms, supplies, equipment, materials, and trained teachers and specialists.[2] This state of affairs, exacerbated by a population growth in Egypt during the past seven years or so estimated to be about 2 per cent to 3 per cent per annum, has made it difficult for Egyptian officials to expand the infrastructure to meet evolving special education needs in an organized manner – that is, in a manner that is organized, consistent, and coherent from a western perspective. Thus, changes are continually experienced as officials try to find ways to serve more children when there are only limited increases in the resources necessary to do so.

Egypt is a 7,000-year-old country undergoing constant development while being in a constant state of transition. It is not oil-rich and its cash resources are used for many things, other than education, to meet more pressing needs (for example, water, electricity and shelter). Presently, Egypt's economy is in flux, with significant unemployment; the need for more housing, human services, and trained personnel to provide those services; and with political and cultural customs that influence all aspects of life in ways that are much different from those to which westerners are accustomed. It is within this context that we developed our participatory approach to evaluation.

Challenges in the Development of the Evaluation Method

The program evaluation method used by us was guided by the principles of participatory evaluation as explicated by Cousins and Earl (1992) in that a partnership was formed between trained evaluation personnel from the US and a small number of Egyptian teachers and administrators who were involved throughout the planning and implementation of the evaluation. The evaluators in the Egyptian Training Project coordinated evaluation activities and provided support, training, and quality control during the evaluation process.

In the Egyptian training project, the training, consultation and evaluation that was planned changed in response to needs that emerged over time. This evolving nature of evaluation is in contrast to that described by Lee and Cousins (chapter 5 of this volume) who noted that the success of the participatory process is enhanced by having a clear and detailed plan. In this specific international context, the watch-words were 'flexibility' and 'responsiveness'. Adherence to a clear and detailed plan would have been detrimental to implementation in that it was essential to modify training and evaluation plans to meet newly identified needs of the Egyptian educators as the project progressed, and cultural and communication differences contributed to the challenges in planning and implementing the evaluation.

The complexity and challenges inherent in this context led us to examine the philosophical assumptions of our approach.

> *A deaf American instructor signed his words in American sign language. His signs were voiced in English by an American hearing interpreter. Then, they were repeated out loud in Arabic by a hearing Egyptian interpreter. They were enunciated silently in Arabic by another hearing Egyptian interpreter who sat in front of a deaf woman who is able to read lips. The deaf woman signed the words in Egyptian sign language for the other deaf participants in the training class.* (Field notes, Cairo, Egypt: May 24 1992)

Underlying Assumptions

In part, our approach was grounded in the constructivist paradigm described by Guba and Lincoln (1989). Three of the underlying assumptions of the paradigm were particularly relevant for us in the choice of the participatory approach. First, in the constructivist paradigm, the ontological assumption is made that reality is a social construction. For example, terms such as 'evaluation', 'curriculum', 'lesson planning', and 'autism', had different meanings for the American and Egyptian trainers. This interpretation of the meaning of important concepts was complicated by cultural differences, as well as differences in knowledge. Gaining a common understanding of concepts could, at times, be quite difficult.

Second, the epistemological assumption in the constructivist paradigm holds that the evaluator and the primary users are engaged in an interlocking process with each affecting the other. In order to break through cultural barriers, it was necessary to establish a human connection of common bonds. Thus, conversing informally, sharing pictures and stories about one's family and children, and eating together under the trees in the school courtyard were common ways to collect data.

Third, in the constructivist paradigm it is posited that facts are products of social constructions and reflect values. For example, concepts – such as using sign language to teach deaf students, training deaf people to teach sign language to hearing teachers, or accepting the language of the local deaf community – were value-laden and were discussed quite a bit over time. These discussions took place in many meetings of the members of the training team and in many conversations between and among the parties to the agreement in the United States and in Egypt.

Methodology

Needs Assessment

In June 1991, three US staff members from Gallaudet University went to Egypt to meet with MOE officials and with US AID staff to conduct a needs assessment. The purpose of the needs assessment was to determine who the training participants would be (i.e., the characteristics of the group to be trained), what training topics should be included in the training, and what training strategies could be used most effectively in Egypt. As a result of this needs assessment, a program of training was devised and an evaluation plan established. Project operations began in September 1991, when twelve Egyptian MOE representatives came to the US for training.

To further develop the training plan, another needs assessment was conducted with the twelve MOE representatives who had come to the United States for training. This needs assessment consisted of a four-page form that participants completed. The purpose of this assessment was two-fold: first, trainers would be provided with reliable and detailed information about the individual participants (i.e., their educational and professional backgrounds); and, second, information would be provided to indicate the participants' perception of their proficiency in a number of topical areas related to special education and program development and evaluation. Then, based upon the results of this second needs assessment, trainers would be able to develop their presentations to address the educational, professional, and perceived level of proficiency of the training participants. Trainers would meet these needs in a number of different ways. For example, trainers might allot a greater amount of time to a topic based upon what was learned in the needs assessment. Or, they might add or delete topics previously considered. It should be noted that the trainers always had to be prepared to adapt their presentations to meet the emerging needs of the participants as identified through daily evaluations.

Purposes of the Evaluation

The purposes of the evaluation, therefore, were:

  (a) to provide a means for determining ongoing training needs;
  (b) to provide a rationale for modifying training while it was in progress;
  (c) to revise the training plan for upcoming training;
  (d) to respond to concerns of the primary users and participants during the train-
       ing periods; and
  (e) to provide a source of information for reporting on project activities and
       progress to officials at US AID, the Egyptian Ministry of Education, and
       Gallaudet University.

Participants

Alkin's (1991) definition of primary users was used to describe the participants in this
project: primary users are those who assume responsibility for program implementation
or those who are vitally interested in the program. The primary users of the evaluation
were two training teams: seventeen Americans and eighteen Egyptians. The American
team, based at Gallaudet University, consisted of project staff and consultants skilled
in various aspects of special education, educational administration, research, policy
analysis, program evaluation, program development, and curriculum. The Egyptian team
consisted of six administrators from the MOE, three administrators from the National
Curriculum Centre (a quasi-independent organization of the Ministry), four teachers in
schools for students with disabilities, and five deaf individuals who were being trained
to teach sign language to hearing teachers of Egyptian deaf children. Fifty teachers from
schools in five governates in Egypt also were recipients of the training; however, they
were not considered to be 'primary users' of the evaluation data.

Data Collection

Data was collected principally using qualitative methods, including observations of the
training sessions, interviews with primary users, small group meetings on a daily basis
with primary users, document review and analysis, and daily assessments administered
as written surveys to all primary users and recipients of the training (hereafter referred
to as 'participants'). Each day of training began with a review of comments (which had
been translated from Arabic overnight) from the daily assessment forms for the previous day, in which participants were asked to identify what they had learned that was
important to them, topics on which they still needed additional information or clarification, and any problems or concerns that they had regarding the training. The comments were discussed with the primary users in order to determine their perspectives
regarding the training. Data was collected during four training sessions: a month-long
training session in the United States; and three training sessions in Egypt that were
either two weeks or three weeks in length.

In addition to the daily evaluations, pre-training data were collected to determine
training needs and attitudes towards students and people with disabilities. At the conclusion of each of the four training sessions a summative evaluation was conducted to

determine the effectiveness of the training. To complement the daily and summative evaluations, project staff, consultants, and a random sample of participants were interviewed regarding their opinions and perspectives about the training. Again, the intent was to gather data that could be analyzed in order to enhance the training and to empower those involved in the training.

Data Analysis Procedures

Content analysis procedures, following the tenets prescribed by Goetz and LeCompte (1984) and Patton (1980), were used to organize and examine the open-ended questions of the daily and summative evaluations, interview data, and field notes. The data was analyzed in the field, and the preliminary results were shared with the primary users in the morning staff meetings each day before the training sessions began. Formal analysis of the qualitative data was accomplished by entering the data in *The Ethnograph*, a computer software program in which the evaluator is able to code, recode, and sort data files into analytic categories (Qualis Research Associates, 1988). The initial categories were based upon the evaluation questions and, when they had been modified as transcripts, were read more closely so as to identify emerging themes and relationships between and among categories. Data bearing up on each category was physically separated and reviewed again to determine results so that the implications of the data could be examined.

Impact and Implications of the Participatory Model

Guiding Questions

Several questions were formulated to guide the analysis of the impact of using a participatory model of program evaluation in Egypt. The questions are as follows:

1 What were the effects of the participatory model on program changes, substantive learning, and the development of evaluation skills by the primary users?
2 What factors are related to empowerment of participants and utilization of evaluation results?
3 What are the implications for conducting participatory evaluations in an international context?

These questions provide the framework for our reflections on the effects of the participatory evaluation process, factors that contributed to meaningful participation, and implications for conducting participatory evaluations in international contexts.

Effects of the Participatory Model

Evaluation utilization   Cousins (chapter 4 of this volume) identifies three dimensions of evaluation utilization: discrete decisions, substantive learning, and development of research skills. In the evaluation of the Egyptian training project, the discrete decisions that resulted from the evaluation process led to program changes. For example, on a day-to-day basis, changes would occur in training content, presentation, and/or emphasis. The substantive learning that occurred represented a confirmation of prior knowledge and new insights gained by the primary users. For example, the Egyptian trainers and the participants retained information learned from one training session to the next and they were able to apply that information to new training topics. The development of evaluation skills is reflected in changes witnessed in the primary users relative to their attitudes and understanding of program evaluation. For example, at the beginning of the project, the Egyptian training team had little concept of and appreciation for program evaluation. During the initial training in September 1991, these educators were provided with theoretical training in program evaluation. Then, during that and subsequent training sessions, they observed and participated in the evaluation process. From this training and experience, they developed an understanding of and appreciation for program evaluation as evidenced by their interest in daily evaluation results, inquiries about program evaluation, and utilization of program evaluation in the replication training that they did in their own governates after the Gallaudet team completed their work in Egypt.

Empowerment through attitude change   While Cousins (chapter 4 in this volume) discusses discrete decisions, substantive learning, and development of research skills, we found that observation of attitude changes provided powerful evidence of the effects of participation in the evaluation process in this international context. Webster (1992) professed that it is necessary to reformulate the image and expectations of vulnerable persons to empower them. The primary users in the Egyptian training project established that one of the goals of the evaluation was to determine the change in participants' attitudes towards persons with disabilities. The behavioral observations of changes that occurred throughout the training process support the empowering effect of a reformulation of the image of persons with disabilities. Through this process the deaf trainers became empowered in a way previously unknown in Egypt, in that sign language had not been used much in schools for the deaf there and deaf people for the first time were officially allowed to train hearing people in sign language.

In a sense, being at Gallaudet and receiving instruction in sign language served as an 'awareness training' for the Egyptians at the first session. The need to incorporate sign language training and to involve deaf people was discussed at length at daily staff meetings with the primary users, and it was decided that deaf people should be included in the next training to train the Egyptian educators in techniques of teaching sign language. As a result of this identified need, five deaf Egyptians were recruited to participate in subsequent training sessions. In the remaining training sessions, the deaf Egyptians spent the morning training period with one or two deaf American instructors

---

At the first training session, one hearing Egyptian administrator asked the American trainers to stop using sign language because it was 'distracting'. In addition, he said that they did not use sign language with their deaf students because they 'knew' that it would impede learning. After observing the signing deaf people on Gallaudet's campus and after participating in the training on a 'new vision' of persons with disabilities, the Egyptians expressed, through the evaluation process, a need to know more about sign language.

A comment made by one of the Egyptian teachers at the end of the last training session illustrates the change of attitude reflected by many of the training recipients: 'We need more training in sign language. This has not been enough. The project needs to be extended. If not, we have not gone far enough. We need more deaf people trained in teaching sign language.' (Field notes, Cairo, Egypt May 27, 1992)

developing strategies for teaching sign language to hearing teachers; during the afternoon training period, they taught sign language to the hearing Egyptian teachers. Thus, as a result of the evaluation process, the hearing Egyptian special educators became empowered in their ability to express a need that had not been formerly recognized, and the deaf Egyptians became empowered primary users of the evaluation data as they participated in the daily morning meetings and all the activities associated with the training.

As we learned about the history, tradition, and importance of national administrators in the implementation of Egyptian special education, we observed another area related to attitude change and empowerment in terms of the primary users' perceptions of program evaluation. Our hope was to 'move' attitudes from an implicit 'good–bad' orientation to one in which evaluation could provide a forum in which ideas are presented, heard, and, then used, even by people who are unaccustomed to having such influence in their work. We observed changes, for example, to the extent that training participants could support the training, yet empower themselves by making suggestions that were immediately discussed and used by all training team members, including officials from the ministry. This empowering effect helped to build credibility among the partners in the training process, especially the teachers who were being trained. In our view, this is crucial in those international contexts in which teachers' voices are rarely heard.

Factors Related to Empowerment and Utilization

Cousins (chapter 4 in this volume) specified three factors that explain variation of evaluation impact:

(a)   decision or policy setting, such as administrative support and timing in the decision stream;
(b)   evaluation implementation that includes the credibility, relevance, methodological quality, and communicative quality of the data; and
(c)   interactive processes, such as involvement of participants and plans for distribution of the results.

Factors related to empowerment and utilization are discussed in terms of strategies that were used during the project to incorporate meaningful participation for the primary users at three stages of the evaluation: planning and training, data collection, and data interpretation and use. These stages correspond, with some variation, to the three factors identified by Cousins, as follows:

(a) planning and training parallel administrative support and timing in the decision stream;
(b) mechanisms for data collection parallel evaluation implementation; and
(c) the mechanism for interpretation and implementation of changes parallels involvement and plans for distribution of results.

Planning the evaluation and training the primary users   For us, a critical aspect of the participatory model is the focus on the training of primary users in evaluation to enhance their confidence in empowering themselves. Training in evaluation began with a briefing by the project evaluator of the American team at two staff meetings prior to the arrival of the Egyptian team, as well as an entire day of training in program evaluation that was integrated into the first training program for the Egyptians who were in the United States. The following vignette illustrates the initial training activity with the Egyptian team:

> *The US evaluators from Gallaudet University began their training with a 'brainstorming' activity to determine the meaning of program evaluation to the participants. We discovered multiple meanings of this term, such as attainment of instructional objectives, assigning of grades for school work, and administering standardized tests to students. The evaluators discussed the concept of evaluation as it was envisioned for this project: a means of systematically collecting information for the purpose of improving decision making; in this specific context, decisions about the training project in which they were engaged.*

The evaluators used a modification of the Brinkerhoff, Brethower, Hluchyl and Nowakowski (1983) framework for planning an evaluation to guide the training process, which included the following steps: identification of the object of the evaluation, audiences (primary users), purposes, and constraints and opportunities; development of an evaluation design (theoretical framework and evaluation questions); formulation of plans for data collection, analysis, interpretation, use and reporting; and formulation of plans for project management and meta-evaluation.

The evaluators explained each step in the evaluation process and provided MOE officials with examples of their application, and then provided them with time to work in small groups to determine how this step applied to the Egyptian training project. They were given the opportunity to share ideas from their small group, and an evaluation plan was developed based upon the shared ideas. The results of the training session were shared with the American trainers in a staff meeting the next day. Their comments were shared with the Egyptian team members and modifications were made to the evaluation plan.

The strengths of this process are that it enhanced the shared understandings of the meaning of evaluation and it empowered the primary users in the development of the evaluation plan. The input of the primary users was particularly helpful with regard to the appropriateness of data collection strategies to be used with the Egyptian teachers in later training sessions. Two problems were associated with this process. First, it was not possible, due to logistics, to have the entire American and Egyptian teams in the evaluation training sessions at one time. Therefore, the training/planning process was

> *During the fourth training session in Egypt, only five of the twelve trainers' daily assessment forms in one disability area were returned. This non-response problem was raised at the daily staff meeting, and the lead trainer in that area (who had entered the project after the initial training in evaluation) expressed the opinion that there was 'too much' evaluation.*
>
> *Evidence of the 'empowering' effect of involvement came from the response of the primary users to this person who commented that it was the attitude of the leader that determined how seriously the other participants would take the evaluation. One Egyptian trainer said, 'We have a very short period of time to do tremendously important work. We need feedback every day to be sure that we resolve any problems and so we can have the most effective training possible. The leaders need to stress the importance of evaluation in this because we only have you here for a short time.' This opinion was backed up by the leader of the American training team. As a follow-up to that discussion, the lead trainer in that disability area explained the importance of evaluation to all the participants and the daily assessments were completed satisfactorily for the rest of the training session.*

somewhat disjointed. However, the Americans and Egyptians were fairly close in their thinking about the evaluation plan, so this did not become a major obstacle.

Second, a more significant problem was represented by the changing of staff members during the project. The members of the American and Egyptian teams moved in and out of the project as dictated by instructional needs and personal considerations. Thus, while some members of the team continued throughout the duration of the project, others did not. Some of the people who were involved in the initial planning of the evaluation did not continue, and others who came in later had a different 'stake' in the evaluation. The implications of this are discussed more in the next section.

Mechanisms for data collection   Based upon the evaluation plan, the data collection strategies worked fairly smoothly. Daily assessments were completed, observations were recorded, interviews were conducted, and the results were used almost immediately to make changes in the program. As the participatory evaluation unfolded it became clear that people who were involved in the evaluation process supported those activities necessary for meaningful data collection and data use.

Mechanism for data interpretation and implementation of changes   The daily feedback loop was used as a way to empower the primary users in the interpretation and use of the data. The effect on primary users of this feedback loop was quite powerful. The complexity of the situation in terms of language, culture, and training issues underscores the importance of the feedback loop in allowing the trainers to be empowered in the interpretation of the data and in developing recommendations for action. In addition, the teachers received more effective training and the evaluators were able to make more intelligent interpretations of the results.

King (chapter 6 of this volume) also reported on the importance of supporting collaborators by showing a true interest in what they are saying and thereby earning their respect and trust. This was accomplished by responding to the daily feedback for

> *Comments on the daily assessments indicated that the recipients of the training were disturbed because all the signs they learned in Cairo were not the same as the signs that deaf people used in their home schools. If this comment had been ignored or interpreted without input from the primary users, a number of different actions might have occurred: possibly, the recipients might have returned home thinking how useless the training was that they had received in Cairo; the evaluator might simply have reported that the training that was offered did not meet the needs of the participants who attended the sessions; the deaf Egyptians, who were new sign language trainers, might have been frustrated and stymied in their attempts to bring sign language into the classrooms of deaf Egyptian students. Instead, the evaluator brought up the comment at the small group meeting with the primary users and the instructor in sign language discussed their comments in the next training session. He told the teachers: 'You have to accept the signs of the deaf community. It is a fact of life. There will be different signs.' A discussion followed on the importance of respecting the local language, the common practice of having more than one way of expressing an idea in sign language and to respect deaf culture.*

the evaluations even when we could not change things (such as translation of materials into Arabic, an activity which was not included in the funding of the training). At least we could say to the Egyptians that we had heard them even when we did not have power to control certain aspects of the project.

International Implications

Soon after the project began, the implications of our work became apparent. For example, in the design of the program evaluation we did not believe the Egyptians would be interested in learning about evaluation or about helping us in its planning. Thus, the initial assumptions we held, generally, about different cultural contexts needed to begin, not end, with an adherence to Rogers' (1965) ideal of 'unconditional positive regard' since we had to learn that all project activities were important to our Egyptian partners. We also learned very quickly that people with limited content area expertise in special education and instructional methodology – for example, the teachers we trained – had a great desire to be 'full' participants in the planning and implementation of other project activities as well. While this may have made the program evaluation process much more labor intensive, the success of the project, we believe, was enhanced through attention to commonly understood details. Thus, the evaluation was quite useful.

Empowerment is intertwined with utility. Program evaluation efforts, on one hand, can be empowering if that which is done creates the ambience for the active use of program evaluation data. On the other hand, it is possible that program evaluation can be enhanced through a process that begins and concludes with the notion that utility is only a reflection of that which is stated in the data. The more often that specific perspectives are found to exist that parallel the positions, views, and opinions of those who are to be empowered, though, the greater the possibility that true empowerment can occur. Such empowerment would be reflected in a subsequent positive change in the conditions that caused program needs to arise in the first place.

While we believe that the work done in evaluating the training activities of the Egyptian training project has implications for other developing nations in what is known as the 'Third World', we also are realistic enough to understand that the great variability of characteristics from one nation to the next, just in the Middle East itself, will obfuscate some aspects of what we find in one place while heightening an awareness about that same characteristic in another place. For example, in Egypt, training can be, and was, interrupted many times during the course of any one-hour period with participants entering and leaving the training room for a variety of personal and professional reasons. In another example, there was considerable participation by a group of people being trained, even when the responses given allowed a trainer to assume that everything being taught was understood and, of course, would be implemented with little difficulty when the training was completed and the participant had returned home. Therefore, the implications we are describing need to be thought of as *guides* to planning participatory evaluation in developing countries.

Impetus for change   In a sense, the impetus for participatory evaluation in the United States has been more on 'bottom-up' educational reform efforts. This contrasts sharply with that in Egypt, whereby efforts to make change only occur because of 'top-down' stimuli from the Ministry of Education. Thus, teachers and students who are supposed to be the beneficiaries of training do not appear to be allowed to benefit unless the ministry explicitly allows this benefit to be officially sanctioned. This means that the teachers who participated in the training – who were to have been empowered through evaluation and participation in the training itself – in some cases were not thought of as being key people by those responsible for overseeing the delivery of special education who work at the national level. Yet, informally, we frequently were told by teacher participants that they have been empowered because they have implemented some of what they learned during the training because it was important for them to do so for professional and personal reasons.

Emancipation   Brunner and Guzman (1989) noted that participatory evaluation can be problematic in an international setting because empowerment might only be successful when the institution that promotes it wants to emancipate dominated groups. And, further, emancipation can only occur when the groups strongly identified with the project are prepared to assume responsibility for it and have the means to become emancipated on their own. The lack of involvement of local school administrators in the training was an impediment to the teachers' implementation of what they learned during the training.

   In some ways, this effect was diminished as local school administrators in Egypt because their role is not viewed in terms of providing instructional leadership in their schools. Rather, Egyptian administrators are responsible for personnel attendance, ordering supplies, and for attending to those issues that parents raise in terms of their children's daily living needs. They also serve as the contact for the school with officials in the ministry. Emancipation, thus empowerment, would have been enhanced, we believe, if administrators were thought of as being equally important to teachers even with the 'different' role they undertake in contrast to American school administrators.

Participation of primary users   King (chapter 6 in this volume) noted that one cannot require someone to participate in an evaluation who chooses not to, therefore, one needs to find people who want to participate. Most of the primary users of this evaluation, we believe, wanted to participate, but there were people at other, higher levels in the organization that were not as interested in participating in this kind of activity. The primary interests of those individuals were in procuring more equipment and receiving more training for more people about the use of that equipment.

At the outset, as we planned project activities, our decisions were based upon what we learned after the brief site visits to 15 schools in 5 governates for students with disabilities three months prior to the commencement of the project. Our proposal included an evaluation plan designed to provide a sense of understanding about what we were to do in as objective a manner as possible to US AID officials, especially since we were interested in utilizing the data as a basis for program continuation after the original project period was completed.

As we have mentioned, ideas about evaluation quickly changed upon project implementation. Two things happened that caused us to alter our perceptions about the importance of program evaluation for this project. First, when the Egyptian team came to America for training in September 1991, our initial ideas about what they knew and did not know about special education and teaching methodology significantly changed. After some very frank discussions that we had because we did not initially receive useful information on the daily program evaluation forms, we began providing daily reviews of the evaluations. Thus, we demonstrated our commitment to the empowerment of this group of people both in the design of training and in the planning process, since we were able to show them how their comments resulted in changes. This is rarely done in Egypt.

Second, we used the daily evaluations and daily summary of those comments each time we conducted training in Egypt. In this way, program evaluation became a habit and the daily summaries of the previous days' training that we reported were eagerly anticipated by the primary users and by the training participants. Further, we asked US AID officials to visit the Egyptian training site and, when it was feasible, they stayed for the meetings where the daily evaluation summaries were presented. In this way, deviations from our proposal were more readily accepted because US AID staff saw, at first hand, what was being requested by the Egyptian training participants and how we responded to their comments.

From the perspective of conducting program evaluation in a developing nation, especially in Egypt, the daily evaluation activity became institutionalized because there was observable perceived worth by almost all of the primary users who were doing it. And, it seems to us, that this daily formative evaluation activity was more important and more powerful than the other formative and summative program evaluation activities that were conducted for this project.

Respect for cultural differences We believe that it is important to respect the multiple meanings attached to cultural differences. Some cultural differences, we found, impeded full participation by primary users in the evaluation process. For example, there was an initial reticence on the part of the Egyptian teachers who were being trained, to disagree with ministry officials during training sessions, or to speak with us about their professional concerns, or to volunteer ideas that had not been approved by those who were more senior to them in their schools. After we observed what occurred in the training in the United States and noted the need for 'frank talk', and after we had demonstrated our respect for their opinions and perspectives by altering the training to meet their needs, the data we received on the daily evaluations became more useful.

Generally, it is considered risky to endorse a western innovation that conflicts with an idea from the host culture (Azuma, 1984; Seo, Oakland & Hu, 1992). In Egypt, the educational system is based upon a national curriculum that is supposed to be followed by all teachers, with information learned by all students in all Egyptian schools at the same general pace throughout the academic year. We advocated for a position in special education that educational planning, and thus instruction, should be individualized; based upon the developmental and educational needs of students. Rather than be disrespectful of the tradition of implementing a national curriculum, our perspective was to offer training that did not interfere with the national curriculum, but recognized individual differences among students with disabilities and ways to address those differences in the classroom. The curriculum, or the national tradition, was respected, and the daily task of teaching students with disabilities also was given greater importance.

Prohibitions From the outset, project administrators felt that every member of the Gallaudet team had to subscribe to a prohibition on discussing religion and politics. In a country such as Egypt these are significant aspects of daily life. Often it was difficult for us not to comment upon daily events about which we heard or that were introduced in our conversations with our new Egyptian colleagues. However, we did not discuss these issues. Further, it was important to be respectful of different religious and political traditions. As a result, we altered our training schedule to allow for prayer, to honor holidays and other religious celebrations, and to be tolerant of the 'ways' in which Egyptians go about doing their work on a daily basis. It is our belief that by being respectful we were more successful in terms of the training we conducted and the evaluation of that training as we did not focus on issues outside of the training that might be construed by our hosts as discourteous.

Limitations or Challenges of this Evaluation

As one might imagine, there were limits to our work. Only now are we beginning to understand the complexities associated with three of what we believe are the most important of those limitations. We think of these limitations as challenges.

First, our study provided the basis for an indirect examination of the effects of participatory evaluation, not a formal study like those conducted by other authors in this volume. The data sources did not provide direct responses to inquiries about participatory evaluation, as were included in some of the other studies. Rather, our perspectives were obtained from open-ended questions meant to evaluate the training in special education and instructional methodology; demonstrations of substantive knowledge gained through observations of critical incidents; reactions to evaluation procedures and the importance of evaluation; as well as from observing the transfer of the process of evaluation to replication efforts by some of the training participants with other sets of Egyptian teacher and administrator participants. From this set of perspectives, we believe that participatory evaluation meets the objectives set forth by those who have previously examined this and other interactive models of evaluation.

Second, we found the primary users were able to effect changes in the training program in Egypt through their involvement in this participatory evaluation. The primary users, especially most of the ministry officials, wanted to know the results of all of our evaluation efforts. Yet, they were not included in the development of quarterly

Donna M. Mertens, Terry R. Berkeley and Susan D. Lopez

and other project evaluation reports. In some sense, as we have suggested elsewhere in this chapter, these written reports had less impact than did the daily evaluations in that they contained little new information that had not been previously discussed with the primary users. Under ideal conditions, it would have been preferable to have the primary users react to these other reports. Ziegahn (1989) noted a similar problem in an evaluation in a developing nation. She reported that her evaluation had a limited impact because of the physical and structural separation of the program and its evaluation which limited communication.

Third, because of language differences, we were dependent upon the quality of translations in the training and in the interpretation of program evaluation data. While we are sure that some meanings were confused or lost, we are confident that there is consistency in our findings due to the many opportunities that we had for face-to-face interaction between the evaluators and the primary users on a daily basis during the training program and in formal meetings of the three parties.

Conclusions

Many of the requirements for an effective participatory evaluation, mentioned by Cousins and Earl (1992), we found occurred here. Further, in our work, we tried to emphasize the need for training primary users about program evaluation and the value of program evaluation work. For us, this implies the value of incorporating into our training such strategies as 'brainstorming', cooperative learning, and application exercises about the development of an evaluation plan. As we discovered and discussed, there is a need to be sensitive to the fluid, dynamic nature of international evaluation efforts and the implications of the need for continued training about evaluation for primary users. In this regard, the best allies of the evaluator may be the primary users who have felt the power of their involvement in the evaluation by witnessing that changes they suggested can be implemented in a training program in which they were participants. In our view, flexibility is a key variable in the successful establishment of a participatory evaluation design in developing nations.

Finally, we feel that there are long-term effects associated with conducting participatory evaluation in an international context; that is, primary users can be empowered 'on location' (i.e., what they said was heard and listened to during the training sessions), and this information can be heard by officials responsible for supervision. However, the extent of the effects on the primary users is not clear since we are unable to stay on site for long periods of time. For example, we had the following question: to what extent are the ideas that were taught being implemented in the home schools of the primary users? To us, though, our approach to participatory evaluation in Egypt provides some direction for the future.

Future Directions

As we implemented this model of program evaluation, we came to understand more about the dynamics associated with a participatory design. We believe that these dynamics are 'future directions', and that they are provocative in terms of what happens in evaluating human service efforts in developing countries. These dynamics include:

1   Questions about the application of how the information from the training is transferred to practice by teachers in their classrooms. At present, there is not sufficient information to address this issue. Future plans call for a follow-up with the teachers and administrators on site. The training design, then, needs to be modified to respond to the literature about the transfer of skills learned during in-service training.

2   As in any evaluation, we found the information provided to decision makers from the evaluation constitutes only one source of information. We believe additional research is needed to determine the effect of other sources of information, such as budget and cost analyses, commitment of senior staff, competing priorities, and workload, on the utilization of evaluation findings. These variables were mentioned by Cousins (chapter 4 in this volume) and Lafleur (chapter 3 in this volume) as being useful in their evaluations. In Egypt and in similar developing nations, we think this list might include safety considerations, travel, and cultural factors.

3   Additional data needs to be collected and analyzed on the broader impact of program evaluation, generally, and participatory evaluation, specifically, on funding agencies such as US AID, the World Bank, and agencies of the United Nations. Each of these organizational bodies sponsors programs in which participants can be empowered so that their roles and functions can be more widely understood and respected in their home countries.

4   Participatory evaluation from our experience, as we have reported, is more labor intensive than other, more traditional approaches to program evaluation (see also Lee and Cousins, chapter 5 in this volume). The impact in time, financial considerations, and utility needs to be studied, especially in developing nations where program evaluation is a luxury in contrast to the greater need for program space, trained personnel, supplies, materials, and even basic, non-technical equipment.

The conduct of program evaluation adhering to theoretical propositions like those of participatory evaluation must, we think, begin with an assertion that western and non-western views about evaluation are different. Thus, the use of a participatory design in the United States, Canada, Australia, and western Europe seems to be very different from that conducted in Egypt, Kuwait, Ghana, or Brazil. This is not to imply that program evaluation cannot be conducted in developing countries; we have done so. However, cultural, programmatic, political, sociological, and historical contexts have to be understood and respected before an evaluation is designed and implemented. And then, the characteristics of the culture may further impinge on program evaluation efforts that will result in positive change and real empowerment. Still, these designs must be developed, used, and reported – even ones in which there are significant obstacles – if more and more people in all nations are to be served effectively and respectfully.

Notes

1   For conversations about similar dynamics in Japan and South Korea (perhaps, the only examples in the literature), please see Azuma (1984) and Seo, Oakland, and Hu (1992).

2   This is a reason for US AID support of basic education programs.

Donna M. Mertens, Terry R. Berkeley and Susan D. Lopez

References

ALKIN, M.C. (1991) 'Evaluation theory development: II', in McLAUGHLIN, M.W. and PHILLIPS, D.C. (eds) *Evaluation and Education: At Quarter Century*, Ninetieth Yearbook of the National Society for the Study of Education, Chicago, University of Chicago Press, pp. 91–112.

AZUMA, H. (1984) 'Psychology of a non-western country', *Journal of Psychology*, **19**, 1, pp. 45–55.

BRINKERHOFF, R.O., BRETHOWER, D.M., HLUCHYL, T. and NOWAKOWSKI, J.R. (1983) *Program Evaluation*, Boston, Kluwer.

BRUNNER, I. and GUZMAN, A. (1989) 'Participatory evaluation: A tool to assess projects and empower people', in CONNER, R.F. and HENDRICKS, M. (eds) *New Directions in Program Evaluation: International Innovations in Evaluation Methodology*, (No. 42, pp. 9–17), San Francisco, Jossey-Bass Publishers.

COUSINS, J.B. and EARL, L.M. (1992) 'The case for participatory evaluation', *Educational Evaluation and Policy Analysis*, **14**, 4, pp. 397–418.

GOETZ, J.P. and LeCOMPTE, M.D. (1984) *Ethnography and Qualitative Design in Educational Research*. Orlando, FL, Academic Press.

GUBA, E. and LINCOLN, Y.S. (1989) *Fourth Generation Evaluation*, Newbury Park, CA, Sage.

PATTON, M.Q. (1980) *Qualitative Evaluation Methods*, Beverly Hills, CA, Sage.

QUALIS RESEARCH ASSOCIATES (1988) *The Ethnograph*, Corvalis, OR, Author.

ROGERS, C.R. (1965) *Client Centered Therapy: Its Current Practice, Implications, and theory*, Boston, Houghton Mifflin.

SEO, G.H., OAKLAND, T. and HU, S. (1992) 'Special education in South Korea', *Exceptional Children*, **58**, 3, pp. 213–218.

WEBSTER, A. (1992) 'Images of deaf children as learners', in CLINE, T. (ed) *The Assessment of Special Educational Needs: International Perspectives*, London, Routledge.

ZIEGAHN, L. (1989) 'Internal evaluation in a developing organization: Impediments to implementation', *Studies in Educational Evaluation*, **15**, pp. 163–81.

Part 4

Themes and Conclusions

Much ground has been covered and we have learned many lessons. In this final section we critically revisit our notion of participatory evaluation and endeavor to derive recommendations for its application in schools and school districts. In doing so we take a systematic look at observed impact and consequences of the applications that were studied and then give direct consideration to explaining those findings. In our discussion and interpretation we are informed significantly by a variety of sources: specifically, our reading of the research literature; our own ideas grounded in past practice; and the insights and points offered by Michael Huberman and Marvin Alkin. We end the chapter, and indeed the book, with our own thoughts about integrating participatory evaluation into the educational change puzzle and then challenge readers to apply the principles and lessons inherent in the collection to their own organizational circumstances.

Chapter 10

Participatory Evaluation in Education: What Do We Know? Where Do We Go?

J. Bradley Cousins and Lorna M. Earl

Introduction

This is a book about change in schools and school systems. We began by building a case for a particular approach to change, one defined by the collaborative involvement of researchers and educational practitioners. We call the approach participatory evaluation and locate it within a conceptual landscape of teacher professionalism as inquiry-mindedness and organizations as learning entities as the backdrop, and teachers' joint work as the foreground. These fundamental elements, in our view, are key to sustained organizational improvement and educational reform. The purpose of this book has been to study closely a variety of applications of participatory evaluation and to critically assess their impact and viability as elements of the educational reform picture.

The authors contributing to this volume, all well-seasoned evaluators in their own right, have provided their own reflections about participatory evaluation within the context of their own original empirical investigations. Michael Huberman (chapter 7 of this volume) graciously provided a critical synthesis of a subset of these studies and shared with us his insights and interpretations. Marvin Alkin (personal communications, April 1993 and June 1993) similarly provided critical comments. Armed with this array of data and critical perspectives we now revisit the concept of participatory evaluation as an approach to educational change. Our purpose is not only to take stock of what we know, but to consider what that knowledge says about the future of collaborative research in schools.

Bang for the Buck? A Mixed Review

'Given that decision making in educational organizations is necessarily diffuse, it seems desirable that all parties involved in or affected by decisions share a common information base, such as that provided by an evaluation' (Burry, Alkin and Ruskus, 1985, p. 148). Participatory evaluation projects, through the direct involvement of educational practitioners in the process of constructing them, strive to provide that shared knowledge base.

The explicit goals of participatory evaluation, in our terms, are utilization-oriented; in Patton's words *'intended use by intended users'* (1988, p. 14, emphasis in original).

But historically, the use of evaluation data has been defined in terms of support for decision making and the learnings of an undifferentiated 'decision maker', whereas contemporary approaches to organizational change are more directly aligned with decision-making models that are inclusive, engaging and otherwise participatory. If applied research or evaluation is to support a more contemporary approach to change it makes sense that the research process is equally involving and engaging. After all, practitioners are far more likely to learn from one another and 'researchers can support the organizational learning process by helping to organize human networks that stimulate and facilitate this process of learning' (Whyte, 1991, p. 238). This is precisely what participatory evaluation, of the sort that we advocate, intends to do. But how do we know if it's done it? What are the indicators? Support for curriculum decision making? New insights into cause and effect relationships? The development of understandings that are common among organization members about school and district operations? Elaborated communication and dissemination networks? Development of a sense of inquiry-mindedness among organization members and, within organizations, the skills to carry out deliberative acts of systematic inquiry? Indeed, in some measure, we subscribe to each of the forgoing as the utilization-oriented goals of participatory evaluation. Admittedly, at the outset, we looked forward to an abundance of celebratory consequences emerging from our collection of studies. But, taken as a whole, though calls for celebration are certainly audible they are partially obscured by the noticeable rumbling of marginal impact and forgone opportunities to take advantage of emergent, contextually relevant evaluative data.

Program Decision Making and Program Learning

'The chief task in both evaluation and research utilization fields is enacting transfer in such a way as to affect levels of practitioners' understandings, perceptions, decisions, and actions either individually or institutionally' (Huberman and Cox, 1990, p. 157). While it is generally agreed that the litmus test for evaluation impact ought not to be whether recommendations were implemented, whether action plans were followed, or whether otherwise rational observable consequences were apparent (Alkin, 1991; Huberman, chapter 7), such consequences by their very nature, if in evidence, do give cause for celebration.

Opportunities to observe evaluation impact were premature in at least one study (Lee and Cousins, chapter 5), but most others were forthcoming in this regard. Good news stories were in evidence. Earl showed how the evaluation process dovetailed nicely with ongoing school-based efforts to implement curriculum management plans. Huberman calls this 'double dipping' since those charged with carrying out the evaluation were also being held accountable for the implementation effort. What is not clear from the Earl study, however, is the extent to which teachers bought into the evaluation process and the knowledge that it generated. Given the enthusiasm that school-based staff took in the dissemination process, it seems likely that these data were, in fact, useful to teachers in making sense of who they are and what they need to do. Cousins' Rockland site provides further evidence of desirable instrumental consequences. Here, needs assessment data were legitimately used by all key stakeholder groups in implementing the many changes associated with the transition years initiative. Mertens, Berkeley and Lopez showed how an evolutionary evaluation design supported ongoing changes in the content and emphasis of the training program for Egyptian special education teachers.

Self-reported evidence of learning about program operations and consequences was also in evidence. In the Mertens *et al.* study, as in Cousins' Rockland case, evaluative data provided both confirmation of prior knowledge and reaffirmation of current directions as well as new insights into program operations and functioning. 'Thus, as a result of the learning process, the hearing Egyptian special educators became empowered in their ability to express a need that, heretofore, had not been recognized' (p. 147). In Cousins' words about his own study, 'The research process appears to have given staff pause to reflect on patterns of evidence and to begin to question some deeper assumptions about the teaching and learning process' (p. 62). Earl, too, showed conceptual benefits attributable to the participatory process. In particular, administrator and curriculum coordinators found participation in the interview data collection process to be especially illuminating in terms of informing their own practices and the practices of others. Lafleur offered similar sentiments expressed by principals, department heads and teachers participating in the curriculum review process.

But not all of the news was good news. Several of the studies revealed severe limitations on the use and impact of evaluation data which was manifested, generally, in the lack of commitment to evaluation follow-up or in the use of the information for blatantly political and/or non-rational decision making. In Cousins' study, needs assessment data provided by the participatory research team at the Lakeview site were just ignored by the senior administrator who was in the key position to do something about them. This turn of events had rather significant ill effects on the attitudes and motives of at least some of the research team members (teachers). The chances of building on this initial collaborative research effort were, as a consequence, virtually eliminated. A similar scenario emerged in Lafleur's data. Participating school administrators and consultants were manifestly frustrated by the lack of commitment of senior administration to action plans emerging from their efforts of systematic inquiry. Huberman interprets Lafleur's data as follows:

> . . . [participants in the research process] probably came to grips with programs they had administered or taught but had not examined for several years. This has always been the forté of evaluation research: a look square in the face, warts and all, at a program that has been taken for granted, despite limitations. If, however, there is no follow-on activity, that look square in the face will have been largely gratuitous. (p. 108)

In two of King's case examples, politics centered around fiscal needs and priorities causing evaluation data to be either blatantly ignored, discredited or selectively interpreted by policy makers in support of obvious political agendae. As we have espoused, an alleged advantage of participatory evaluation is that it leads to research products that are locally relevant and responsive to organizational needs. However, King's OEL case example where the report, and indeed the evaluation effort, were dismissed out of hand for failure to include standardized outcome-based data (a conscious decision by participants), shows how the power of politics can easily override the rationality inherent in the process. We shall return to this issue subsequently in our discussion of stakeholders.

Organizational Learning

We discussed learning at the level of the program or the object being evaluated, learning that is done by individuals or groups of individuals. But what of learning at the organizational level? Was there evidence of wider changes in organization culture, propensity to question basic assumptions, development among school or district staff of shared representations of organizational operational processes and relationships among them? Is participatory evaluation truly a powerful route to cultural change in this direction?

A sensible place to begin is with the question of whether school and district staff are willing and able to continue applied research activities with researchers either out of the picture or in much more of a background support role. In short, was there evidence of enhanced capacity of staff to embrace the research function? While the results were by no means uniform, several studies provide rather compelling evidence that this capacity was indeed fostered. King reported that 'the practice of action research was integrated into the teachers' work, and is now, they report, an ongoing part of their practice' (p. 95). Clearly, success of this sort is by no means guaranteed. After all, the choice to participate at all is part of the free and informed choices that practitioners make in participatory action research (Argyris and Schön, 1991). Indeed, the choice not to continue was exercised in King's other action research site where personal matters led to teachers' decisions to 'take a break' from such activities.

In both Cousins' case sites, most participants reported feeling confident in their abilities to carry out subsequent research tasks in the absence of continued intensive support, but at Rockland, this actually happened. One of the teachers involved on the original research working team was promoted to a curriculum coordinating post and immediately launched a follow-up study extending into the elementary panel using a similar design methodology. Participation in focus interview data collection and analysis activities, for some, led to unbridled enthusiasm in Earl's system partners approach to applied research on curriculum management. In her words,

> Whatever else has occurred as a result of these participatory formative evaluations of school improvement, focused interviewing has become a system pastime. It is sometimes difficult to convince committee members that it is not always necessary and certainly not efficient to use interviews for data collection. Even the newly appointed CEO engaged the assistance of the research department and conducted his own focused interviews with a broad-based sample of key stakeholders as a basis for his 'entry plan'. (p. 31)

Earl also noted the spread of the system partners approach from the secondary to the elementary panel and that at least one school staff independently applied for and received external funding for continued research activities.

In Lee and Cousins' study, considerable dependency on the evaluator by school improvement project personnel was not only in evidence but it extended beyond evaluation issues to project implementation ones. However, the authors noted that when it became necessary for the evaluator to retreat due to increasing time limitations, project staff were able to survive and to continue reasonably independently with their evaluative functions. Ongoing acceptance of and engagement in program evaluation activities was also observed by Mertens *et al.* regarding participants in the special education training process they studied: 'From this training and experience, [participants] developed an understanding of and appreciation for program evaluation as evidenced by their interest in daily evaluation results, inquiries about program evaluation, and utilization of program evaluation in the replication of training that they did in their own governates' (p. 146).

As was the case concerning the use of evaluation data within the context of specific programs; several studies yielded rather glum indications that organizational learning was even a remote possibility. Generally speaking, either the non-use of evaluation data (suppression) or its misuse contributed to particularly dim prospects of continued activities. As mentioned above, Cousins' Lakeview site and Lafleur's study of prior participants in program review projects each clearly showed deleterious effects of non-use of data by those, usually senior administrators, in a position to do something about them. The apparently unavoidable net effect of such inaction seems to have been the precipitation of dismal conclusions about the costs of the research effort (and the costs were almost invariably high in terms of time and human resource energy) cast against the perceived lack of benefit to the system. Why participate? We concur fully with Huberman's question, What was learned if their was no follow-up? Although not explicitly reported by King, one can easily imagine a similar perspective developed among participants in her CPIP and OEL research processes whose products were used toward political ends or otherwise conveniently misrepresented.

The Shulha and Wilson narrative (chapter 8), while representing a special case of participation, is a particularly salient example of organizational non-learning. The authors worked hard over a protracted period, using methods of systematic inquiry, to determine the need for and foster commitment to a school–university partnership in a significant research and development initiative. But like a house of cards, the project quickly came crashing down, with administrators and teachers, each for their own reasons, distancing themselves from the project at virtually the first signs of non-acceptance/non-support by the organizational hierarchy. What is particularly illuminating, if not disturbing, in this story is the teachers' manifest frustration in the researchers' inability to come through with the apparently much awaited student evaluation deliverables. This project worked toward the explicit goal of fostering the development of a sense of inquiry into classroom practices on the part of teachers. In the ideal, school staff would not only have been developing a shared picture of, and questioning basic assumptions about, student evaluation and reporting, but they would have been developing hypotheses and testing them out in ways that were designed by them and made sense to them. What ended up happening bore little, if any, relationship to this scenario.

And so what do we conclude about participatory evaluation as a route to organizational learning? Yes, it has potential. Yes we saw some movement toward such ends. Yes, we need to keep things in perspective. Organizational learning, like most cultural change, will not happen over night. It will happen as a consequence of sustained activity on behalf of organization members that foster if not create the conditions necessary for social interaction and collective sense making of organizational phenomena. Participatory evaluation has such potential but it seems to us that certain conditions must be in place and that real organizational pay off will happen only when participatory research mechanisms become more fully integrated into organizational life. We elaborate on supporting conditions later, but before we present them, and before continuing with our appraisal of participatory evaluation's bang for the buck, we pause at this point to address three conceptual considerations about the relationship between participatory evaluation and organizational learning.

First, the very nature of program evaluation holds with it implications for the appropriate 'unit of analysis' when thinking about organizational learning. Evaluation most often has as its focus a particular innovation or program and such entities invariably have finite numbers of people whose attention they draw. It is unreasonable to think about, at least in the early stages, organizational impact outside of those in some way connected to the focus for evaluation. This means, then, at least in the short run, the logical unit of analysis for learning is the program or innovation project. This line of argument is not dissimilar to that offered by researchers in business and industry who focus on the new product development project as the appropriate unit for learning (Clark and Fujimoto, 1991). It should be noted, however, that the project can be the school, say, if the focus for evaluation is a school improvement initiative. In this instance, and depending very much on the scope of the initiative, learning might be anticipated in the sub-organization (school) as opposed to the larger organization (district).

A second consideration has to do with the nature of the innovation being evaluated and the type of learning that might be expected. Recent evidence suggests that the existence of knowledge structures may pave the way to learning. According to Forss, Cracknell and Samset

> in a situation characterized by well-developed and dominating knowledge structures and little diversity, then organizational learning can be high. The people in the organization learn by getting involved in evaluation work themselves – and evaluation will thus be one of the major instruments of learning. (1994, p. 583)

But this is relatively low level or incremental learning and has more to do with fine-tuning rather than rethinking the phenomenon in question. Is this the sort of learning we might expect from educational participatory evaluation? Indeed, much of what we observed related to reaffirmation and continuation in particular directions rather than deeper issues of program redesign. But it is interesting to note that educators, including those referred to in the studies in this volume, are rarely confronted with highly developed and widely shared knowledge structures. Educational innovations and programs are, almost by definition, relatively abstract, and carry with them considerable political, social and cultural baggage in need of sorting. What are the prospects for organizational learning in schools? Might we expect deeper, more penetrating sorts of learning outcomes? We raise these observations as food for thought since the data generated here are unable to provide definitive answers.

Finally, a response to Huberman's comments about rationality inherent in the participatory evaluation process. He observes 'that information that is rationally delivered may not be rationally received' (p. 106). We concur. But we need to revisit a central feature of the participatory process. Some of the practitioners involved in the process are also, at least in the ideal, the ones in a position to do something about the information that is delivered. Indeed the data that are discussed and deliberated are done so by the people expected to use them. The 'emotional, haphazard, politically sensitive information flying around' is as likely to be flying around the research project meeting room as it is in the classroom or principal's office. This is where the structured, 'hyper-rationalized' research process gives way to interpretation, consensus building and sense making *within the non-rational context* of schools. In our own view, it is fairer to think of participatory evaluation as a *rationalizing* process rather than a 'hyper-rational' one. To be sure, however, issues concerning of the uneven distribution of power among organization members and direct versus indirect involvement in the research are germane to these considerations. We shall consider them more directly below.

What's In It For Me? Effects on Practitioners

'What's in it for me?' counts among the most fundamental and crucial questions surrounding participatory evaluation in education. Weiss (1991) and others remind us about the mismatch between the world of research and the world of practice, and the horrific challenge confronting those who would attempt to bridge the two. Life in schools is such that even thinking about adding to the already bursting-at-the-seams list of things to do for teachers and administrators, is likely to get one into trouble faster than can be imagined. And so, what *is* in it for practitioners? Why on earth get involved? Our collection of studies provides at least some answers.

Virtually every study presented in this volume has something to say about effects on practitioners, and most of the things said are good. Perhaps most celebratory are aspects of professional development concerning the acquisition, reactivation or fine-tuning of a variety of skills associated with acts of systematic inquiry. Participants in several of the projects, especially those involving them in nuts and bolts research activities eagerly articulated their appreciation. It gave them a new perspective and a sense of accomplishment in a job well done; no one raised concerns about the validity or credibility of the research products. Involvement helped some folks to sharpen their critical eye, presumably a skill that would spill into other aspects of their practice. But, as already mentioned, and it bears repeating, frustration mounted when inaction was the main follow-up (see especially the chapters by Lafleur, Cousins and King). There was an affective element as well. Several of the participants reporting talked about pride, enjoyment and gratification and in some cases (e.g., Lafleur) personal and professional enduring friendships formed.

In a very real sense, involvement in these projects translated into professional and personal empowerment for many of the participants. Cousins reported that participation raised the visibility within the system for some and ultimately led in some degree to their being promoted to positions of added responsibility or transferred into different roles within the system. Earl noted that the process helped to develop the leadership capabilities of staff participating on the needs assessment committee. She remarked that members of the committee were never reluctant to make presentations of study findings and rarely called on research staff to assist with dissemination activities. In some cases the empowering consequences of participation translated into giving voice to practitioners not accustomed to participating in policy-shaping matters. For Shulha and Wilson this was reflected in the creation of teacher leadership roles within the school (although the continuing consequences of such roles since the project was disbanded remains to be known). In the Mertens *et al.* study of cross-cultural participatory evaluation, deaf teachers were recruited as active participants in the training process and teachers' voices were heard by those who do not often listen. In their words,

> We observed changes, for example, to the extent that training participants could support the training, yet empower themselves by making suggestions that were immediately discussed and used by all training team members, including officials from the ministry . . . this is quite crucial in those international contexts in which teachers' voices are rarely heard. (p. 147)

'What's in it for me?' can also spell, as will be no surprise to Weiss (1991), for example, aggravation, headaches, and fatigue for participants playing a very direct role in the research process. This is particularly the case where release time from ongoing organizational duties is either inadequate or not provided. Earl reported research team members working after hours when organizational responsibilities were pressing: although they did so happily, one can easily imagine undesirable consequences of sustained extra effort of this sort. Shulha and Wilson reported that in the process of negotiating the school–university partnership, concerns about the implications of increased workload due to the project were clearly articulated by teachers and needed to be answered. In Cousins' study, time away from ongoing responsibilities was provided but some concerns lingered about being absent from normal duties. Project managers in Lee and Cousins' study complained vehemently about the severe underestimation they had made regarding the necessary commitment of time. Time for evaluation activities was particularly problematic since some of these individuals carried the weight of responsibility for managing their school-based projects while simultaneously maintaining other core functions. Similar concerns were raised by teachers in one of King's action research sites. Observations of this sort prompted Huberman to suggest that 'commitment matters less than [the] time out' provided in order to carry out the project. We concur with this view. It seems paramount that projects of this nature receive adequate support (including release time) if they are to be viable. The real benefit here is not so much the extrinsic reward but the realistic demands of the applied research enterprise, particularly in the face of developing research skills on the fly.

Continuing our focus on the downside, two of the studies observed real concerns of teachers working on these projects within schools. As reported by Lee and Cousins, the funding of the school improvement projects led to awkward circumstances for some participants in relation to the remaining school staff. Particularly where funding meant visible resources, the creation of elitist 'have' versus common 'have not' subcultures within the school was in danger of becoming an issue. Often, such results flew in the face of the espoused objectives of the projects. King noted a similar phenomenon regarding her action research development activities:

> The teacher researchers report feeling like 'elite lepers', rebuffed, on the one hand, because others see them as the chosen few when they garner special favors from administration, yet ostracized, on the other hand, because they appear overly enthusiastic about school improvement and professional development. (pp. 96–97)

Similar findings have been observed in studies of teacher leadership (Smylie, 1992) and participatory decision making in schools (Weiss, Cambone and Wyeth, 1992).

Researcher's Perspective

While organizational commitment and resources are fundamental to successful participatory evaluation, the role for researchers is less than traditional and, as seen in some of our studies, more than demanding. Probably one of the most significant findings, and one that was noted across sites, is the (necessary?) adoption of an evolutionary planning focus for the research. Of course this approach is naturally required in a process where researchers and practice-based personnel are to be working in partnership. It becomes even more important in a cross cultural context where many factors cannot be anticipated as noted by Mertens *et al*. Nonetheless, the transition provides somewhat of a challenge, as Earl reported: her staff found it difficult getting used to dealing with 'freewheeling' educators and relinquishing control over the process. On the other hand, Earl expressed some gratification with a sense of new-found respect for her department throughout the system. While evolutionary planning mostly means not coming in with a set agenda, on occasion, as King's OEL case demonstrated clearly, it can mean putting out fires. In this very large collaborative effort all sorts of problems emerged, ranging from the questionable credibility of research support staff to refining the research decision-making process to facilitate communication and limit unwieldiness.

As shown in chapter 5, Lee's role in the research activities was somewhat unique since, given her background and prevailing circumstances, she found herself up to her elbows in project implementation activities and problem solving. Huberman quite rightly notes that this role – evaluator being all things to all people – will not generalize. Nevertheless, it does raise fundamental questions about the evaluator's role in program and innovation affairs. Notably absent from many of the chapters (e.g., Cousins, King, Lafleur) was sustained involvement of evaluators in follow-up activities. Whether this was, in fact, due to time constraints, negotiated arrangements or other reasons, it runs counter to what some (e.g., Burry *et al.*, 1985; Huberman and Cox, 1990) would suggest to be a key force in increasing the chances that a study will be used.

Explanatory Themes: Considerations of Process and Context

Above, we have alluded to several factors, circumstances and conditions that either support the participatory process and increase its chances of having impact within educational organizations or that get in the way. We now move from the foreshadow into the light; we turn to a more direct analysis of themes running through the studies that help to explain the impact that was observed. At the outset, we acknowledge that definitive answers are not available. Rather, our posture is one of taking best guesses on the evidence provided as to what happened and to note, as appropriate, what remains to be learned, further investigated or otherwise studied.

King and Huberman each provide thoughtful analyses of how we might situate participatory evaluation, as we have defined it, within the larger context of collaborative and action-oriented research perspectives. Indeed, we attempt to provide clarification in chapter 1 depicting participatory evaluation as utilization-oriented in *interest* and joint researcher–practitioner control-oriented in *form*. Now that we have presented a series of independently conducted studies carried out across a wide array of educational contexts it would be useful to take a close look at how participatory evaluation was operationalized. To what extent did the authors' images of collaborative research match with our own? How much variation was observed and along which dimensions? Is it worth revisiting central features of our own scheme based on what the studies are telling us?

Participatory evaluation, the reader will recall, is portrayed here as an extension of the conventional 'stakeholder-based' approach to evaluation; a more restrictive and intensive version of it according to Alkin (personal communication). Three central features define the process we advocate. First, participatory evaluation involves a rather small number of 'primary users' in the research process as opposed to the wide array and mix of stakeholder groups normally associated with the conventional model. Second, control of the research process is to be shared between researchers and members of the participating organization. By contrast, the evaluator maintains control of the research process in the conventional approach; stakeholders are consulted for insights into their views, opinions, values positions and practical wisdom. Finally, in the conventional approach, stakeholders are most heavily involved in start-up and follow-on activities; they help to define the scope of the evaluation and to specify the objectives for it and they participate directly both in the interpretation of accumulated data and in developing implications for action. In our approach, primary users participate in all phases of the evaluation. In addition to those just mentioned, they collaborate in preparing data collection instruments, and collecting, analyzing and reporting data. Using this template as a guide we now take a close-up look at the studies, their fidelity of implementation of the model, and the implications of their findings for the model.

User Involvement

In chapter 1 we defined the term 'primary users' rather loosely. We made allusions to Alkin's (1991) use of the term but specifically meant 'organization members with program responsibility or people with a vital interest in the program' (p. 8). In retrospect, we find that our use of this definition does not fit well with Alkin's. His (and indeed others', notably, Patton) use of the term is much more restrictive and focused. Whereas our perspective allows for variations around the user table in organizational power and status, Alkin is more deliberate. In his words

> Not only are individuals designated as 'primary user', interested and engaged with the evaluation (and participation is certainly a high form of engagement) but they also must be *likely* users. And, participants are not to be considered as likely users unless they are in some sense empowered. Both Michael Quinn Patton and I agree that utilization is the goal, and given that goal the skilful engagement by evaluators of primary users in the process is important. But, 'participant' does not necessarily equate with primary user. (Personal communication, emphasis in the original)

Table 10.1 shows how the individual studies stack up against Alkin's definition of primary user. We see here considerable variation across studies. Three studies (Earl; Lee and Cousins; King, CARP case) appeared to involve pretty much exclusively those with primary program responsibility and in a position to do something about findings emerging from the evaluation. Most studies, however, involved a broader mix of users. That is, primary users in Alkin's terms and 'second tier' primary users, if you will. These are individuals who have responsibility for program – usually implementation – and, as such, a vested interest in it. In our view, they are indeed considered primary users to the extent that they are intended users and their use of the data is very much in line with the central purposes of the evaluation. Generally, however, when 'push came to shove' we note that members of the second tier did not have at their disposal the organizational clout of the primary user, traditionally defined. Some studies (e.g., Lafleur; Cousins, Lakeside case; King, CPIP case; Shulha and Wilson) reflected participation that was virtually, if not entirely, devoid of empowered primary users. In most of these cases, the consequences, in terms of bang for the buck, were disastrous.

Table 10.1   Primary user[a] involvement by study

Study (chapter)	Primary user involvement	Description
Earl (2)	high	• Needs assessment committee: school administrators, central office administrators, department heads, curriculum coordinators Interview data collectors: central office staff, school administrators
Lafleur (3)	mod-low	• School administrators, department heads, curriculum specialists, teachers; senior administrators uninvolved
Cousins (4)	mod-high	• ROCKLAND: Steering committee: senior administrator, school administrators, teachers Research work team: teachers
	low	• LAKESIDE; Steering committee: senior administrator, computer coordinator, principal, teachers; limited involvement of senior administrator Research work team: teachers
Lee & Cousins (5)	high	• Funded school improvement project directors and participants, school administrators
King (6)	low	• CPIP: program staff development personnel; limited involvement of senior administrator, personnel change
	moderate	• OEL: site school administrators, teachers, OEL personnel; senior administrator tangentially involved
	high	• CARP: teacher pairs
Shulha & Wilson (8)	moderate	• School administrators, teachers; indirect involvement by senior administration, personnel change
Mertens, Berkeley, & Lopez (9)	mod-high	• Administrators, teachers, Ministry of Education personnel; limited participation by US AID

[a] Defined according to Alkin (1991).

And so we have what appears to be rather compelling evidence favoring the participation and involvement of the primary user, traditionally defined.

Huberman, too, was sensitive to the implications of who it was that made up the participant group. He talks about administrators, principals and program coordinators as being 'second-layer stakeholders' and the implications of hierarchical structure for the validity and credibility of the data.

> When a central office administrator comes in to interview teachers on a sensitive instructional or organizational issue, it puts those teachers on a tightrope, no matter how benevolent each party may be. It also, incidentally, casts some shadows on the trustworthiness of the data that have been gathered with virtually no opportunity to assess the nature and degree of any resulting bias. (p. 106)

He goes on to acknowledge the potential for illumination and awareness-heightening qualities of collaborative research but suggests that such experiences are surrealistic if the artists are members of the organizational power elite. We begin to see now the potential downside of collaborative endeavors that involve as organizational particip- ants *only* those primary users who are organizationally empowered. McTaggart (1991), operating from a critical theorist's perspective, puts it this way

> People can be required to work out ways of implementing policy developed on the basis of knowledge produced by research *on* them rather than by them. This is *not* [participatory action research] but is rather the cooption of people into the research, development, and dissemination approach invented by a coalition of policy makers and social scientists whose primary interest is in maintaining control. (p. 172, emphasis in original)

And so we have, on the one hand, the likelihood of non-participation of 'empowered' primary users opening the door to political misuse, mischievous use or unjustifiable non-use of evaluation data, and on the other, exclusive reliance on such participants as being problematic in terms of threats to the quality of the research enterprise and, perhaps more significantly, limiting the professionalization of teachers. It is fair to say, then, that we have strengthened our case for a more balanced approach; one that in- cludes members of the empowered primary user group working in concert with mem- bers of the second tier of interested users. Indeed this was most often the operationalization of participatory evaluation in the present set of studies where impact was observed. What's more, where a balanced approach *was* adopted, it was most often the case that second tier users assumed joint responsibility with researchers for much of the research workload, an observation which in our view answers Huberman's concern about tech- nical adequacy and bias, assuming respondents would be more forthcoming with peers as opposed to superiors. Brandon, Wang and Heck (1994) provide additional support in their look at school level needs assessment activities. They concluded that staff tended to buy-in to selected needs more convincingly in schools where teachers were involved in decision making about the research (needs assessment) process itself.

If we accept that a balanced approach to participation is sensible, the issue of how people end up participating becomes an important one. As Alkin observed, in the present studies the selection process seems to have been a mixture of selection, representation of various units and volunteering (personal communication). Whatever the method, a more deliberative focus on involving empowered primary users more directly in the research and ensuring involvement of second tier users seems likely to be profitable.

Depth of Participation

A second central feature of our brand of participatory evaluation is that participants become directly involved in as many of the technical research activities as is possible and/or feasible. The rationale for this feature is twofold. First, if applied social research is to become fully integrated into the organizational culture it will be necessary for organization members to develop the skills required to carry a study from start to finish. Second, direct participation in the 'nuts and bolts' operations of research, enhances the likelihood of practitioners seriously coming to terms with the meaning of the data collected and its implications for program and organizational practice. If we adhere to

Table 10.2 Depth of participation by study

Study (chapter)	Depth of involvement	Description
Earl (2)	high	• Involved in all phases. Needs assessment committee: designing, training, coordinating reporting. Interview team: data collection and summary
Lafleur (3)	high	• Involved in all phases. Technical services laid on by researcher
Cousins (4)	high	• ROCKLAND: Steering committee: planning, instrument development, interpretation of findings Research workteam: data collection and analysis, interpretation of findings, reporting
	mod-high	• LAKESIDE: Steering committee: planning Research workteam: data collection, analysis, interpretation of findings, reporting
Lee & Cousins (5)	high	• Involved in all phases. Technical services laid on by researcher
King (6)	moderate	• CPIP: design, question generation, determination of methods, interpretation of findings
	mod-low	• OEL: planning evaluation principles and process, interpretation of data
	high	• CARP: Involved in all phases. Researcher available for consultation
Shulha & Wilson (8)	low	• Reflection on focus group data
Mertens, Berkeley, and Lopez (9)	mod-high	• Involved in all phases. Planning, data collection, interpretation

the maxim 'you never really learn about something until you teach it' the parallel slogan here would be 'you never really know your data until you write about it'. Table 10.2 provides an indication of the extent to which participants truly participated in the full gambit of research activities. As can be seen, depth of participation was variable across studies and cases.

In several cases (Earl; Lafleur; Cousins; King, CARP case) technical research skills were, in some sense, laid on by the researcher but virtually all tasks were carried out by the participant research team. In others (Cousins, Rockland case; Lee and Cousins) technical aspects of the process, especially 'number crunching', were farmed out to agencies with the appropriate expertise. Other approaches were more similar to the traditional stakeholder-based orientation where most of the technical work is accomplished by the researchers, and the participants play a significant role in planning and interpretation phases (King, OEL case; Mertens *et al.*). In Shulha and Wilsons' study, data collection and analysis was carried out by the researchers in parallel with activities surrounding the negotiations of collaboration. Of course, these data were fed back to the school staff as the project progressed.

An overriding concern – and we acknowledged it above – was the labor intensity of the research process and its associated implications. These implications took two forms. First, to recap, in cases where some impact of the research was observed, demands on time did not appear to be a major concern (Earl; Cousins, Rockland case). However, where perceived impact was negligible or inappropriate, participants seriously questioned the time spent (Lafleur; Cousins, Lakeside case). Lafleur put it this way, 'with limited resources, there was a feeling that the evaluation took too much time and required labor intensive involvement. This was especially true when compared to the seemingly limited time, resources, and energy devoted to implementing follow-up activities related to the action plans' (p. 51). A second manifestation of time–labor related problems concerned the underestimation of required time upon agreement to be involved (to be sure, no one overestimated). Often this was expressed as frustration in not being able to carry out research functions while at the same time accomplishing primary functions at an acceptable personal standard. Alkin (personal communication) reminds us that time commitments are contractually obligated when an external evaluator is brought in, but a reasonable facsimile did not seem to be the case for internally recruited participants. This observation underscores the necessity for educational organizations to come to terms with the realities of participation and to support participation with appropriate resources and release time.

Given the prevalence of the labor intensity issue, it may be prudent to rethink depth of involvement. In particular, would it be beneficial for organization participants to be more heavily involved with the less technical aspects (planning, interpretation, dissemination) of the process than the highly technical ones (data collection, analysis)? Our experience suggests three conclusions. First, it will likely not pay to involve participants in highly technical activities such as quantitative data analysis if these tasks can be delegated. Certainly, however, it will be important to train participants in the skills involved in making sense of the products of such effort (e.g., statistical output, summary tables and figures). Second, participation in interview data collection and the content analysis of qualitative data, though labor intensive, appears to be worth the effort, at least sufficiently so as to warrant budgeting for its inclusion if resources permit.

A third conclusion is that participation in dissemination seems vitally important. In several instances, participants not only embraced such opportunities with alacrity, but were in some sense empowered by them (Earl; King, CARP case; Mertens, *et al.*). Forss *et al.* (1994) underscore the importance of wide-reaching communication systems in support of extending learning beyond the limited numbers of participants in the actual research act. From another perspective, Huberman warns that the act of feeding back is a delicate one – 'one wrong sentence and you are out' (p. 106) – a position that we both agree with and take as support for relying on the credibility of local actors in spreading the word. But we also note in the forgoing studies a relatively minor role in dissemination and follow-up activities for researchers. This gives us cause to wonder just how much impact may have been improved had evaluators taken a more active role? Undeniably the literature is replete with variations of this message (Bickell and Cooley, 1985; Burry *et al.*, 1985; Huberman and Cox, 1990; Huberman, 1990).

Shared Control

A final distinguishing feature of participatory evaluation is the notion of shared control of the research agenda and the research decision-making process as distinct from researcher-controlled approaches (e.g., conventional stakeholder model) and practitioner controlled activities (e.g., various forms of action research). In this sense we

Table 10.3 Shared control by study

Study (chapter)	Control of research	Description
Earl (2)	shared	• Researcher provided technical support but decisions made by group
Lafleur (3)	shared	• Coordinating role for researcher. All committees chaired by school administrators
Cousins (4)	shared	• ROCKLAND and LAKESIDE; Coordinating role for researcher. Steering committees chaired by senior administrator. Work team chaired by researcher
Lee and Cousins (5)	shared	• Coordinating role for researcher. Project coordinators chaired research work teams
King (6)	evaluator	• CPIP: evaluation-specialist chaired and coordinated the study
	evaluator	• OEL: evaluation-specialist chaired and coordinated the study; joint, evolutionary decision making
	shared	• CARP: Researcher in coordinating role, teachers carried out research project
Shulha & Wilson (8)	evaluator	• Researchers controlled evaluation process during invitation to collaborate. Research and development project was to be shared
Mertens, Berkeley and Lopez (9)	shared	• Study chaired and coordinated by researchers. Evolutionary planning and negotiated decision making

advocated 'partnership' in the truest sense of the word, each party contributing specialized knowledge or expertise. Table 10.3 provides a glimpse of the extent to which control was shared in the present set of studies.

A quick perusal of table 10.3 reveals to our satisfaction that, indeed, for the most part, the collaborative arrangements studied were principally creatures of shared control. More often than not the researcher provided technical support and helped shape the research with suggestions grounded in technical training and practical experience. In some cases, shared control may have been somewhat compromised by the heavy dependency on the researcher. For example, in Lee and Cousins' study, dependency on the evaluator was remarkable and extended beyond applied research issues. Nonetheless, successful weaning was subsequently in evidence when limits on the researcher's availability rendered continued dependency impractical. In Cousins' approach, the research report and recommendations included in it were crafted by the researcher, unlike Earl, for example, whose department, as a matter of policy, assumes a reactive role at this stage. Huberman suggests that Cousins' approach is participatory only in the weakest sense and characterizes it as 'a study run with intermediaries' (p. 109). This assessment is inaccurate since it misrepresents the actual role of practitioners. The participants – especially the second tier users as opposed to the senior administrators – constructed and vetted the data collection instruments, collected the data, content analyzed interview and written comment data, and fine-tuned recommendations. What is not participatory about that? And why assume the researcher was in control; he wasn't.

In other examples (King, OEL case; Mertens *et al.*) evolutionary evaluation design features benefited from practitioner input as the project unfolded. Finally, Shulha and Wilson maintained control over the preliminary evaluation activities, but the planned research and development activities on student assessment were to be jointly owned.

In retrospect, it seems to us, and we credit Huberman with the insight, that it is not so much project control that will tip the balance, as it is the 'number, variety and mutuality of contacts' (p. 104), the tighter 'linkages' established between researchers and schools and districts. It seems sensible enough that practitioners with full agendae defined by their core function will never completely outgrow their need for at least consultative input, if not direct participation, on the part of researchers, regardless of how much they choose to invest in the nuts and bolts of these activities. Huberman and Cox (1990) put it well,

> It is the sustained interactivity that allows for the process of mutual education, by which users render evaluators progressively wiser in relation to the work- ings of the local context that actually account for the observed outcomes, and heighten the awareness of users by feeding back this information to users in ways that are locally recognizable yet framed in such a way as to deepen or sharpen local understandings. (p. 168)

Alkin provides some additional insights concerning sustained interactivity. He thinks of the range of skills that the evaluatior brings to the participatory project as far exceeding the narrowly defined technical research skills.

> I believe that the issue of technical skills of evaluators is too frequently very narrowly interpreted. Evaluator technical skills also have to do with interper- sonal relations, understanding organizations, sensitivity, working groups, and the like . . . part of this role relates to teaching and sensitizing practitioners to the *power of evaluation* as part of decision making. (personal communication, emphasis in original)

Participatory Evaluation in your School and District: If the Shoe Fits . . .

Participatory evaluation may not be for every school or school system, but it may be for yours. How would you know? On what would you base a decision to invest human and fiscal resources – and our studies show that the investment is not likely to be trivial – in activities that will, at least in the short run, run parallel to and probably distract from the teaching and learning core activities in which staff are involved daily? We turn our attention to five areas for consideration that we believe members of organizations thinking about participatory evaluation as a route toward change ought to take into account.

Top-down or Bottom-up?

If change in schools is to be authentic and lasting it will require educational practi- tioners to develop new understandings of their work, or some aspects of it. 'Individual members of the school organization must actively reconstruct the meaning they attribute to their work before lasting change will occur' (Cousins and Leithwood, 1993). This brings into question the viability of exclusively top-down or bottom-up approaches to change. Top-down approaches are generally informed by broad-based policy perspectives on the future role of schools and, perhaps to a lesser degree, knowledge about innovative practices grounded in academic research. Typically, their implementation is informed by the practice-based knowledge of those responsible for delivery. But one can easily imagine discrepancies between broad-based political innovations and research-based innovations, and the practical wisdom of, say, teachers. Indeed, history has attested to the failure of reform efforts of this sort (Darling-Hammond, 1990). This is not, however, justification for exclusively bottom-up approaches to change. While grass roots orientations are more likely to be sensitive to local contexts because they provide opportunities for local understanding through social interaction, deliberation and dialogue, they can be often focused narrowly on conservative, low quality changes (Huberman, 1983; Nelson and Seiber, 1976), and they may result in organization members' failure to question basic assumptions and in doing so prevent the opportunity for anything but superficial forms of organizational learning.

It seems likely, as we have argued elsewhere (Cousins and Leithwood, 1993; Earl and Cousins, 1995), that superior approaches to change are ones that involve an appropriate balance between top-down and bottom-up orientations. Recent literature on educational reform (Fullan with Stiegelbauer, 1991; Fullan, 1993; Elmore and Associates, 1990; Murphy, 1991) and educational leadership (Leithwood, 1992; Fullan & Hargreaves, 1990; Sergiovanni, 1992) is replete with strong arguments favoring transformational leadership, collaboration, professionalization of teaching and so forth. But what are the implications for participatory evaluation as a change strategy?

First, we are of the belief that participatory evaluation works best in educational contexts that practice – not just espouse – approaches to reform that respect a balance between top-down and bottom-up considerations. Our studies suggest that when this balance is off the chances of successfully informing the change process with participatory evaluation data are very unlikely. Moreover, the process can have further negative consequences (predominantly motivational) if the mismatch between what is espoused (participation, collaboration) turns out to be quite different than the final result (non-use or mischievous use of data). This suggests to us that an investment, however modest, in some sort of pre-evaluation assessment of the readiness of the organization for this approach or its suitability to it, would likely pay dividends in reducing misspent time and resources. Are decision processes in evidence that truly value input from those responsible for innovation implementation? To what extent are teachers invited to assume leadership roles in schools? How autonomous is school-level decision making? Organizations that are open to input from teachers in combination with administrative input are better suited to meaningful collaborative research activities.

Who Participates?

The process of selecting individuals to participate in the research process is a critical one. Clearly, as King reminds us, participation by those who want to participate is key. The work demands of applied research often tend to be underestimated, and given their typically substantial nature, motivation to participate and to see projects through to completion is extremely important. But beyond this essential feature it is necessary to consider at least two other characteristics of participants. The first characteristic follows from the previous argument. There ought to be a balance of members from different levels within the organization. One reason supporting balanced composition has to do with organizational perspective. As DeStefano (1990) noted 'persons at different positions within or surrounding an organization have different values, purposes and levels of understanding regarding an evaluation of that organization' (p. 257). It makes sense to us to aim to capture the insights and practical wisdom of those with different implementation responsibilities. Another reason for a balanced approach is to ensure that at least some organization members who participate are primary users of evaluation data in the way thought of by Alkin and Patton. Who is in an organizational position to enact recommendations or organizational imperatives that are likely to follow the research? Without the sincere involvement of those in a position to do something about the findings, the data are susceptible to the same sort of demise as those generated by more traditional approaches involving researchers who are external to the organization. That is, evaluation data are more likely to be less fully understood and consequently used selectively or otherwise not used to their maximum potential.

The second consideration that extends beyond motivation, and King touched on this as well, is expertise. Yes, dependency on researchers for the successful completion of technical research tasks is an unavoidable reality. But given the workload demands of such projects and the considerable coordinated effort required to carry them out, organization members with prior experience in activities of this sort are likely to be highly valued members of the team. The less time spent learning on the fly the principles of applied research, the more time spent getting the job done efficiently and effectively. This line of reasoning supports some sort of 'cascade' approach to research projects where at least some members of prior research efforts participate in subsequent ones so as to optimize learning from experience and minimize the re-invention of the wheel.

Partnerships are Rarely Made in Heaven

We also learned from the forgoing studies that the process of developing partnerships is one that ought not to be taken for granted. As Huberman pointed out, under the wrong conditions the researcher will be viewed with suspicion, perhaps as an instrument of those with organizational power. The researcher's role is multifaceted. What does one look for in a researcher likely to be successful in the role? First, as we have identified from the outset, the provision of technical research skills and knowledge is key. While competence in principles of applied research is essential, it is also important that these principles fit the local context. Organization team members will help to ensure this fit, but researchers with some sense of organizational know-how can only help to foster this process. Second, the researcher must be able to communicate effectively; to instruct the uninitiated as the process unfolds; and to serve as translators between the different worlds of research and practice. As observed by Alkin, effective instruction by researchers will not be limited to matters of applied research theory and principles. It will also entail some form of education about the power of evaluation and its potential value to the organizational decision-making process. Third, and not many of the studies in the current collection portrayed this, it seems important that the evaluator maintains his or her involvement after the data are in. That is to say, it seems likely that a stronger role in communicating and disseminating research results throughout the organization would be beneficial in enhancing the impact of the project. Indeed, such activities are more likely to occur as the linkages between researchers and educators are strengthened. Substantial involvement at this point in the process is increasingly endorsed in the literature (e.g., Huberman and Cox, 1990).

How do partnerships begin? Where can a school or district without research services tap into research resources? How can schools or districts with research services in place make better use of these services? These are questions to which no simple answers are available. Nonetheless, it might be prudent to consider the enterprise from the researchers' point of view. In doing so, one will quickly recognize that the challenges and demands placed on researchers are substantial as well (see the chapter by Lee and Cousins, for example).

It is also necessary to think about what researchers stand to benefit from participatory activities – benefits that extend beyond those specified in contractual arrangements. For the in-house research shop, increased involvement in participatory activities carries the potential to enhance the reputation of the research unit's status as an integral component of the ongoing organizational decision-making process. We saw evidence of this in Earl's study. Interestingly, the greater the participation at this level, the more in tune with organizational culture and customs the researcher will become, the result of which will support further involvement of this sort. This enhanced sensitivity to organizational nuances and customs will benefit internal and external researchers alike.

External researchers are an enigma to many educators. Huberman characterizes their role as being inherently ambiguous. What are their motives for participation? Are they the 'hired gun' working for senior administration? Is there a hidden agenda? What's in it for them? Both Cousins' and King's studies revealed instances of practitioners raising one eyebrow on the arrival of the researcher. Are they in pursuit of their own research agenda? Are they trying to sell something?

Indeed, historically the relationship between researchers and practitioners has been anything but symbiotic. The traditional social sciences model of research advocates a detached 'objective' approach to generating knowledge, one that involves practitioners as the objects of researcher rather than partners in it. Researchers would enter the organization, collect their data, then exit to compile, interpret and publish in forums that were distant from the vantage point of the educational practitioner. But, as we have observed, this approach is changing in favor of models that hold in high esteem the practical wisdom of practitioners and value their partnership in the research process. The direction in which Shulha and Wilson were headed serves as the most vivid example in the current context. While academic research interests are distinct from the applied research interests most directly visible in participatory evaluation projects, it is important for practitioners to recognize that it is in the researcher's long- and short-term interest to work in partnership, to establish connections, to strengthen relationships with members of the field of practice. This sort of mutuality of benefit is elaborated here and elsewhere by Huberman (1990).

Time, Energy and Other Costs

One of the most strikingly consistent findings observed across studies was the underestimation of the time involved in actually doing the research. For some participants, this meant add-on work to an already full agenda. For others, it meant limits on their ability to carry out their primary organizational function, a situation generally found to be personally and professionally unacceptable. For others, it meant just plain fatigue. While we recognize that budgetary constraints will limit the extent to which the participatory process can be fiscally underwritten, our view is that under-supported projects run the risk of isolating applied research activities as expensive add-on events that cannot possibly justify their costs. Of what possible value can a process be that leaves participants physically and emotionally bankrupt? The obvious message here is for people to enter the process with eyes wide open to the issues of scope and task demand. There is a role for evaluators here to help school- and system-based personnel to come to terms with just what is involved. It will be especially important for researchers to contribute at this level in systems that are unaccustomed to applied research as a regular process. But there is a responsibility for organization members, too, particularly those commissioning the study, to develop their understanding of what is involved and to lobby in advance for adequate resources to sustain the activities.

Building for the Future

Participatory evaluation ought not to be thought of as a one-shot deal. We observed limits on our ability to conclude that evidence of organizational learning was apparent. Part of these limits were simply a function of bounds on time and experience. Prior to having an impact on the organizational culture, to becoming an integral part of routine organizational processes, several repetitions of participatory evaluation will be required. By implication, the successes and benefits of each project should be celebrated by practitioners and researchers alike. Also, processes ought to be documented such that others may follow increasingly well-trodden paths rather than always blazing the trail. Evaluation activities might also be institutionalized through tie-ins with existing organizational data bases and communications functions. There ought to be some sort of archival system in place such that prior activities are easily accessible. Relationships with researchers might be cultivated through ongoing contact and dialogue.

Final Remarks

Participatory evaluation is not a panacea. There is nothing magical about it or its ability to fuel the educational reform process. It will not apply universally. But it does have potential. It builds on the strength of partnership especially the complementarity of program knowledge and research expertise. It provides a demanding and intensive focus for school and district staff and makes available opportunities for the development of shared understandings of complex educational and organizational phenomena. It fosters the development of intrinsic payoffs for educators and has the potential to be integrated into the culture of schools. This collection of studies has done a lot to further our understanding of participatory evaluation, its impact and the conditions under which it is likely to thrive. But much remains to be known. It is our hope that ongoing research and practical wisdom will continue to shed light on important issues, concepts and relationships among them. It is especially our hope that researchers and practitioners will work together to generate that light.

References

ALKIN, M.C. (1991) 'Evaluation theory development: II', in MCLAUGHLIN, M.W. and PHILLIPS, D.C. (eds) *Evaluation and Education: At Quarter Century*, Chicago, IL, The University of Chicago Press, pp. 91–112.

ARGYRIS, C. and SCHÖN, D.A. (1991) 'Participatory action research and action science: A commentary', in WHYTE, W.F. (ed.) *Participatory Action Research*, Newbury Park, CA, Sage, pp. 85–96.

BICKELL, W.E. and COOLEY, W.W. (1985) 'Decision-oriented educational research in school districts: The role of dissemination processes', *Studies in Educational Evaluation*, **11**, pp. 183–203.

BRANDON, P.R., WANG, Z. and HECK, R.H. (1994) 'Teacher involvement in school-conducted needs assessment', *Evaluation Review*, **18**, 4, pp. 458–71.

BURRY, J., ALKIN, M. and RUSKUS, J. (1985) 'Organizing evaluations for use as a management tool', *Studies in Educational Evaluation*, **11**, pp. 131–57.

CLARK, K.B. and FUJIMOTO, T. (1991) *Product Development Performance: Strategy, Organization, and Management in the World Auto Industry*, Boston, Harvard University Press.

COUSINS, J.B. and LEITHWOOD, K.A. (1993) 'Enhancing knowledge utilization as a strategy for school improvement', *Knowledge: Creation, Diffusion, Utilization*, **14**, 3, pp. 305–33.

DARLING-HAMMOND, L. (1990) 'Instructional policy into practice: "The power of the bottom over the top"', *Educational Evaluation and Policy Analysis*, **12**, 3, pp. 233–41.

DESTEFANO, L. (1990) 'Evaluating effectiveness: Federal expectations and local capabilities', *Studies in Educational Evaluation*, **16**, pp. 257–69.

EARL, L.M. and COUSINS, J.B. (1995) *Classroom Assessment: Changing the Face; Facing the Change*, Toronto, The Ontario Public School Teachers Federation.

ELMORE, R. and ASSOCIATES (ed.) (1990) *Restructuring Schools: The Next Generation of Educational Reform*, San Francisco, Jossey-Bass.

FORSS, K., CRACKNELL, B. and SAMSET, K. (1994) 'Can evaluation help an organization to learn?', *Evaluation Review*, **18**, 5, pp. 574–91.

FULLAN, M.G. (1993) *Change Forces: Probing the Depths of Educational Reform*, London, Falmer Press.

FULLAN, M.G. and HARGREAVES, A. (1991) *What's Worth Fighting For? Working Together for your School*, Toronto, Ontario Public School Teachers' Federation.

FULLAN, M.G. with STEIGLEBAUE, S. (1991) *The New Meaning of Educational Change*, New York, Teachers College Press.

HUBERMAN, M. (1983) 'Recipes for busy kitchens: A situational analysis of routing knowledge use in schools', *Knowledge: Creation, Diffusion, Utilization*, **4**, pp. 478–510.

HUBERMAN, M. (1990) 'The social context of instruction in schools', Paper presented at the annual meeting of the American Educational Research Association, Boston, MA.

HUBERMAN, M. and COX, P. (1990) 'Evaluation utilization: Building links between action and reflection', *Studies in Educational Evaluation*, **16**, pp. 157–79.

LEITHWOOD, K.A. (1992) 'The move toward transformational leadership', *Educational Leadership*, **49**, 5, pp. 8–12.

MCTAGGART, R. (1991) 'Principles of participatory action research', *Adult Education Quarterly*, **41**, 3, pp. 168–87.

MURPHY, J. (1991) *Restructuring Schools: Capturing and Assessing the Phenomena*, New York, Teachers College Press.

NELSON, M. and SIEBER, S. (1976) 'Innovation in urban secondary schools', *School Review*, **27**, pp. 101–19.

PATTON, M.Q. (1988) 'The evaluator's responsibility for utilization', *Evaluation Practice*, **9**, 2, pp. 5–24.

J. Bradley Cousins and Lorna M. Earl

SMYLIE, M.A. (1992) 'Teacher participation in school decision making: Assessing willingness to participate', *Educational Evaluation and Policy Analysis*, **14**, 1, pp. 53–67.
SERGIOVANNI, T.J. (1992) 'Why we should look for substitutes for leadership', *Educational Leadership*, **49**, 5, 41–5.
WEISS, C.H. (1991) 'Reflection on 19th-century experience with knowledge diffusion', *Knowledge: Creation, Diffusion, Utilization*, **13**, 1, pp. 5–16.
WEISS, C.H., CAMBONE, J. and WYETH, A. (1992) 'Trouble in paradise: Teacher conflicts in shared decision making', *Educational Administration Quarterly*, **28**, 3, pp. 350–67.
WHYTE, W.F. (ed) (1991) *Participatory Action Research*, Newbury Park, CA, Sage.

Exercises

In this section we list a number of exercises useful for helping to consolidate thinking about participatory evaluation, its possibilities and its potential. The exercises are divided into 'knowledge' and 'applications' categories. Applications exercises pertain to schools or school systems and are written from the point of view of educational practitioners. They can be tackled individually or in groups but they are likely to be most potent if treated as a basis for discussion.

Knowledge Exercises

1   What is participatory evaluation? How is it different from other forms of applied research? How is it different from conventional stakeholder-based evaluation? How is it different from various forms of action research?

2   What are some likely benefits of participatory evaluation to:
    a)   individual members of an educational organization?
    b)   educational organizations?
    c)   researchers?

3   What are some possible drawbacks to participatory evaluation?

4   What factors are chiefly responsible for the successful implementation of participatory evaluation?

5   What factors inhibit the success of participatory evaluation?

Applications Exercises

1   Think of an applied research project that was recently carried out in your school or school district.
    a)   Describe the project. What were its main objectives? What were its intended uses? Who were its intended users? What sorts of information were collected? How was this information compiled, analyzed and reported?
    b)   Could the study be considered a participatory evaluation? Why or why not?
    c)   What impact did the study have?
    d)   What factors enhanced the usefulness of the study? What factors limited its usefulness?

2 Think now about the school or district in which you work.
   a) How are decisions made about educational innovations, programs, curriculum and the like? Who is involved in the decision process? How much input do teachers have into the decision-making process?
   b) How often does your school or district rely on applied research data as a source of information about program decision making? What other sources of information are used for decision making? What barriers prevent your organization from making greater use of evaluation and applied research?
   c) How would you characterize your district's or school's orientation toward leadership? Are teachers formally or informally invited to participate in leadership activities? Do senior administrators consult professional teaching staff over important curriculum or management decisions?
   d) Is your school or district ready for participatory evaluation? How would you know?

3 Think of a researcher who has worked on applied research projects in your school district.
   a) What sort of rapport does he or she have with administrators? With teachers?
   b) Is he or she viewed as being credible within the school system? Why or why not?
   c) What could the researcher do to improve his or her credibility in the system?

4 Imagine that you have been approached by senior administration in your district to coordinate an applied research project. The project might be a system-wide review of math, a school level evaluation of cooperative group learning, or a needs assessment survey of rate-payers. Your initial task is to formulate a proposal for the research project that will include clear indication of what you intend to do, who will be involved and how much it will cost.
   a) Describe the intended research project. What is its purposes and objectives? Who are its intended users? Who are the primary stakeholders (specify your definition)? What are the relevant secondary interests in the research?
   b) Who of the following would you involve in the project? Provide a rationale for members of each group. What role would each play? Senior administrators; central board office coordinators or curriculum specialists; school administrators; teachers; students; parents; other members of the school or district community; internal research staff; external researchers.
   c) How would decisions be made on the research project?
   d) Would you constitute an executive or steering committee and a research workgroup? Why or why not? Who would sit on each?
   e) What internal research expertise is available within the school district? What prior applied projects have been carried out, and how can they be of use to you?
   f) If external research expertise is needed, how would you go about obtaining it? Who would you contact? What sorts of issues might enter into a negotiated agreement to participate with an external researcher?
   g) Make explicit each of the following. Who would you involve in decision making about each component? How much time would each step take? Defining the scope of the study (breadth of questions asked, sources of data); designing the study; determining the methods used to collect data; deciding how data would be compiled and analyzed.

h) How would the findings be reported? Informal ongoing reports as data come in? Formal written report at the end of the process? Executive summary for wide distribution?

i) How and to where would the report(s) be disseminated? Who would be involved in disseminating the information from the study? Why?

j) How much would the study be likely to cost? Be sure to figure in personnel and release time if necessary. What non-personnel items would you need to budget for? Would the study be worth the money budgeted? How would you know?

k) How would you know if the study had its intended impact? What other benefits are likely to occur as a consequence of the study?

l) What might be some obstacles that are likely to intrude on the successful completion of the project? What strategies might help to overcome these obstacles?

Notes on Contributors

Terry R. Berkeley is Associate Professor and Department Chair for Early Childhood Education at Towson State University. He has taught courses in disabilities, program development and evaluation, budgeting and cost analysis, policy analysis, and the politics of education. He served as director of the Egyptian Training Project. His publications can be found in *Rural Special Education Quarterly*, *Topics in Early Childhood Special Education*, *Educational Administration Quarterly*, and chapters in various books on education and early childhood education.

J. Bradley Cousins is Associate Professor of Educational Administration at the Faculty of Education, University of Ottawa. His research program and graduate teaching reflect a strong commitment to educational field development. Throughout his career he has participated in many funded and unfunded research and development projects in collaboration with teachers and educational administrators. Recent books are *Developing Leaders for Future Schools* (co-authored with Ken Leithwood and Paul Begely, 1992, Falmer); and *Classroom Assessment; Changing the Face; Facing the Change* (co-authored with Lorna Earl, 1995, Ontario Public School Teachers Federation).

Lorna Earl is Research Director for the Scarborough Board of Education and a sessional lecturer at the Ontario Institute for Studies in Education. A leader in the field of assessment and evaluation, she has been widely involved in consultation, research and staff development with teachers' organizations, ministries of education, school boards and charitable foundations. In 1994, she was named 'Distinguished Educator' by OISE. Recent books include *Classroom Assessment: Changing the Face; Facing the Change* (co-authored with Brad Cousins, 1995, Ontario Public School Teachers Federation); and *Triple Transitions: Educating Early Adolescents in the Changing Canadian Context* (co-authored with Andy Hargreaves, forthcoming, Falmer).

Michael Huberman is Professor of Education at the Harvard University Graduate School of Education and Senior Research Associate at The Network, Inc. Right now, he scuttles between teaching (qualitative data analysis, life histories of administrators), large scale research (multiple case studies in middle-school science, math and technology), and a Spenser grant of special interest here: the effects of interactive dissemination on researchers.

Jean A. King is Associate Professor in the College of Education and Human Development, University of Minnesota. Former Director of the Center for Applied Research and Educational Improvement (CAREI), her research interests include long-term school change, action research, and evaluation use.

Clay Lafleur is Chief Research Officer with the Simcoe County Board of Education and is responsible for system-wide research and evaluation activities as well as program development and implementation. He is Past President of the Association of Educational Research Officers of Ontario and the University of Toronto chapter of Phi Delta Kappa. His research interests include leadership, school improvement, learning environments, individual and group development, communication, collaborative action research, complementary research methods and participatory program evaluation.

Linda E. Lee is Vice-president and partner in the consulting company Proactive Information Services Inc. A former evaluation consultant for a large urban school division and a senior research analyst for the Manitoba Department of Education, Ms Lee currently works in areas of evaluation, social research, and program development for a range of clients in the not-for-profit and public sectors. Her publications include *Management Tools: Options for Guidance for Grades 1 to 8* and *The Guide Program: For the Fun and Challenge of It!* (the national program for Girl Guides of Canada).

Susan D. Lopez is an Adjunct Professor in the Department of Educational Foundations and Research at Gallaudet University. She has taught courses in program evaluation, educational research, statistics, and educational psychology. She served as the Associate in Training and Evaluation for the Egyptian Training Project. She also served as evaluator for a training project for Kuwaiti teachers. In addition to her work at the International Center on Deafness at Gallaudet University, she has conducted numerous evaluation and research studies for government and private industry on a variety of educational and social science projects.

Donna M. Mertens is Professor in the Department of Educational Foundations and Research at Gallaudet University where she teaches courses in program evaluation, research design, and educational psychology. She served as the first chief evaluator for the Egypt Training Project. She is the author of a forthcoming book, *Diversity in Research Methods in Education and Psychology* (Sage, 1996), and co-author of *Research Methods in Special Education* (Sage, 1995) with John McLaughlin. Her publications appear in a number of books and journals, including *Evaluation Practice, American Annals of the Deaf, Studies in Educational Evaluation, Educational Evaluation and Policy Analysis, and New Directions for Program Evaluation.*

Lyn M. Shulha is Assistant Professor of Curriculum and Evaluation at Queen's University, Kingston, Canada. She is currently investigating, through site based studies, the potential of program evaluation designs to contribute to program implementation, organizational renewal and re-structuring. As well, she works directly with teachers and administrators in constructing frameworks and action plans for curriculum planning and student assessment. Lyn is a regular presenter at the American Evaluation Association annual meeting.

Robert J. Wilson is Professor of Measurement and Evaluation at Queen's University in Kingston, Canada. His interests are in classroom teachers' assessment practices. He has published several research articles about Canadian practice which have served as a basis for a text for teachers entitled *Assessing Children in Classrooms and Schools* (Allyn & Bacon Canada). He is also serving on the Technical Sub-committee for Canada's participation in the Third International Mathematics and Science Study having worked on several large-scale assessment programs in Canada both in and out of government.

Author Index

Subject Index

action research 8, 10, 75, 86, 87–9, 93–5, 98, 99, 100–1, 104–5, 162
  emancipatory 10, 101, 105
  historical perspective on 86, 100
  practical 87–9, 105
  process issues in 93–5, 98
  social justice and 10
  variations in form 87–9, 100, 104
applied social research (*see* evaluation)

charitable foundation 72, 78
classroom assessment 115–38
conflict model 105
curriculum review, development and implementation 22, 33, 89–91, 160, 161

dissemination competence 103

educational change 1, 159, 174–5
educational research 103, 115–38
educational researchers 128
evaluation 8, 9, 10, 34, 79, 86–7, 89, 96–7, 103–6, 108, 115, 140–55
  as a political activity 34, 90, 96–7, 106, 108
  constructivist paradigm in 142–3
  democratization of 34
  focussed interviews for 22, 31
  international context for 140–55
  hyper-rationality and 106, 164
  methodological diversity in 34
  purposes 33, 79, 86, 106, 144
  responsive 87, 104, 105, 142
  technical rigor 8, 89, 105
  utilization 9, 10, 86–7, 103
  theory 115
evaluation process 21–6, 33, 41–3, 46–9, 51, 56–9, 63–4, 67, 69, 76–81, 82, 91, 92, 118–25, 143–5, 149–50
  data analysis 23, 25, 42, 56, 58, 63–4, 67, 92, 120, 145, 172

data collection 23, 25, 42, 56–7, 58, 92, 119–22, 144, 149
dissemination 29, 43, 56, 58, 78, 79, 80, 81, 167, 172, 177
planning 22, 25, 42, 76, 79, 91–2, 118–9, 143–4, 148–50, 166–7
reporting 23, 25, 56–7, 58, 64, 91, 124–5
ownership of 23, 25, 26, 38, 62, 82, 91, 118–9, 149–50
team building 38, 56–9
evaluation utilization (*see* utilization of evaluation data)
evaluation of training 140–55
evaluator's role 8, 9, 99, 104, 106, 128–9, 177
emancipation 151
empowerment 9, 39, 44, 45, 50, 53, 63, 64, 105, 127, 140, 146–53, 165, 168, 170, 172
  factors influencing 147–50
external evaluation 55–71, 72–85, 91–95, 108–9, 113–38, 172, 177
  charitable foundation involvement 72–85, 109
  field centre involvement 55–71, 108
  centre for applied research involvement 91–5
  university-based evaluator involvement 55–71, 91–5, 115–38

field centres 55

human learning 5, 105

influences on schools 4, 33, 93
internal evaluation 21–32, 33–53, 107–8, 172, 177
  district research unit 21, 107
  requirements of effective 31
  model of 33